The Signless and the Deathless

The Signless and the Deathless

On the Realization of Nirvana

Bhikkhu Anālayo

Foreword by Bhante Gunaratana

Wisdom

Wisdom Publications
132 Perry Street
New York, NY 10014 USA
wisdomexperience.org

Library of Congress Cataloging-in-Publication Data
Names: Anālayo, 1962– author.
Title: The signless and the deathless: on the realization of nirvana / Bhikkhu Anālayo.
Description: First edition. | New York: Wisdom Publications, 2023. |
Includes bibliographical references and index.
Identifiers: LCCN 2023006245 (print) | LCCN 2023006246 (ebook) |
ISBN 9781614298885 (hardcover) | ISBN 9781614299011 (ebook)
Subjects: LCSH: Nirvana. | Enlightenment (Buddhism)
Classification: LCC BQ4263 .A53 2023 (print) | LCC BQ4263 (ebook) |
DDC 294.3/423—dc23/eng/20230308
LC record available at https://lccn.loc.gov/2023006245
LC ebook record available at https://lccn.loc.gov/2023006246

ISBN 978-1-61429-888-5 ebook ISBN 978-1-61429-901-1

27 26 25 24 23
5 4 3 2 1

Cover design by Jess Morphew. Interior design by Tony Lulek. Set in DGP 11.25/14.9.

The index was not compiled by the author.

As an act of Dhammadāna, Bhikkhu Anālayo has waived royalty payments for this book.

Wisdom Publications' books are printed on acid-free paper and meet the guidelines for permanence and durability of the Production Guidelines for Book Longevity of the Council on Library Resources.

Printed in the United States of America.

Whose pasture is emptiness
And signless concentration—
Their track is hard to trace,
Like that of birds in the sky. (Uv 29.31)

Contents

Foreword by Bhante Gunaratana

The Buddha's teachings on Nirvana, the ultimate goal of the Buddhist path, are subtle, and understanding them can be quite challenging. The meaning of Nirvana is often completely misunderstood and misinterpreted, particularly in the West, where it has become a cliché for something ultimately desirable and pleasant in the mundane realm. In the East, on the other hand, while synonymous with liberation from *saṃsāra*, it remains connected in people's minds with the notion of the immortality of a permanent soul or self. Therefore, a clear exposition on this profound subject is of utmost importance.

In this book, renowned scholar and teacher Venerable Anālayo sheds welcome light on this topic by offering a new perspective: that the descriptions of Nirvana in the early Buddhist texts convey a complete "stepping out," as Venerable Anālayo puts it, of our usual modes of the construction of experience. In doing so, he skillfully corrects a tendency in the West to view Nirvana in terms of the extremes of eternalism and nihilism. In addition, Venerable Anālayo shares valuable insights into the concept of deathlessness as laid out in the scriptures—and presents it as a state of total freedom from suffering that can be attained in this very life.

Venerable Anālayo is a brilliant scholar whose works exhibit a profound precision and clarity. His extensive knowledge of early Buddhist literature and logical exposition of the Buddha's teaching make this book an invaluable asset for all Dhamma seekers.

Acknowledgments

I AM INDEBTED to Bhikkhu Bodhi, Chris Burke, Bhikkhunī Dhammadinnā, Linda Grace, Sarah Kirchberger, Yuka Nakamura, and Lambert Schmithausen for commenting on a draft version of this book and to the staff, board members, and supporters of the Barre Center for Buddhist Studies for providing me with the facilities needed to do my practice and writing.

Introduction

IN THE FOLLOWING PAGES I survey selected passages from the early Buddhist texts in order to provide a perspective on the significance of the realization of Nirvana.[1] My attempt to do justice to this topic is based on what—to the best of my knowledge—is a new approach. Said simply, this approach considers descriptions of the breakthrough to Nirvana to convey a complete stepping out of the way the mind usually constructs experience.[2]

The first part of this book serves as a preparation for the type of perspective I intend to present, by way of examining indications offered in the early discourses on the topic of the construction of experience.[3] In order to approach this matter from a practice-related viewpoint, a central concern in my exploration is the notion of the signless (*animitta*), in particular its meditative development as a form of concentration, which appears to have a counterpart in some later traditions in the cultivation of nonattention (*amanasikāra*).

The second part of my exploration then turns to the deathless. As an epithet of Nirvana, the idea of the deathless in its early Buddhist use can be understood to involve a departure from notions of immortality held in the ancient Indian setting, instead offering the promise of complete freedom from being afflicted by mortality while still alive.

The two main parts of my study fall into twelve subsections each, with a summary of the basic points at their respective ends. In the conclusion that follows these two main parts I apply the idea of a transcendence of the construction of experience to a textual description of the awakening of the Buddha's son, Rāhula.

Whereas the topic of signlessness does not seem to have garnered much scholarly attention so far, the realization of Nirvana and passages related to this topic have been taken up in a vast number of publications, both scholarly and popular. Although I have tried my best to take into account a fair range of these, I have not been able to do that in a fully comprehensive manner. To do so properly would require a book in itself.[4] Moreover, any attempt at comprehensive coverage would need to take up not only relevant scholarly assessments but also the different positions and perspectives on Nirvana that have emerged in the course of time in the various Buddhist traditions, which would require another book in itself.[5]

Rather than attempting such broad coverage, the present book has the much humbler purpose of formulating my current understanding of selected early Buddhist passages in the hope of offering a meaningful perspective. For the time being, I have minimized critical observations, except for a few remarks in my notes.[6] As a result, what I propose here comes with no claim of superseding previous discussions and presenting the final word on the matter. Instead, what I present is simply a new way of approaching the topic of Nirvana, based on the viewpoint of the construction of experience as recognized in early Buddhist thought. The resultant perspective is therefore just one out of many, although hopefully being at least internally coherent and relevant to actual meditation practice.

In order to make my exploration as accessible as possible to readers from various backgrounds, I have tried to refrain from referring to texts by their Indic names and instead provide references to reliable translations of the relevant Pāli versions in inline quotation for passages that I do not translate myself.[7] Although the main text of my exploration is geared toward a general audience, my annotations in turn are meant to cater to readers with a more scholarly inclination; hence, I provide quotations of the relevant originals and some further discussions. When translating from any of these originals, although in general I attempt to be fairly literal, I tend to change singular verb forms to plural in order to maintain a gender-inclusive writing style.

I. The Signless

THIS FIRST PART of my exploration is dedicated to a detailed study of the "sign" and its absence. I begin by exploring the function of the sign in perception and its relation to the construction of experience. Then I turn to the practice of bare awareness as a way of forestalling the arising of defilements due to grasping at signs, and to the potential of a similar type of practice in relation to the experience of pain. Another related topic is the role of the sign in relation to overcoming unwholesome mental states, in particular conceit. This leads me to the topic of signless concentration, which takes the absence of signs as its object and involves an approach to mental composure based on a form of attention that can be called "nonattention." In the final part of my exploration, I turn to the role of signless concentration in relation to meditation on emptiness.

1. The Sign

The word "sign" renders the Pāli and Sanskrit term *nimitta*,[8] which stands for the characteristic mark of things: that which in a way "sign"-als to the perceiver what that thing is, thereby enabling its recognition. Due to this function, the sign has a causal nuance: taking up a sign *causes* the process of making sense of experiences through the operation of perception. In other words, the sign stands right at the center of the network of causal factors leading to the arising of perception and is responsible for the type of associations and evaluations that usually come intertwined with the perceptual process.

The basic idea of the *nimitta* that emerges in this way could be related to an analysis of sense perception by the nineteenth-century philosopher Hermann von Helmholtz. He notes that a sign, representative of external influences on what we experience, need not be a completely accurate reproduction of that which it signifies. It suffices if the same object under the same circumstances produces the same sign, and not a different one.[9] The potential inaccuracy of signs is also a central concern in the early Buddhist analysis, where their role in facilitating recognition can be strongly influenced by defilements. As a result of that, their impact can at times be rather misleading.

Helmholtz also reasons that, even though sensory experiences are based on mere signs, these should nevertheless not be dismissed as just illusory, as they are the sign of something, be it something existing or happening.[10] This position also resonates with early Buddhist thought, where a keen awareness of the fabricated nature of experience and the pervasive influence of the mind does not lead to taking an idealist position.

Exploring the function of signs in a practical way, so as to make their role more easily intelligible, could be done, for example, with the type of optical illusions that lead to some form of delayed recognition. A so-called hybrid image—an image that can be perceived in two different ways, depending on the viewing distance—would be particularly apt. Bringing such an image slowly closer or moving it slowly further away until the second perception suddenly springs to mind can offer a good opportunity for noticing the working mechanism of taking up a sign.

The function of the sign, as understood in the early Buddhist analysis of perception, can also be exemplified with a narrative episode in an early discourse. After a long absence, a monastic had reportedly come to beg at the house of his former family and was recognized by a female servant. The Pāli version, in agreement with parallels extant in Chinese, Sanskrit, and Tibetan, indicates that her act of recognition was based on taking up the "sign" of his hands and feet, as well as of his voice (translated by Ñāṇamoli 1995/2005, 682).[11]

This example conveniently reflects key aspects of the operation of the sign. The preceding narrative reports that this monastic had gone forth against much opposition from his family. After a long time, he had come to his former home for a first visit in his role as a monastic. This means that, on following the narrative setting, his outer appearance would have changed drastically, as he was now shaven headed and wearing robes, to which the impact of aging should probably be added. For this reason, the servant's ability to recognize him would have to rely on features that are less amenable to change. If during previous contacts with the son of the household she would have paid much attention to his hair, which in the ancient Indian setting males usually wore long, and to the type of adornment and clothes he wore, based on such features she would not have been able to recognize him now. Someone's voice is a more reliable guide in this respect, although that can also change through aging. But in conjunction with the hands and feet, sufficient characteristic features would have been available for her to take up the sign and recognize that this was the son of her masters. The features of the face, mentioned in some versions, would be an additional aid, although the shift from long hair to bald, perhaps even combined with his having previously had a beard and now being clean shaven, can make it more difficult to recognize these.

This episode conveys that the basic working mechanism of recognition trains the mind to be on the lookout for what is relatively permanent, simply because features less amenable to change work better for purposes of identification. Ñāṇananda (2015, 257–58) explains: "To perceive is to grasp a sign of permanence in something . . . That is to say, a sign stands for permanence. A sign has to remain unchanged until one returns to it to recognize it."

In this way, a tendency to ignore or overlook the fact of impermanence is in a way built into the very way perception appraises the world. An illustrative example would be the so-called change blindness, when observers do not notice that an actual change in a visual object has occurred. The propensity of perception to latch on to unchanging signs is so ingrained that it can even impair the very ability to perceive—that is, to note that something has changed in the meantime.

Due to the tendency of overlooking the impact of impermanence, every successful act of recognition can strengthen the mistaken impression that there is something permanent in things. Hence, there is a need for intentionally directing attention to the aspect of change to counterbalance this tendency. Countering the tendency to perceive as permanent what is changing must be a central reason why contemplation of impermanence features so often in the early discourses as a particularly commendable form of cultivating liberating insight.

According to Theravāda exegesis, sustained meditative attention to impermanence can lead to gaining the signless liberation (translated by Ñāṇamoli 1982, 259).[12] This correlation can be appreciated in the light of the tendency of signs to reinforce the mistaken impression of permanence. When viewed from this perspective, contemplation of impermanence has indeed an important role as a corrective to the potentially misleading input resulting from taking up signs. The way perception operates is to a considerable degree a result of past conditioning, wherefore mental training can change those operational mechanisms.[13] If the taking up of signs has inculcated a tendency to presume things to be permanent, intentionally directing perception to what is impermanent can counter that tendency. Ñāṇananda (2015, 187) reasons that through "the dispelling of the perception of permanence, the tendency to grasp a sign or catch a theme is removed." The point here is of course not to render recognition dysfunctional but only to counter the tendency of the mind to be carried away by signs.

Regarding the above commentarial correlation, this would not imply that a signless form of meditation is in itself a way of contemplating change. The reason is simply that, in order to attend to impermanence, one would have to be aware of signs.[14] In other words, signless concentration, a term to be explored in more detail below, is not about contemplating impermanence, precisely because it involves not paying any attention to signs.

In the above episode of the monastic visiting his former home after a long absence, the signs taken up by the servant were physical features of the person she recognized. In addition to these, however, his present appearance also involved signs chosen by him to "sign"-al, if I am allowed to continue with the wordplay, his status to the world. Wearing robes and having a shaven head are signs to mark the condition of being a monastic, employed deliberately to set a contrast with being a layperson.

This leads me to another instance that involves the signs of a layperson. The relevant Pāli discourse and a Chinese parallel report that the Buddha was once visited by a person holding a parasol and wearing sandals, which in the ancient Indian setting was typical for laity. The Buddha consequently addressed him in the way a monastic speaks to a householder (translated by Ñāṇamoli 1995/2005, 467). Yet, his visitor was upset at being addressed in this way, as he had given up his wealth and responsibilities and for this reason felt he should no longer be reckoned a householder. In reply to this reaction, the Buddha clarified that his form of address simply reflected the fact that his visitor had the marks and signs of a householder.[15]

The Buddha's visitor in this episode had failed to convey appropriately through his outer appearance who he internally believed he was and how he wanted to be regarded by others. This example illustrates how the choice of hairstyle, clothing, and particular modes of behaving are ways in which signs are set up for others so that they form a certain type of impression (and thereby confirm the construction of one's own self-image). Continuing with my wordplay, such signs serve to "sign"-al what people believe to be "sign"-ificant about themselves. Needless to say, signs set up for such purposes are not always understood in the way they are intended; that is, signs can be misunderstood or misinterpreted by others.

In addition to this function of signaling what appears significant, the sign as the basic constituent of perception stands in relation to language and concepts. A discourse extant in Chinese, with a similar presentation found in a Pāli parallel (translated by Bodhi 2012, 962), explains that verbalization is the result of perception (which in turn, as shown above, relies on signs):[16] "Following on perception, one in turn verbalizes. This is said to be knowing the result of perception."

In this way, signs stand at the root of the potential problems caused by language and concepts, be it by introducing an unwarranted evaluation or by encouraging an equally unwarranted reification. The first of these two aspects calls in particular for the practice of sense restraint, whereas the second relates to the topics of bare awareness and the cultivation of signlessness in order to become aware of, and counter, the way one tends to construct one's own experiences.

2. Grasping at Signs

A key dimension of the act of taking up a sign by an unawakened mind is the weaving of subjective evaluations into the process of perception, which usually happens in a way that is not consciously noticed. The early discourses point to such evaluations by speaking of the "sign of attraction" and the "sign of aversion," for example. Whereas paying unwise attention to the former can trigger sensual desire, doing the same with the latter can result in the arising of ill will (translated by Bodhi 2000, 1568).[17] This presentation alerts to the predicament inherent in the basic act of taking up a sign, central to the appraisal of the world through perception. The influence of the sign can trigger an unwholesome mental condition, and this often enough happens outside of the purview of conscious recognition. From the subjective viewpoint, beauty and ugliness, etc., are regarded as features of the objects out there, rather than acknowledged for what they truly are: evaluations that originate in one's own mind.

The problem of evaluations rooted in unwholesome mental conditions comes to the fore in another passage extant in Pāli, according to which sensual lust, anger, and delusion are makers of signs (translated by Bodhi 2000, 1326).[18] The Chinese parallel conveys the same basic idea, although it does not have an explicit counterpart to the idea of a "maker" of signs. The three root defilements are makers of signs (or just signs) in the sense that they can substantially impact how the world is experienced. They do so by influencing which signs are given attention, thereby making these stand out in the overall perceptual appraisal of any object or situation. Unless kept in check by mindfulness, these three quite literally construct one's world. That which arouses sensual lust, anger, and delusion appears to be out there, when in reality it is in here, namely in the way perception has woven those signs into its appraisal of the world. Ñāṇananda (1974/1985, 15–16) reasons that to reckon the three root defilements as makers of signs

> might appear, at first sight, a not-too-happy blend of philosophy and ethics. But there are deeper implications involved. It is a fact often overlooked by the metaphysician that the real-

> ity attributed to sense-data is necessarily connected with their evocative power, that is, their ability to produce effects. The reality of a thing is usually registered in terms of its impact on the experiential side . . . Now, the "objects" of sense which we grasp . . . their significance depends on the psychological main-springs of lust, hatred and delusion.

The role of defilements as makers of signs in turn relates to an elementary stage in the arising and gradual increase of defilements. Usually one does not consciously decide "let me now be lustful" or "be furious" or "be confused." Instead, perception has identified something that triggers a defilement and, as the mind keeps returning to that, the defilement keeps increasing and coloring subsequent acts of perception. In this way, the three root defilements can indeed become makers of signs.

In contrast to this predicament stands the possibility of being "empty of sensual desire, anger, and delusion."[19] This is precisely the goal of early Buddhist meditative training, namely to empty the mind of defilements and thereby arrive at a way of apperceiving the world that better accords with reality and no longer is under the sway of these three signs. I will return to the relationship of such absence of defilements to liberation in the second part of my exploration (see below p. 105).

The need to be wary of the impact of subjective evaluations and to keep the mind increasingly empty of defilements informs a foundational mindfulness-related practice known as sense restraint. Such practice needs to be differentiated from the idea that sense objects should just be avoided. The idea of merely curtailing sense experience comes up for criticism in a Pāli discourse and its Chinese parallel, which feature a young brahmin reporting his teacher's injunctions in this respect (translated by Ñāṇamoli 1995/2005, 1147). According to this teacher, one should just refrain from seeing forms with the eye and hearing sounds with the ear.[20] Yet, the critical reply to this proposal clarifies that the solution is not to pretend to be blind or deaf. Instead, anything happening at a sense door needs to be monitored with mindfulness to avoid any grasping at signs that may cause unwholesome mental repercussions. How this can be achieved can be seen in actual instructions on sense restraint, taken from a discourse preserved in Chinese, which proceed as follows for the sense door of the eye:[21]

> If seeing a form with the eye, however, do not grasp the sign and also do not savor the form . . . guard the eye faculty so that no greed or sorrow, bad and unwholesome states, arise in the mind.

The Pāli parallel (translated by Ñāṇamoli 1995/2005, 875), after similarly warning against grasping the sign, continues by extending this warning also to grasping any "secondary characteristic" (*anuvyañjana*). Such secondary characteristics tend to elaborate further the first impression created by the sign. Their function can conveniently be illustrated with the help of the phrase employed instead in the above-quoted Chinese counterpart, which speaks of "savoring" the object. In other words, the task is to avoid savoring what is being experienced, not keeping it on the tongue of the mind, so to say, comparable to delicious food.

The use of the term "grasping" in both versions can best be taken to convey the sense of latching on to the sign, by way of clinging to whatever associations it calls up. Someone who successfully practices sense restraint still sees, hears, etc. The information seen, heard, etc., is still processed by the mind in order to be understood, which requires reliance on signs. But mindfulness is sufficiently well established at that point to notice when such processing of the sensory data takes up biased signs and veers off into unwholesome territory.

Both versions explicitly highlight that the main purpose of sense restraint is precisely to avoid the arising of bad and unwholesome states. Noticing as soon as possible that a particular sign is triggering such unwholesome reactions would enable the exercise of restraint right there and then, by way of letting go of that type of sign and intentionally directing attention in a way that avoids savoring the corresponding secondary characteristics.

Such sense restraint can enable becoming increasingly conscious of the operation of those signs that potentially trigger an unwholesome reaction, thereby offering a foundational practice for learning to work with signs.

A central implication of cultivating sense restraint in this respect would be an encouragement to realize when something causes strong repercussions within. This can then lead to investigating whether the evaluation underpinning those strong reactions realistically reflects the actual situation or whether it is, at least in part, due to projections and biases. Such projections and biases would be due to grasping at signs and savoring their secondary characteristics. The practice of sense restraint would thus help the practitioner to become increasingly aware of the way the mind is processing things under the impact of unwholesome projections and biases, thereby enabling a stepping out of such habitual patterns of reactivity and their detrimental consequences.

As an illustration of this first and foundational type of practice in relation to signs, lack of sense restraint could be compared to someone aimlessly surfing around on the internet, clicking here and there, at the mercy of whatever happens to appear on the screen. Establishing sense restraint could then be related to the case of someone who uses the web just to find a particular type of information, without getting sidetracked by whatever other things may be popping up here and there. Needless to say, the same contrast between aimless surfing and not getting sidetracked can also take place just in the mind, without any need to go online.

Building on the groundwork laid through sense restraint and standing in continuity with it, meditative training in relation to signs can then proceed to increasing levels of profundity with the practice of bare awareness, to be discussed below, and eventually with signless concentration. These mutually supportive practices can be seen to form part of a continuum of mental cultivation aimed at understanding and working with the way perception appraises the world. Before getting into those practices, however, first a closer look at the construction of experience is required.

3. The Construction of Experience

The basic operation of the sign relates closely to how perception makes sense of, and thereby to a considerable degree constructs, the world of experience. In this respect, early Buddhist thought can be understood to take a middle position between realism and idealism. In short, the existence of things outside of the purview of subjective apperception is not denied, but the way they are actually perceived is considered to be largely influenced by the mind.

A Pāli discourse, with parallels extant in Chinese and Sanskrit, reports the Buddha stating that the end of the world cannot be reached by walking, yet there is no making an end of *dukkha/duḥkha* without reaching the end of the world (translated by Bodhi 2000, 1188).[22]

The parallel versions agree in showing the monastics in the audience to be at first unable to grasp the meaning of the Buddha's succinct statement, presumably because they were taking the term "world" in its ordinary meaning. They reportedly approached the Buddha's attendant Ānanda for clarification. Below is the central part from the Pāli version of his clarification.[23]

> Friends, that by which in the world one becomes a perceiver of the world and a conceiver of the world, that is called "the world" in the noble one's discipline.

In the Pāli and Chinese versions, Ānanda continues by taking up each of the six senses individually—the five physical senses and the mind as the sixth—making clear how they all contribute to the construction of "the world." The parallels report that his elucidation received the Buddha's approval.

This reappraisal of the significance of the term "world" offers a key to understanding the meaning behind the succinct dictum that the end of the world cannot be reached by walking. It reflects a substantial shift of perspective from the assumption, presumably prevalent among the members of the audience of this discourse, that the world is as it appears to be out there. The teaching clearly draws attention to the degree to which the genesis of the world takes place in the mind, without going so far as to assert that there is nothing at all out there. The existence of something out there is in fact implicitly affirmed with the expression "that by which *in the world* one becomes a perceiver of the world." The end of the world, when understood in this manner, will indeed not be reached by travelling to some external location. Instead, it is to be found within, namely by stepping out of the construction of the world.

Another Pāli discourse and one of its two Chinese parallels present what appears to be basically the same perspective by succinctly stating that "the world has arisen in the six."[24] This conveys that any experience of the external world arises through the activity of the six senses. It is precisely because what appears to be out there much rather originates right here that it can also be transcended right here. Tilakaratne (1993, 71) sums up: "The subject is nothing other than a complex of reactions to the world (object); the world is nothing other than what is perceived by the subject."

The same principle holds for the term "all," in that such an expression simply covers the whole gamut of experience that is possible through the six sense spheres (translated by Bodhi 2000, 1140);[25] in other words, "all" stays within the confines of subjective experience.

Yet another Pāli discourse and its Chinese parallel confirm that the term "world" stands for what is encountered through the six senses (translated by Bodhi 2000, 1153).[26] Ñāṇananda (1971/1986, 84) offers the following comment on this notion of the world:

> Thus the world is what our senses present it [to] us to be. However, the world is not purely a projection of the mind in the sense of a thoroughgoing idealism; only, it is a phenomenon which the empirical consciousness cannot get behind, as it is itself committed to it. One might, of course, transcend the empirical consciousness and see the world objectively in the light of *paññā* [wisdom] only to find that it is void (*suñña*) of the very characteristics which made it a "world" for oneself. To those who are complacently perched on their cosy conceptual superstructures regarding the world, there is no more staggering a revelation than to be told that the world is a void. They might recoil from the thought of being plunged into the abysmal depths of a void where concepts are no more. But one need not panic, for the descent to those depths is gradual and collateral with rewarding personal experience.

According to two different Pāli discourses and their parallels, the world is in fact led by the mind (translated by Bodhi 2000, 130 and Bodhi 2012, 554).[27] The leading role taken by the mind in this way also comes up in a verse in the *Dharmapada* collections, whose Pāli version begins by stating that "the mind precedes phenomena," *dharmas*, a proposition similarly found in several parallels.[28] In fact, the Pāli version goes further by also qualifying phenomena to be "made by the mind."[29] The context shows that this is not meant to convey an idealistic sense. The statement in question occurs in two twin verses, which point out that doing evil leads to affliction just as doing good leads to happiness. In other words, the verses in question express in a poetical manner the basic teaching on karma and its fruit that is such a pervasive concern in the early texts.

This basic principle of karma is not confined to rebirth, as it can have repercussions visible in the same lifetime in which a particular deed was done. In fact, to some extent it can be considered to produce some effects immediately. The type of intention with which one approaches a particular situation will influence not only the way one acts but also the way one perceives (and inevitably evaluates) the actions and attitudes of others who are playing a part in the given situation. In this sense, then, the mind can indeed be considered the source of phenomena, and these are mind-made to a higher degree than one would normally be ready to admit.

Another relevant statement, found in a Pāli discourse and its Chinese parallel, presents the diversity observable among animals as a reflection of the diversity of the mind (translated by Bodhi 2000, 958).[30] The Pāli commentary explains this to refer to karma and its fruit,[31] in the sense that the diversity observable among animals reflects the diversity of their deeds done intentionally in former lives. An alternative interpretation, presented by Ñāṇananda (2015, 107–8), proposes that this passage can be taken to refer to the constructing activity by those who perceive such diversity among animals:

> Generally, we may agree that beings in the animal realm are the most picturesque. We sometimes say that the butterfly is beautiful. But we might hesitate to call a blue fly beautiful. The tiger is fierce, but the cat is not. Here one's personal attitude

accounts much for the concepts of beauty, ugliness, fierceness, and innocence of animals.

The nature of perception also comes up in the context of a set of similes, found similarly in a Pāli discourse and a range of parallels, which illustrate each of the five aggregates (translated by Bodhi 2000, 951). Here, perception is comparable to a mirage (of the type that can appear in the Indian hot season).[32] It projects something else on top of what is actually there. The same discourse also takes up the potentially deluding nature of consciousness, which is similar to a magical illusion (created by an illusionist). A mirage and an illusion turn out on close inspection to be void and without any essence. The same holds for these two aggregates, and even more so for their ability to mislead the mind into mistaken conclusions and evaluations.

A Pāli verse with several parallels even goes so far as to commend the understanding, in relation to the world, that "all this is unreal."[33] The indication given in this way needs to be handled with care in order to avoid reading too much into it. It is probably best read in line with the material surveyed so far, in the sense of drawing attention to the lack of reality of what has been constructed by the mirage of perception and the magical illusion of consciousness. Such an understanding can serve as a path to liberation, here expressed as a transcendence of both this shore and the other shore (a topic to which I will come back subsequently, see p. 62). The ensuing four verses in this Pāli collection keep returning to the significance of understanding that "all this is unreal," relating such insight to freedom from greed, sensual lust, anger, and delusion, respectively.[34] The context suggests that this serves as a strategy to wean the mind from taking things too seriously, something that is particularly prone to happen when defilements manifest. A brief reminder of the lack of reality of what has been conjured up by the mirage of perception and the magical illusion of consciousness can offer substantial help to sap the power of the forces of greed, sensual desire, anger, and delusion.

The construction of experience appears to be the main theme of a passage that puts a spotlight on the role of the fourth aggregate (*saṅkhāra*s or *saṃskāra*s) in this respect. According to the relevant Pāli version, whose presentation in this respect finds confirmation in counterparts extant in Chinese and Tibetan, the fourth aggregate performs the following role in relation to each of the five aggregates:[35]

> Monastics, "they construct the constructed," therefore they are called volitional constructions. And what is the constructed which they construct? Bodily form, which is constructed, they construct into bodily form; feeling tone, which is constructed, they construct into feeling tone; perception, which is constructed, they construct into perception; volitional constructions, which are constructed, they construct into volitional constructions; consciousness, which is constructed, they construct into consciousness. Monastics, "they construct the constructed," therefore they are called volitional constructions.

The key term here is Pāli *saṅkhāra* or Sanskrit *saṃskāra*, which can be rendered in a range of different ways.[36] For the purpose of my present exploration, I have chosen the rendering "volitional constructions," without thereby intending to present this as the one and only choice. The Indic term is too multivalent for a single English counterpart to be able to convey all of its nuances, and in other contexts the more commonly used "volitional activities," "volitional formations," or even just "formations" can indeed be the preferable option.

As regards the role *saṅkhāra*s/*saṃskāra*s play in the above passage, one relevant dimension would again be the perspective of karma and its fruit. However, the passage occurs in the context of a survey of characteristic functions of each of the five aggregates, and the operation of the fourth aggregate is not confined to the effect of what has been done in the past. From this perspective, then, it seems meaningful to interpret this passage as pointing to the role of *saṅkhāra*s/*saṃskāra*s in the construction of experience in the present. On this understanding, these *saṅkhāra*s/*saṃskāra*s can be seen to perform their role continuously, that is, in every moment of experience. As long as their constructing activity is based on ignorance (the first link in the standard presentation of dependent arising that leads on to *saṅkhāra*s/*saṃskāra*s as its second link), such construction is inevitably bound to result in the manifestation of *dukkha/duḥkha*.

The need to become aware of the construction of experience, which seems to emerge as a common theme in the selected passages surveyed above, has a counterpart in the findings of modern psychology. Feldman Barret (2017, 130) explains that "we humans are architects of our own experiences . . . We actively participate in constructing our experiences even though we are mostly unaware of that fact." Although this may at first sight seem counterintuitive, the truth of the matter is that the world of experience is to a considerable degree a construct of the mind (86):

> Your perceptions are so vivid and immediate that they compel you to believe that you experience the world *as it is*, when you actually experience a world *of your own construction*. Much of what you experience as the outside world begins inside your head.

4. Bare Awareness

A major tool for becoming aware of the construction of experience is mindfulness, especially in a role that could perhaps best be conveyed with the English expression "bare awareness" (which is not based on a specific Pāli or Sanskrit term).[37] This role of mindfulness can be illustrated with a cryptic instruction that occurs in two Pāli discourses. The first instance, which has no parallel, is addressed to a non-Buddhist wanderer by the name of Bāhiya (translated by Ireland 1990, 18–21). According to the narrative frame of the instruction, Bāhiya lived in a part of India corresponding roughly to the area of modern Mumbai, where he was much respected and well supported by the local people. He believed himself to be an arahant/arhat or at least on the path to becoming one. A former relative, reborn as a celestial being, out of compassion informed him that he was not even on the path to becoming an arahant/arhat, let alone being one himself. Asked if anyone else in the world was an arahant/arhat or on the path to becoming one, the former relative directed Bāhiya to the Buddha, who at that time was staying at Jeta's Grove.

Bāhiya left right away and walked across half of the Indian subcontinent until he reached Jeta's Grove, located in northern India, southeast of modern New Delhi. Finding out that the Buddha had just gone out to collect alms food, Bāhiya followed him into town. Meeting the Buddha on the streets of Sāvatthī/Śrāvastī, he begged for an instruction. The Buddha pointed out that this was not the proper time for him to give instructions, as he was walking for alms. Bāhiya insisted, stating that he could not be sure of the length of their respective lives. Being requested thrice, the Buddha gave Bāhiya a brief instruction, which led to Bāhiya becoming an arahant/arhat on the spot.

His apprehension of the uncertainty of life turned out to be well founded, as soon after his encounter with the Buddha he reportedly had an accident and passed away. The Buddha told his disciples that they should take care of Bāhiya's remains as one of their fellow practitioners and informed them that Bāhiya had passed away as a fully awakened one.

The instruction with the remarkable potential of enabling someone up to that point unacquainted with Buddhist teachings to become an arahant/arhat on the spot proceeds as follows:[38]

> Therefore, Bāhiya, you should train yourself like this: In what is seen there will be just what is seen, in what is heard there will be just what is heard, in what is sensed there will be just what is sensed,[39] in what is cognized there will be just what is cognized. Bāhiya, you should train yourself like this.
>
> Bāhiya, when for you in what is seen there will be just what is seen, in what is heard there will be just what is heard, in what is sensed there will be just what is sensed, in what is cognized there will be just what is cognized, then, Bāhiya, you will not be thereby (*na tena*). Bāhiya, when you will not be thereby, then, Bāhiya, you will not be therein (*na tattha*). Bāhiya, when you will not be therein, then, Bāhiya, you will be neither here, nor beyond, nor between the two. Just this is the end of *dukkha/duḥkha*.

This cryptic instruction can conveniently be related to the construction of experience. In terms of different meditative approaches related to the sign, it takes sense restraint a step further. The task is not only to avoid clinging to any evaluative sign that could trigger unwholesome mental reactions but also to remain with bare experience as such. Just seeing what is actually being seen, without adding any further elaborations to that. This points to a bare noting of what is being perceived, leaving a sustained pause before taking any other step in the mental realm, in particular avoiding any reification of what is experienced. Ñāṇananda (2016, 146) explains:

> The implication is that at whatever time one stops short at the seen and takes it only as a seen and not something seen, and likewise in the case of heard, only as a heard and not something heard, in the sensed only as a sensed and not something sensed, and in the cognized only as a cognized and not as something cognized, that is to say, there is no imagining a "thinghood," then one would not be thinking in terms of it. One would not imagine "by it" (*tena*) in the instrumental sense or "in it" (*tattha*) in the locative sense.

To achieve that requires stepping back from the ingrained tendency to participate fully in whatever is taking place at any sense door, instead of which one adopts the attitude of an uninvolved observer. Ñāṇananda (2015, 319 and 537) explains the implications of putting into practice this instruction as follows:

> The basic principle in this training seems to be the discipline to stop short at bare awareness . . . The latter half of the discourse seems to indicate what happens when one goes through that training . . .
>
> That is to say, when, Bāhiya, you have gone through that training of stopping at just the seen, the heard, the sensed and the cognized, then you would not be imagining in terms of them. The algebraic-like expressions *na tena* [not thereby] and *na tattha* [not therein] have to be understood as forms of egoistic imagining . . . When you do not imagine in terms of them, you would not be in them. There would be no involvement in

> regard to them . . . then, Bāhiya, you are neither here, nor there, nor in between the two . . . In other words, you would have realized voidness.

The suggested relationship to a realization of voidness can be related to the void nature of the mirage of perception and the magical illusion of consciousness in particular, and thereby to insight into the construction of experience. On this understanding, the instructions to Bāhiya can be taken to convey that remaining with bare awareness of what actually happens provides the foundation for no longer being carried away by what is perceived: *not thereby*. When one is no longer carried away by whatever is perceived, it becomes possible to remain free from taking a firm stance on it: *not therein*. By no longer being carried away or taking a firm stance on what is seen, etc., the underlying current of diminishing a sense of self can issue in no longer being caught up in even a trace of identification with the sense (*here*), its object (*there/beyond*), and their interaction (*between the two*). In this way, increasing degrees of freedom lead to stepping out of *dukkha/duḥkha*.

Based on freedom from the automatic processing of data by way of various associations and evaluations, there comes increasing freedom from reactivity, and the inner distance created by pausing rather than reacting enables no longer taking a firm stance on what is experienced. As a result, it becomes possible to remain free from identifying with the subject, from clinging to the object, and from appropriating the experience that results due to their interrelation.

The second instance featuring the same succinct instruction involves a Buddhist monastic. The narrative in the relevant Pāli discourse and its parallels in Chinese, Sanskrit, and Tibetan proceeds quite differently from the case of Bāhiya. In fact, according to another episode that must be meant to reflect an earlier occasion, this monastic appears to have been quite obsessed with speculative viewpoints current in the ancient Indian setting (translated by Ñāṇamoli 1995/2005, 533).[40] This reportedly motivated the Buddha's delivery of the famous simile of being shot by a poisoned arrow and not allowing the physician to remove the arrow unless all kind of irrelevant details related to the shooting have been clarified.

An apparently stubborn character would explain why on the present occasion, when he reportedly requested guidance from the Buddha for his meditation practice, this monastic's request was at first met with some reluctance. Eventually, however, the Buddha gave him the same instruction as the one addressed to Bāhiya. Fortunately, the discourse does not stop at this point, as the Buddha is on record for checking if his instruction had been properly understood. To explain his understanding, the monastic presented a set of verses. As these verses met with the Buddha's approval, they can be relied on as a guide to decode in particular the first part of the cryptic instruction itself. The Chinese version of these verses begins as follows:[41]

> [If] on seeing a form one does not grasp its sign,
> And the mind conforms to right mindfulness
> Craving will not defile the mind with what is detrimental,
> And the bondage of attachment will also not arise.
> Not giving rise to cravings
> For the countless forms that manifest,
> Thoughts of lustful desire, ill will, and harming
> Will be unable to afflict the mind.
> Diminishing [what] fosters a host of afflictions,
> One gradually draws close to Nirvana.

The parallel versions agree in applying the same understanding to the other sense doors (translated by Bodhi 2000, 1176). Although this monastic did not become an arahant/arhat on the spot when hearing the Buddha's penetrative instruction, the parallel versions also agree in reporting that he reached the final goal after a period of practice.[42] This confirms that his explanation was indeed based on understanding the basic implications of the practice the Buddha had described to him in brief.

At the same time, however, when giving the above explanation, he would still have been a worldling. In fact, his explanation seems to be mainly a gloss on the first part of the instruction regarding the training in bare awareness as predominantly a form of sense restraint. As this exposition does not offer any comment on "thereby," "therein," or "neither here, nor beyond, nor between the two," it seems fair to assume that the implications of these references will only become clear after having successfully implemented the basic training in bare awareness and made substantial progress toward, or even reached, the final goal. Perhaps for this reason, the above explanation corresponds mainly to working with signs at the level of avoiding unwholesome reactions, in line with the practice of sense restraint, whereas the deconstructing potential of bare awareness beyond merely holding craving in check is not fully evident. Nevertheless, having understood the main point about working with signs would be sufficient for putting the instruction into practice successfully. In other words, even if the implications of some parts of the instructions on bare awareness are not immediately evident, it suffices for getting started with the practice if the basic impact of grasping signs is clear.

In principle, it would even be possible to read the instruction to convey that by cultivating bare awareness of just the seen in the seen, etc., one is not thereby, not therein, and neither here, nor beyond, nor between the two. Yet, just bare awareness will hardly suffice to lead the average practitioner to an experience of the end of *dukkha/duḥkha*. For this reason, it seems to me preferable to assume that, based on the foundation laid in bare awareness, liberating insight deepens progressively in such a way that one is increasingly not thereby, then in turn evermore not therein, and eventually neither here, nor beyond, nor between the two. In fact, the narrative setting of the instruction to Bāhiya is one that calls for as succinct an instruction as possible. It follows that the explicit indications regarding not being thereby, not therein, and neither here, nor beyond, nor between the two must be meant to fulfill a specific purpose by way providing indications how the practice of bare awareness should be taken further.

The gist of the main task of bare awareness, to be undertaken so that in the seen there is just the seen, etc., can be explored further with the help of comments made by Ñāṇaponika (1962/1992, 30). His explanation, which uses the expression "Bare Attention" to refer to what I prefer to express with "bare awareness,"[43] proceeds as follows:

> Bare Attention is the clear and single-minded awareness of what actually happens *to* us and *in* us, at the successive moments of perception. It is called "bare," because it attends just to the bare facts of a perception as presented either through the five physical senses or through the mind which, for Buddhist thought, constitutes the sixth sense. When attending to that six-fold sense impression, attention or mindfulness is kept to a bare registering of the facts observed, without reacting to them by deed, speech or by mental comment, which may be one of self-reference (like, dislike, etc.), judgement or reflection. If during the time, short or long, given to the practice of Bare Attention, any such comments arise in one's mind, they themselves are made objects of Bare Attention.

Ideally building on a first exploration of the impact of the sign by cultivating sense restraint during any activities, the practice of bare awareness can be cultivated as a specific application of mindfulness. This can take the form of establishing mindfulness in a modality of open receptivity to whatever happens at any sense door, with an eye out for the arising of any mental comment and the onset of some form of reactivity. Whenever these happen, the task is simply to let go of the respective sign and relax into being with bare experience as such.

In another publication, Ñāṇaponika (1968/1986, 4) adds:

> Particularly in an age like ours, with its superstitious worship of ceaseless external activity, there will be those who ask: "How can such a passive attitude of mind as that of bare attention possibly lead to the great results claimed for it?" In reply, one may be inclined to suggest to the questioner not to rely on the words of others, but to put these assertions . . . to the test of personal experience.

5. The Sign of Pain

The potential of bare awareness has considerable relevance to facing the challenge of being in physical pain. An illustrative episode involves the Buddha himself, at a time when he was apparently in his old age. According to a Chinese version of this episode, he described how he dealt with pain in the following manner:[44]

> My body is just like an old cart which, by being expediently patched up and adjusted, reaches the place to which it is going; by expedient strength I can maintain it alive a little [longer], through my own strength and effort, putting up with these painful feelings. When I do not give attention to any signs and enter signless concentration, then my body is at ease and there are no afflictions.

Another parallel also extant in Chinese simply indicates that the Buddha's physical condition recovered to some degree due to "no longer keeping mental attention on the disease."[45] Although this is the only one out of a range of parallel versions that does not explicitly mention signlessness, it still can be taken to convey a significant perspective on the actual practice, namely encouraging a dropping of the sign of being "sick" or of having a "disease."

The relevant passage in another version extant in Chinese, which in this case is found in a text on monastic discipline rather than in a discourse, indicates that the Buddha "relied on contemplating signless concentration to bring about an appeasement of his physical sickness."[46] In what way such an appeasement could come about can be gathered from the Pāli parallel, which explains that "with the cessation of certain feeling tones, by way of not giving attention to any signs, he dwelled having attained the signless concentration of the mind."[47] This relates the cultivation of signless concentration to the topic of feeling tones (*vedanā*), showing how their impact can be substantially reduced in this way. The same can be seen in a Sanskrit fragment parallel, according to which the Buddha, "having made an effort to calm certain feeling tones and by not giving attention to any signs, dwelled having accomplished the direct realization of the signless concentration of the mind."[48] In other words, the parallels surveyed so far suggest that the impact of the feeling tones when being sick can be substantially reduced by letting go of the sign of "pain," in the sense of just being aware of the occurrence of sensations without solidifying this into being "pain."

The formulation in the Sanskrit version also throws into relief the elevated nature of signless concentration by speaking of a "direct realization" that is being "accomplished." Another discourse extant in Chinese reports that the Buddha was able to bear up "by entering such a kind of concentrative attainment, a concentration in which attention is not aware of the multitude of signs."[49] The reference to "such a kind of concentrative attainment" is a phrase often used in the early discourses to convey the sense of a meditative accomplishment that requires a considerable degree of meditative expertise. This fits the present episode of the Buddha's own management of physical pain, which clearly involves someone whom the early discourses present as having had a superb degree of meditative proficiency.

Nevertheless, the same potential can also be tapped, to a lesser degree, by those who are not as proficient in meditation, namely by not taking up the elaborations of "I am so sick" or "it is so painful." This does not mean that one should pretend to be healthy when afflicted by a disease. Whatever can reasonably be done in terms of taking medicine and adjusting behavior, food intake, etc., should certainly be done. Instead of encouraging the turning of a blind eye to health problems, the suggestion is much rather a call for bare awareness of the sensations that make up the pain. Through bare awareness it becomes possible to remain without making it "my pain," by just remaining mindful of it as "changing sensations."

This potential of bare awareness in facing pain and disease has been successfully tapped by Mindfulness-Based Stress Reduction and related programs, whose implementation precisely requires a basic training in mindfulness. Kabat-Zinn (1990/2013, 374) explains:

> Several classic laboratory experiments with acute pain showed that *tuning in* to sensations is a more effective way of reducing

> the level of pain experienced when the pain is intense and prolonged than is distracting yourself . . . the sensory, the emotional, and the cognitive/conceptual dimensions of the pain experience can be *uncoupled* from one another, meaning that they can be held in awareness as independent aspects of experience. Once you see that your thoughts about the sensations, for instance, are not the sensations themselves, both the experience of the sensory and the cognitive dimensions of the pain experience may change independently. This is also true for our emotional reactions to unpleasant sensory experience. This phenomenon of uncoupling can give us new degrees of freedom in resting in awareness and holding whatever arises in any or all of these three domains in an entirely different way, and dramatically reduce the suffering experienced.

A key aspect in the cultivation of such mindfulness appears to be the potential of bare awareness by way of not latching on to the sign of "pain" or of being "sick."

A Pāli discourse and its Chinese parallel illustrate this potential with the example of being shot by an arrow (translated by Bodhi 2000, 1264).[50] Reacting to the pain with aversion and grief compares to being shot by a second arrow. The additional pain of the second arrow, representing mental suffering, can be avoided through the cultivation of mindfulness.[51] Another relevant instruction can be found in a Pāli discourse and its two Chinese parallels, which report an instruction to an elderly and ailing lay disciple (translated by Bodhi 2000, 854). The relevant succinct injunction takes the following form in one of the Chinese versions: "even though the body is sick, let the mind not be sick!"[52]

The basic procedure for successfully avoiding the second arrow and not letting the mind become sick along with the body appears to be bare awareness, in the sense of a cultivation of mindfulness in such a way that grasping at the sign of "pain" or "disease" is avoided. Once again, this is not to say that the fact of being sick will no longer be recognized; the idea is not to ignore health problems. Instead, the task is to train in such a way that, in the words of the instruction to Bāhiya, in the sensed there will be

just the sensed. In terms of the explanations offered by the other monastic who reportedly received the same instruction, by practicing in this way the mind can learn to avoid being in bondage to attachment and bypass the tendency to give rise to various kinds of craving.

6. Unwholesome Thoughts and Conceit

The transformative potential of mindfulness directed to the mind's tendency to take up signs can also help to counter mental defilements. A Pāli discourse and its Chinese parallel relate this potential to the three types of unwholesome thoughts (translated by Bodhi 2000, 920). These three types are modes of thinking that are under the influence of sensuality, ill will, and harming. An antidote to these three modalities of detrimental rumination takes the following form in the Chinese version:[53]

> The mind being well settled in the four establishments of mindfulness or dwelling in concentration on the signless, cultivating it, cultivating it much, bad and unwholesome states will thereby cease and be forever eradicated without remainder.

A particularly significant aspect of this indication, found similarly in the Pāli parallel, is that this type of practice is not just a temporary remedy, a way of getting out of or avoiding the arising of unwholesome reactions in the mind. Instead, the present passage envisages the eradication of such thoughts, based on the mind being "well settled" in the four establishments of mindfulness (or "well established" according to the Pāli parallel) or else by way of cultivating concentration on signlessness.

The Chinese discourse translated above continues by indicating that someone who "cultivates concentration on the signless, having cultivated it, cultivated it much, dwells at the door of the deathless and proceeds to the supreme deathless of Nirvana."[54] Although the Pāli parallel is less explicit in this respect, it does encourage the cultivation of signless concentration, proclaiming that such practice will be of great fruit and great benefit.[55]

A minor point worth mentioning, given the pervasive tendency of Buddhist traditions from ancient to modern times to foreground the experience and practice of males, is that the Chinese version explicitly mentions female practitioners together with males as cultivators of concentration on the signless, done in such a way as to stand at the door of the deathless.[56] This indication is well in keeping with an episode in which a highly accomplished nun dismisses the silly idea that women are not as capable as men when it comes to reaching meditative realization. Her reply, reported in a Pāli discourse and two Chinese parallels, clarifies that the distinction between being a female and a male is irrelevant once the mind has reached concentration (translated by Bodhi 2000, 222).[57] The present passage confirms this indication, showing that the cultivation of signless concentration also goes beyond the type of sign sometimes associated with being a female or male.

Returning to the case of Bāhiya, according to Ñāṇananda (2015, 537) his practice of bare awareness would have issued in a realization of voidness or emptiness. In the early discourses, emptiness often refers in particular to the realization that there is no permanent self anywhere in experience. Another passage extant in Pāli and in several parallels takes up the related topic of conceit (translated by Bodhi 2000, 284). The relevant instruction in a Tibetan version of the discourse proceeds as follows:[58]

> Cultivate the signless,
> Quell the underlying tendency to conceit.
> Fully understanding conceit,
> The end of *dukkha/duḥkha* will be achieved.

Conceit in its various forms of hubris, arrogance, and selfing differs from other defilements like sensuality, ill will, and harming, as the latter are more easily discerned and often also create a more palpable state of affliction within. This makes it comparatively easier to recognize them and therefore to emerge from them. The same does not hold for conceit, especially in its more subtle manifestations, which in the early Buddhist scheme of progress to liberation will only be overcome completely when full awakening is attained. The reverse side of the same situation would then be that a penetrative understanding of conceit can lead to full awakening. In other words, although conceit features in early Buddhist meditation practice as a remarkable challenge, at the same time it also affords a remarkable opportunity.

In addition to cultivating signlessness, a method to counter conceit, presented in a Pāli discourse and its Chinese parallel, is perception of impermanence (translated by Bodhi 2000, 961).[59] Its effect in this respect compares to cutting through rootlets when ploughing or to taking hold of a rush that has been cut and shaking it (to get rid of its dry parts). In the same way, one takes hold of whatever has become the building block for being conceited and cuts it off or shakes it thoroughly with the help of contemplation of impermanence. The potential of perception of impermanence in overcoming conceit appears to be fulfilled best if directed specifically at what arouses conceit. For example, if one mindfully notices that conceit has arisen in relation to one's physical appearance, a reminder of its impermanence becoming manifest with the onset of old age can help set things into perspective.

The antidote of signlessness, however, would be operating in a more general manner. The very act of not paying attention to signs would prevent a precise targeting of whatever is the particular support for conceit. Instead, becoming aware of the constructed nature of experience in general, and hence by implication of the constructed nature of conceit, appears to fulfill the same purpose of overcoming it.

7. The Basics of Signless Concentration

The ability to gain signless concentration is not in itself a mark of being a liberated person. This becomes evident in a passage extant in Pāli and Chinese (translated by Bodhi 2012, 949). The latter proceeds as follows:[60]

> Suppose there is a person who attains signless concentration of the mind. Having attained signless concentration of the mind, they in turn dwell being at ease themselves and do not strive further with a wish to attain what has not yet been attained, with a wish to gain what has not been gained, with a wish to realize what has not been realized.

> At a later time, they in turn associate much with secular people, make fun, become conceited, and engage in all sorts of boisterous talk. As they associate much with secular people, make fun, become conceited, and engage in all sorts of boisterous talk, sensual desire in turn arises in the mind. Sensual desire having arisen in their mind, the body becomes in turn heated up and the mind becomes heated up [with passion]. The body and the mind having become heated up [with passion], they in turn abandon the moral precepts and stop [practicing] the path.

The passage describes a practitioner who has gone forth but then gives up the monastic life, which in the ancient setting was considered a dire misfortune. The two versions illustrate the inability of the mere practice of signless concentration to prevent such a misfortune with a simile. When a king and his army arrive in a forest, because of the resultant noise the chirping of the crickets will no longer be heard. It does not follow, however, that the chirping will never be heard again, which will be the case once the king and his army have left. In other words, the cultivation of signless concentration can have quite a powerful effect, comparable to the arrival of an army in a quiet forest. Yet, once the actual experience is over and its aftereffects have waned, the chirping of defilements can recur in the mind. Such potential recurrence holds as long as defilements have not been removed for good. Although signless concentration can become a powerful tool for accomplishing such removal, it does not ensure freedom from defilements on its own. In principle, it is possible for its remarkable effects to remain temporary, without resulting in a lasting transformation of the mind.

The discourse as a whole sounds a warning for the purpose of countering any mishandling of profound meditative experiences. An experience of signlessness as such falls short of being an awakening event. It would be misleading to believe that, because of having had such a profound meditation experience, there is no longer a need for wholehearted dedication to the practice of liberating insight, let alone of regular meditation. In fact, even the Buddha and his fully awakened disciples are on record for having continued their regular practice of meditation.[61] Meditation is not just a means to gain some attainment or other; it is a way of life, and for one who has reached the acme of inner purification this way of life is natural, even inevitable.

The early discourses mention two basic conditions for the actual practice of signless concentration. These already came up implicitly in relation to the Buddha managing pain by entering signless concentration through not giving attention to any signs (see above p. 24). A Pāli discourse and its Chinese parallel explicitly take up the two conditions required for attaining signless concentration or the signless liberation of the mind (translated by Ñāṇamoli 1995/2005, 393). The Chinese version proceeds as follows:[62]

> There are two causes, two conditions for arousing signless concentration. What are the two? The first is not being mindful of any sign, and the second is being mindful of the element of signlessness.

Whereas this passage speaks of being "mindful," the otherwise similar Pāli version instead uses the term "attention." This is not the only occasion where these two textual traditions show this type of terminological variation.[63] Strictly speaking, at least in early Buddhist thought these two mental qualities are distinct, as attention stands for something present in any state of mind, whereas mindfulness is not invariably present and therefore needs to be aroused.[64] Hence, with attention the main question is how to deploy it, in the sense of what is being attended to, whereas with mindfulness the basic task is to establish and cultivate it. However, this perspective changes in later times, and in the Sarvāstivāda tradition(s) mindfulness comes to be seen as a factor present in every state of mind,[65] thereby sharing the role played by attention in early Buddhist texts. Perhaps some such perspective influenced the Chinese translations (or the Indic originals). Such conflation of attention with mindfulness can also be seen in a quotation of the same basic indication in a later work, which also speaks of attention to the signless element, additionally qualified in the Chinese version of this work as being of the "right" type, a qualification not employed in its Tibetan counterpart.[66] The idea of "right attention" as such would correspond to "penetrative attention" (*yoniso manasikāra*) in Pāli terminology.[67]

Another point worth noting is that all versions explicitly mention the signless element as what the practitioner should be attending to. In the present context, attending to the signless element features as a condition in its own right. However, this is not invariably the case for other passages concerned with signless concentration. For example, in the case of the Buddha being sick, mentioned above (see p. 24), the parallels just mention his entering signless concentration, at times additionally explained as requiring not paying attention to any sign. It seems that in such contexts a reference to the signless element was not considered necessary, presumably due to it being implicitly covered by the idea of not attending to any signs.

The underlying rationale could be that, since attention is present in every moment of mental experience, once one does not attend to any sign, one must be attending to the absence of signs—that is, to the signless element. In order to provide a doctrinally exhaustive account of this type of meditative experience, listing attention to the signless element as a second, distinct condition serves to clarify that the absence of attention to any sign does not refer to a state in which perception no longer functions properly, such as, for example, being in the attainment of neither-perception-nor-nonperception or else being just unconscious.[68] In order to distinguish signless concentration from states in which perception no longer operates, it would indeed be necessary to stipulate two conditions: nonattention to signs and attention to signlessness. Nevertheless, from a practical viewpoint it is possible to speak just of the single condition of not taking up any sign at all.

The above-quoted presentation of entry into signless concentration continues by exploring the causes or conditions for remaining in it and for emerging from it. In these respects, the two versions differ. Besides the need to avoid taking up any sign and to keep attending to the signless element to remain in signless concentration, the Pāli version additionally stipulates "prior determination."[69] Among Pāli discourses, the particular phrasing used here seems unique. Such a reference is not found in the parallel and may be a later addition.

The two parallels agree that emergence requires the opposite to the procedure for entry, in that attention is no longer paid to the element of signlessness and instead is directed to any sign. The Chinese parallel adds to this as a third condition the existence of the body with the six sense spheres conditioned by the life faculty.[70] A comparable reference occurs in a discourse on emptiness to be taken up in more detail later, which is extant in Pāli, Chinese, and Tibetan. Here, such a reference occurs in relation to the realization of full awakening, based on a meditative trajectory that incorporates signless meditation (translated by Ñāṇamoli 1995/2005, 969).[71]

Although it remains questionable how far such a reference fits the present case, perhaps it could be related to the fact that, with signless meditation properly practiced, awareness of the body and the six sense spheres is to some extent left behind, as cognizing these would require taking up signs. When emerging from signless concentration, it would take at least a moment before the standard process of mental operation gets back into full swing, and at such a time a practitioner may indeed be just aware of the body and the receptivity through the senses as basic factors of being alive.

In sum, besides the interesting additional points that emerge from only one of the two versions, what they have in common is the need to avoid signs and direct the mind to (the element of) their absence as the conditions for entry and continuous abiding in signless concentration; emerging from it then requires the exact reverse.

The challenges of putting these indications into practice come up in a discourse that involves a chief disciple of the Buddha, Mahāmoggallāna/Mahāmaudgalyāyana, who describes his own practice. The Chinese version records this as follows:[72]

> I had this thought: "If a monastic is not mindful of any sign and attains the mental state of signlessness, dwells being endowed with its direct realization, that is called a noble abiding." I had this thought: "I shall [enter] this noble abiding of not being mindful of any sign and, attaining the mental state of signlessness, dwell being endowed with its direct realization, dwelling

> much in it." Having dwelled much in it, the taking up of signs arose in the mind.

The Pāli version does not employ the qualification "noble" or speak of a "direct realization." It also phrases the arising of distraction in a slightly different manner, namely in terms of consciousness following after signs (translated by Bodhi 2000, 1308). According to both versions, the Buddha approached Mahāmoggallāna/Mahāmaudgalyāyana personally to encourage him to avoid any negligence, which apparently had caused his taking up of signs.

In the Pāli textual collection, this event is part of a series of such interventions by the Buddha to guide and support Mahāmoggallāna/Mahāmaudgalyāyana in the cultivation of each of the four absorptions as well as the four immaterial spheres.[73] Since his cultivation of signless concentration is the last of these, this form of presentation could thus give the impression that such signless concentration requires previous mastery of these eight concentrative attainments. The standard description of the four absorptions makes it quite clear that these build on each other, and the same holds for the four immaterial spheres. Moreover, a Pāli discourse and its Chinese parallel indicate that the fourth absorption is the basis for cultivating the first immaterial sphere, confirming that the series of eight involves attainments that build on each other (translated by Ñāṇamoli 1995/2005, 558).[74] However, in the present case the Chinese version precedes Mahāmoggallāna/Mahāmaudgalyāyana's cultivation of signless concentration with only one such episode, in which he similarly receives the Buddha's help in stabilizing the attainment of the second absorption.[75]

In fact, listings of other concentrative attainments do not invariably imply that these must build on each other. An example is a listing of the four divine abodes (*brahmavihāra*) after the four absorptions and before the four immaterial spheres (translated by Ñāṇamoli 1995/2005, 454).[76] This does not imply that one needs mastery of the fourth absorption to cultivate the divine abodes, nor does it follow that a cultivation of the divine abodes is an indispensable prerequisite for attaining the immaterial spheres. In other words, although the four absorptions and the four immaterial spheres do form a series of practices that build on each other, the mention of other forms of concentration after the four absorptions does not necessarily intend the former to be an indispensable precondition for the latter. The same would apply to the episode discussed earlier, according to which a cultivator of signless concentration may still regress and eventually disrobe, an indication that in both versions occurs after a similar treatment has been applied to cultivators of the four absorptions.[77] Here, too, the mode of presentation need not be taken to imply that mastery of the four absorptions is indispensable for cultivating signless concentration.

In fact, there appears to be no explicit indication that previous mastery of the absorptions is indispensable for the practice of signless concentration. The term "concentration" as such can refer to a fairly broad range of experiences and does not invariably denote absorption. For example, *samādhi* designates the cultivation of walking meditation in a Pāli discourse (translated by Bodhi 2012, 651), an indication similarly found in the parallels.[78]

At the same time, however, the difficulties experienced by Mahāmoggallāna/Mahāmaudgalyāyana make it clear that concentrative abilities are quite an asset when attempting to stay free from taking up signs. The point of this brief exploration is thus certainly not to dismiss the benefit of being able to gain deeper levels of concentration. Instead, the suggestion is only that cultivating signless concentration does not appear to come with explicitly stipulated prerequisites and thus need not be considered confined to those who have already mastered absorption. What such practice appears to require above all is a high degree of mindfulness and experience in working with the mind's tendency to take up signs, such as can be developed through sense restraint and the cultivation of bare awareness.

The description of Mahāmoggallāna/Mahāmaudgalyāyana getting distracted by taking up signs has a counterpart in another statement made in a Pāli discourse and its parallels, according to which an abiding in signlessness will not be lost by someone who has developed signless concentration well (translated by Walshe 1987, 501).[79] The two passages, considered together, can be taken as conveying two complementary points: If even a highly accomplished practitioner like Mahāmoggallāna/

Mahāmaudgalyāyana got lost by taking up signs, the same is only to be expected for anyone who takes up the same practice. At the same time, however, with continued dedication to this form of practice, such distractions will occur less and less often, until eventually it becomes possible to dwell for sustained periods of time in signlessness.

8. Nonattention or Attending to Absence

The circumstance that signless concentration does not really have a circumscribed object implies that here the term *samādhi* would not stand for cultivating some form of an exclusive mental focus. Instead, it appears to involve a meditative stance in which mindfulness as a mental condition of open receptivity would be prominent, enabling letting go as soon as the mind reaches out for any sign in an attempt to get back into its usual rut of mental activity. At the same time, however, any floating around also needs to be avoided, which can be achieved through a penetrative attention to the element of signlessness. In combination with the open receptivity of well-established mindfulness, such attention can be directed toward the absence of processing any sign.

Further support for the idea of cultivating a type of concentration that does not involve an exclusive focus can be garnered from a recurrent definition of the faculty (*indriya*) of concentration in Pāli discourses, although it needs to be kept in mind that this is not found in parallel versions. According to this definition, on "having made letting go the basis, one will gain concentration and will gain unification of the mind."[80] From a practical perspective, this could be taken to convey a helpful indication for cultivating a type of *samādhi* that is not dependent on focusing on a particular object.

The Pāli discourse with the above quote describes how such concentration through letting go builds on the previous cultivation of the other three faculties of confidence, energy, and mindfulness (translated by Bodhi 2000, 1694). It then leads on to cultivating the faculty of wisdom in the form of understanding that the cycle of birth and death, *saṃsāra*, is without a discoverable beginning point: one cannot identify a starting point for the predicament of being under the influence of ignorance and craving.[81] Yet, one can bring about the cessation of ignorance and realize Nirvana, or the deathless. This concords with the general position in early Buddhism of not conceiving of the realization of awakening as some form of a return to a primordial source or ground of existence.

The description provided in this discourse gives the impression that such *samādhi* need not be seen as confined to the experience of Nirvana itself.[82] Instead, it seems to have a preparatory role in bringing about liberating wisdom. This role appears to be based on inculcating the principle of letting go. In addition to eventually fostering the actual breakthrough to awakening, letting go can indeed be cultivated when developing concentration. Needless to say, such a form of concentration would not be without its challenges, as it apparently does not rely on focusing on a specific circumscribed object and thereby differs from the usual approaches for cultivating mental stability. It may be for this reason that another Pāli passage states that only few sentient beings gain such concentration, compared to the many who do not gain it (translated by Bodhi 2012, 122).[83]

The need to develop the ability to let go, apparently required for this particular approach to concentration, would hold all the more for the specific case of signlessness, which calls for letting go of any sign. This is thereby a form of "nonattention" (*amanasikāra*), or else, to put it differently, a form of meditatively attending to what is absent. Taking some form of an absence as a meditation object is indeed a significant dimension of early Buddhist mindfulness practices in general.[84]

A basic modality of such attending to absence can take place when someone or something is arousing resentment and irritation in oneself, in particular when one's own reactivity becomes somewhat obsessive. In such a case, it can be very helpful to make an intentional effort not to attend to those features or activities of the other that trigger such reactions. The Pāli instruction (translated by Bodhi 2012, 774) speaks of cultivating "nonmindfulness" (*asati*) and "nonattention" (*amanasikāra*).[85] Needless to say, this is neither a strategy of in principle trying to avoid all difficulties or challenges nor an encouragement to dwell in a mental condition of utter distraction bereft of mindfulness. To the contrary, firmly established mindfulness in its monitoring function would be required to maintain a nonreactive mental condition. This would also ensure that the lesson to be learned from whatever challenge has presented itself will not be missed. At the same time, the continuous presence of mindfulness can alert one to excessive importance being given to irritating traits, which can potentially trigger unwholesome reactivity. Noticing this soon enough can result in letting go of these particular signs and in no longer paying attention to them.

The benefits of an intentional cultivation of a type of nonattention are not confined to encountering difficult people. The same form of practice can also be turned to good use when having to face difficult conditions in one's own mind. Such a type of nonattention features as one in a series of five methods for dealing with unwholesome types of thoughts (translated by Ñāṇamoli 1995/2005, 212). The recommendation here is that one should no longer give attention to what triggers those unwholesome thoughts. The Pāli version of the relevant instruction again speaks of "nonmindfulness" and "nonattention"; the Chinese parallel only mentions "nonmindfulness."[86]

If such an approach for emerging from obsessive unwholesome thoughts has been successful, a continuity in meditatively attending to absence could take the form of mindful contemplation of mental states in accordance with the instruction given in the *Satipaṭṭhānasutta* and its parallels. In addition to encouraging the recognition of sensual lust, anger, and delusion in the mind, the three parallel versions make it a task of mindfulness to recognize their absence as well. Hence, mindfulness practice can take the form of knowing that, for example, anger is (at least temporarily) absent from the mind (translated by Ñāṇamoli 1995/2005, 150).[87] Such a form of mindfulness is not just about the momentary recognition of the absence of a particular defilement; it can also take the form of a prolonged awareness of the usually very agreeable condition of the mind, its texture and quality, when not overpowered by defilements. In fact, alongside the important task of honestly recognizing defilements in one's own mind, the instructions equally accord importance to an acknowledgment of their absence. The role of mindfulness here is to be aware of the "presence" of such absence.

The notion of absence can be taken further through the formal cultivation of deep states of mental tranquility, where in particular the third immaterial sphere of nothingness involves a meditative experience of total absence. Although this profound attainment requires considerable meditative expertise, the perception of nothingness as such is also part of a gradual meditation on emptiness, to be explored in more detail below (see p. 53).

Another meditative approach toward nothingness, which also resonates with emptiness in the sense of the absence of a self, emerges from a Pāli discourse and its Chinese and Tibetan parallels whose main teaching revolves around the topic of imperturbability (*āneñja/āniñjya*). Together with the discourse describing a gradual meditation on emptiness, the present discourse on imperturbability reflects a fascinating interplay between tranquility and insight. The gradual meditation on emptiness employs perceptions related to tranquility, in particular to the immaterial spheres, as a means of cultivating insight into emptiness. The discourse on imperturbability employs perceptions from the domain of insight to cultivate tranquility.[88] For example, alternative approaches to gaining the meditative imperturbability of deep concentration are based on insight into the nature of material form and into the impermanent nature of perceptions. Another example of employing insight to cultivate tranquility, proposed in this discourse, concerns progress to attaining the immaterial sphere of nothingness. Such attainment is here based on the insightful contemplation that the present experience is void of a self and what belongs to a self (translated by Ñāṇamoli 1995/2005, 871).[89] Attending to this type of absence would go right to the heart of early Buddhist doctrine.

With these different approaches for meditatively attending to absence, or else for cultivating nonattention, it becomes possible to turn a whole range of daily life situations and meditative experiences into preparatory work for dwelling in signless concentration. This is of considerable significance, since not everyone lives in a situation that affords the freedom of dedicating as much time as one would want to formal practice. Taking advantage of the potential of daily life situations as learning opportunities can go a long way in preparing the mind so that, when the occasion for formal meditation manifests, this can unfold its full potential. The key aspect throughout is to learn to let go of latching on to signs, thereby becoming increasingly at ease and comfortable with the presence of an absence.

9. Characteristics of Signless Concentration

More information relevant to the practice of signless concentration can be gathered from a passage that describes its actual undertaking. The Chinese version of the relevant discourse, which involves a nun querying the Buddha's attendant Ānanda about the outcome of a certain type of meditation practice, offers the following description:[90]

> If not rising up and not sinking down [when being in] signless concentration of the mind, having become freed, one is stable, and having become stable, one is freed.

Ānanda explains that the Buddha had declared such meditation to have (liberating) knowledge as its outcome. A quotation of this type of description in a later exegetical text extant in Chinese provides more details:[91]

> If there is no rising up and no sinking down [when] attaining signless concentration of the mind, gathering and keeping all volitional constructions like a water dike, one is stable because of being freed, and one is freed because of being stable.

The same work explains that the outcome to be expected from such meditation is liberation and the destruction of the influxes, adding that Ānanda's reply served as an encouragement to the nun that she will soon attain this lofty goal.[92] The exegetical text also offers comments on the idea of gathering and keeping all volitional constructions. It indicates that arousing much application to volitional constructions would result in much employment of exertion. Apparently by way of providing a contrast, the passage continues by pointing out that it is rather due to a superbly skillful deployment of attention that one attains such concentration.[93]

According to the information provided in this way, signless concentration involves a reciprocally conditioning interrelationship between being freed and being stable. Here, being freed appears to intend temporary mental freedom rather than perpetual freedom. In fact, the reported exchange conveys the impression that the nun had not yet attained complete freedom. For this reason, she was asking about the outcome of such practice, otherwise she would have already known the answer from her own practice.

The early discourses in general employ the term "freedom," or "liberation," (*vimutti/vimukti*) in a range of different ways, with considerable room for temporary liberation of the mind in the form of abiding in states of concentration that do not require or imply the attainment of any level of awakening.[94] In the present case of signless concentration, the mind would have been freed from distraction by way of not taking up any sign. This very freedom supports the stability of the meditative abiding. As already mentioned above, the absence of a circumscribed object prevents one from relying on a focused type of concentration to attain mental stability. Instead, stability of the mind relies on the condition of being freed, and that condition of being freed from getting distracted by taking up signs in turn relies for its continuity on the very mental stability gained in this way.

The discourse passage translated above precedes the interrelatedness of freedom and stability with a reference to neither rising up nor sinking. The exegetical work extant in Chinese provides an additional specification, which appears to convey a sense of effortlessness. All volitional constructions are kept in check in a way comparable to a dike that keeps water from spilling over.

Turning from these Chinese sources to the Pāli parallel, the latter reports the nun's description in this way:[95]

> Not leaning forward and not leaning backward, concentration is reached without exertion by holding in check and restraining. Through being freed, one is stable; through being stable, one is contented; and through being contented, one is not agitated.[96]

Ānanda replies that the Buddha had declared such meditation practice to have liberating knowledge as its fruit. Note that the Pāli version does not qualify this concentration to be of the signless type.[97] Nevertheless, in a groundbreaking study of signless meditations in Pāli texts, Harvey (1986,

26) considered the present Pāli discourse as "indicating something of the nature of *animitta* states."

In fact, closer inspection of the Pāli version supports the indication made explicitly in the Chinese discourse that the concentration under discussion would indeed be of the signless type. The first part of the Pāli discourse, which has no counterpart in Chinese, sets out on a description of a conscious state wherein the five senses and their objects are present but are not being experienced (translated by Bodhi 2012, 1301).[98] The ensuing explanation then lists the three lower immaterial attainments, followed by the above description. The context provided in this way makes it safe to propose that the Pāli version has indeed the signless concentration in mind. Besides, the awakening potential of signless concentration is also recorded in another Pāli discourse (translated by Bodhi 2012, 1053).[99]

The Pāli commentary on the present passage considers the concentration described to be the fruition attainment of an arahant/arhat. In order to arrive at this interpretation, the commentary assumes that the nun had been asking about something she did not understand.[100] This fails to take into account the preceding description in this Pāli discourse of the five senses and their objects being present but not experienced. Such a description does not fit an experience of Nirvana, which involves the cessation of all six sense spheres (to be discussed in more detail in the second part of my study). The context provided by the Pāli discourse rather seems to confirm the explicit indication given in the Chinese version that the topic is signless concentration.

Another significant difference between the parallels is that, instead of an interrelation between mental stability and being free, the Pāli version presents a conditional sequence that leads from being freed via stability to being contented, which in turn results in being without agitation. In addition, the Pāli discourse has a somewhat complex reference to volitional constructions, which is not found in the Chinese version.

The same reference occurs in several other Pāli discourses. In one case the parallels have no corresponding expression, and in another instance no parallels are known (translated by Walshe 1987, 515 and Bodhi 2012, 647, respectively).[101] In yet another case (translated by Bodhi 2012, 336), a similar expression does occur in a parallel version, which conveys the sense of attaining a concentration that "is not being controlled by volitional constructions" or else perhaps not "kept" up or "maintained" by them.[102]

Turning to an interpretation of these descriptions, the need to avoid any leaning forward or backward could in principle be taken to point to the need to keep the mind balanced, neither too lax nor too loose. With other types of concentration, some degree of suppression or control has precisely this function. Given that the present case quite explicitly rescinds such an approach, it would be meaningful to indicate explicitly that the proposed modality of cultivating concentration needs to beware of a loss of balance. According to the *Yogācārabhūmi*, the idea of not leaning forward or backward conveys that not giving attention to signs takes place without repulsion toward them and without clinging to the signless element.[103] On following this meaningful indication, with the mind well established in the present moment, the task would then be to avoid taking up signs without arousing a sense of negativity toward them and to maintain attention on their absence (the "signless element") without clinging to that absence.

The Pāli commentarial tradition, however, understands this phrase to refer to the absence of defilements in one who has eradicated them and hence does not need to make an effort to keep them at bay.[104] This gloss appears to be based on the assumption that the concentration described intends the fruition attainment of an arahant/arhat. As already mentioned above, this identification does not provide a convincing understanding of the main passage under discussion, which appears to refer to a concentration experience accessible by those who have not yet eradicated all defilements.

In actual practice, the appropriate attitude toward signs could perhaps be illustrated with deciduous trees at the time of shedding their leaves in autumn. This is an active shedding; in fact, the difference between a tree getting ready for winter and a tree that has just died is precisely that in the latter case the leaves stay on. But this active shedding is not a forceful act; it involves no repulsion. Instead, it is just a letting go of something that is of no further use. Similarly, the taking up of signs, which is central to the normal functioning of perception comparable to the role of the leaves for the functioning of a deciduous tree during spring and summer, is at this stage of no more use. Like those leaves, it can be allowed to drop off to the ground, as it were.

Although directing the mind toward signlessness is inevitably an active process, at the same time it need not be forceful at all. It appears to require simply a letting go of signs as soon as these are taken up and then relaxing into their absence—that is, into the presence of their absence. This should then be done without turning the resultant experience of inner freedom into something that is clung to or grasped.

The sense of inner freedom to be expected from such practice stands, according to all versions, in a direct relationship to mental stability. Two different perspectives emerge here. One perspective is the reciprocal relationship between freedom and stability, where the one supports the other. The other perspective shows how stability leads to contentment, which in turn fosters the absence of agitation. The indications offered in this way are quite helpful from the viewpoint of actual practice. In particular contentment appears to be rather crucial. Cultivating an attitude of contentment can arouse a pleasant feeling tone, a subtle sense of quiet joy, which in turn can help increase mental stability. Moreover, it can safely be assumed that discontent would be a major force making the mind turn away from the absence of signs and reach out for something more entertaining. Hence, contentment can be expected to offer substantial help for abiding in the total absence of signs, and therewith in the absence of the usual mental operations of making sense and conceptualizing, without succumbing to distraction.

Another dimension is the relationship of signless concentration to volitional constructions. These become as if gathered by a water dike, something achieved by diminishing mental exertion. This must be intending a rather subtle type of practice. Although forceful application of the mind may have had its place earlier, in case defilements manifested, at this point any such exertion needs to be left aside and practice evolves into becoming increasingly effortless, free of suppression or restraint. In a way, the very tendency of the mind to fabricate experience is called into question.

10. Subdued Perception and Unestablished Consciousness

Additional perspectives that may in one way or another provide further background to the cultivation of signless concentration can be gathered from a few selected passages related to the attainment of neither-perception-nor-nonperception, the highest in the series of four immaterial spheres, and from the notion of consciousness as unestablished.

The concentrative attainment of neither-perception-nor-nonperception shares with signlessness a stepping out of the usual functioning of perception. Whereas signlessness achieves this by dropping the sign, the attainment of neither-perception-nor-nonperception, as its name indicates, involves subduing perception up to a point where one can no longer really speak of being perceptive but at the same time also not of being in a state of nonperception. The successful attainment of neither-perception-nor-nonperception appears to require previous mastery of the four absorptions and a meditative progression through the preceding three immaterial spheres (infinite space, infinite consciousness, and nothingness). This much does not appear to be required for signless concentration, which does not need concentration of such a depth as to enable a subduing of perception to the extent that it becomes difficult to say whether it is present or absent. Instead, signless concentration maintains perception in its full clarity, only with the mind no longer processing sense data.

During his quest for liberation, the Buddha-to-be reportedly mastered the attainment of neither-perception-nor-nonperception.[105] Yet, he realized that it did not lead to the type of complete freedom that he was searching for. This could be taken to imply that the path to liberation does not require interfering with the basic operational mechanism of perception to such a degree that one is no longer perceptive. Although the early Buddhist meditative path can lead to some extraordinary experiences, progress to liberation requires above all insight into the way perception constructs the world. Even the attainment of the most refined of the four immaterial spheres is subordinate to such insight, which is the key factor in leading to liberation.

A passage related to the attainment of neither-perception-nor-nonperception could be briefly taken up, as its main import is also relevant to signless concentration. This is the following recommendation in a Pāli discourse:[106]

> The Blessed One has commended nonidentification even with the attainment of neither-perception-nor-nonperception.

The Pāli term translated here as "nonidentification" refers literally to "the condition of not being made of that" (*atammayatā/atanmayatā*). Such nonidentification, in the sense of not turning meditative experiences into building blocks for the construction of an ego as a meditator, is of central relevance to signlessness or any other type of practice.[107]

An additional tool that points in the same direction would be an aspiration apparently related to the attainment of neither-perception-nor-nonperception. One out of several occurrences of a Buddhist rewording of this aspiration takes the form of an inspired utterance (*udāna*) attributed to the Buddha, in the sense of being a short statement expressing some form of inspiration. The Sanskrit version proceeds as follows:[108]

> One in whom in every respect
> Mindfulness of the body is continuously established [reflects]:
> "It might not be, and it might not be for me.
> It will not be, and it will not be for me!"
> Dwelling thus progressively,
> One will in time transcend attachment.

The reference to "it" requires a bit of exploration. Before coming to that, it could be noted that the closely similar Pāli parallel precedes the actual inspired utterance with a narrative (translated by Ireland 1990, 105). According to this narrative, the inspired utterance was occasioned by the Buddha seeing a monastic cultivating such mindfulness of the body.

The dictum given in the above form apparently presents a reformulation of an aspiration employed by some ancient Indian practitioners who considered neither-perception-nor-nonperception to be the final goal.

The practitioners in question seem to pertain to the category of annihilationists,[109] in the sense that they apparently took the cultivation of the meditative attainment of neither-perception-nor-nonperception to result in the annihilation of the self at death. The decisive difference, compared to the dictum in the above instruction, is that the annihilationist version reads "I might not be" and "I will not be."[110] From a Buddhist perspective, there is no self in the first place that needs to be annihilated, therefore what should be annihilated is much rather clinging to self-notions.[111] The successful completion of such annihilation with full awakening also does not require waiting for the time of one's death. Hence, in the Buddhist version of the dictum, the "I" is dropped and the aspiration becomes simply "it might not be" and "it will not be," presumably referring to the absence of clinging.

The above inspired utterance relates the Buddhist formulation of this dictum to mindfulness of the body. In the present context, given that such mindfulness is to be combined with an insight reflection, the idea would probably be for awareness of the whole body to be held in the periphery of the sphere of attention, rather than being its main object. In this way, mindfulness of the body could serve as a sort of backdrop that does not interfere with the main practice and instead supports it by ensuring continuity through being mindfully rooted in the presence of the body.

Another significant feature of the inspired utterance is that it qualifies the main practice as a progressive (*anupubba/anupūrva*) type of dwelling. This could be taken to imply that at first the appropriate reflection would be "it might not be, and it might not be for me." With substantial progress accomplished, a change to the more affirmative and confident "it will not be, and it will not be for me" would fall into place. As the inspired utterance indicates, both aspirations equally serve to "transcend attachment." This is the target toward which they are to be aimed.

The same dictum recurs in another Pāli discourse, which in agreement with its Chinese parallel contrasts clinging to self-notions to seeing the true nature of the five aggregates of clinging (translated by Bodhi 2000, 892).[112] The two parallels continue by depicting progress from nonreturn to full awakening, which leads to consciousness no longer being established on any of the five aggregates of clinging. The resultant condition finds description in the following excerpt, taken from the Chinese version:[113]

> Because consciousness is not established anywhere, it does not increase; because of not increasing, it is not active anywhere; because of not being active anywhere, it is stable; because of being stable, it is contented; because of being contented, it is freed; because of being freed, there is no clinging to anything in the whole world; because of not clinging to anything, there is no being attached to anything. Because of not being attached to anything, one personally realizes Nirvana.

The reference to the unestablished consciousness in the above description, found similarly in the Pāli version, concerns progress from nonreturn to full awakening. Both versions incorporate indications that elsewhere relate to signless concentration. This holds particularly for the interrelation between inner stability, contentment, and freedom. In view of this similarity, it seems worthwhile to explore briefly the notion of a type of consciousness that is unestablished (*appatiṭṭhita/apratiṣṭhita*).

An illustration of the nature of an unestablished consciousness can be found in a passage whose Chinese version proceeds as follows:[114]

> [The Buddha said to the monastics:] "Monastics, [take,] for example, an upper room in a palace which is wide [along] its northern and western [axes] and which has windows on the eastern and western [walls]. The sun arising in the eastern direction, where will it shine?"
>
> The monastics said to the Buddha: "It will shine on the western wall."
>
> The Buddha said to the monastics: "If there is no wall to the west, where will it shine?"
>
> The monastics said to the Buddha: "It will shine in empty space, being without a support."

The Pāli version presents basically the same image in more detail, as the question-and-answer exchange leads from the absence of a western wall to the alternative possibilities that the sunbeam will shine on the earth, in the absence of which it will shine on water (in line with the ancient Indian cosmological belief that the earth rests on water), and in the absence of that it will not be established anywhere (translated by Bodhi 2000, 601).

In both versions, the simile illustrates a type of consciousness that, due to the eradication of all lust, will not lead on to a future existence and its inevitable *dukkha/duḥkha*. Other discourses confirm that the notion of an unestablished consciousness expresses an arahant's/arhat's successful gaining of freedom from the prospect of future rebirth.[115] At times, the same expression serves to describe the actual passing away of an arahant/arhat (translated by Bodhi 2000, 214).[116] In fact, an otherwise unrelated Pāli discourse employs the similar qualification of not being established (*appatiṭṭha/apratiṣṭha*) to designate Nirvana.[117]

Of additional significance are references to an unestablished consciousness as part of explicit indications that it is not possible to point out a type of consciousness that is apart from the other four aggregates (translated by Bodhi 2000, 890–94).[118] This type of indication would serve to prevent reifying the idea of a type of consciousness that is unestablished.[119]

In sum, sustained practice of signless concentration can lead to full awakening and thereby to consciousness no longer being established. At the same time, such a consciousness is not something that exists in its own right, apart from the other aggregates. Instead, it simply stands for the mind of an arahant/arhat, or one who is on the brink to becoming one, and hence for one whose consciousness will not become established in another birth.

11. Awakening and Emptiness

A relationship between signlessness and emptiness can be seen in a listing of three concentrations with the potential of leading to awakening, given in a Pāli discourse and its Chinese parallel. The listing includes signless concentration and concentration on emptiness (translated by Bodhi 2012, 376).[120]

Before exploring concentration on emptiness further, I would like to note that, in early Buddhist usage, to qualify something as empty concerns an absence, usually a specific one. This ties in well with the topics explored above, in that such a qualification conveys what something is empty of. For example, a particular place may be empty of people or else a particular person may be empty of a certain quality.[121] The most central concern of such a notion of emptiness, in its early Buddhist usage, is to clarify that all aspects of subjective experience are entirely empty of a self or some kind of permanent entity or substance.

Another point worthy of note is that the notion of emptiness as the absence of a self is not confined to the case of persons but comprises the whole world of experience. A verse succinctly conveys this as follows: "Always mindful, one should contemplate the whole world as empty."[122] Another verse states that all phenomena are not self (translated by Norman 1997/2004, 41).[123] In fact, it is a distinctive quality of arahants/arhats that they see elements representative of material phenomena, together with consciousness, as thoroughly devoid of a self or of a substantial, unchanging entity (translated by Ñāṇamoli 1995/2005, 905).[124]

The relationship between signlessness and meditation on emptiness receives coverage in a Chinese discourse that does not have a Pāli parallel. The discourse sets out by indicating that cultivating emptiness meditation prepares the ground for signlessness:[125]

> If one has attained [concentration on] emptiness, one is able to give rise to [concentration on] signlessness, [concentration on] nothingness, and have knowledge and vision of being free from conceit.

The discourse then expounds concentration on emptiness in this manner:[126]

> Suppose monastics sit down in an empty place at the root of a tree and well contemplate form as being impermanent, being of a nature to wear away and to fade away. In the same way they contemplate feeling tone . . . perception . . . volitional constructions . . . consciousness as being impermanent, being of a nature to wear away and to fade away. Contemplating those

aggregates as being impermanent, of a nature to wear away, to be unstable, and to change, their minds are delighted, purified, and liberated. This is called [concentration on] emptiness. Those who contemplate in this way, even though they are not yet able to be free from conceit, purify their knowledge and vision.

Furthermore, with right attention and concentration they contemplate the abandoning of the sign of forms and the abandoning of the sign of sounds, odors, flavors, tangibles, and mental objects. This is called [concentration on] signlessness. Those who contemplate in this way, even though they are not yet free from conceit, purify their knowledge and vision.

Furthermore, with right attention and concentration they contemplate the abandoning of the sign of lust and the abandoning of the signs of anger and of delusion. This is called [concentration on] nothingness. Those who contemplate in this way, even though they are not yet free from conceit, purify their knowledge and vision.

Furthermore, with right attention and concentration they contemplate: "From where do [the notions] 'I' and 'mine' arise?" Furthermore, with right attention and concentration they contemplate: "[The notions] 'I' and 'mine' arise from whatever is seen, whatever is heard, whatever is smelled, whatever is tasted, whatever is touched, and whatever is cognized."

They further contemplate like this: "Whatever causes and whatever conditions give rise to consciousness, are those causes and conditions for consciousness permanent or impermanent?" They further reflect like this: "Whatever causes and whatever conditions give rise to consciousness, all those causes and those conditions for consciousness are entirely impermanent." Furthermore: "All those causes and those conditions being entirely impermanent, how could consciousness, which arises from them, be permanent?" That which is impermanent is a conditioned construct; it has arisen from conditions, and it is of a perilous nature, of a nature to

> cease, of a nature to fade away, of a nature to be abandoned with understanding.

The passage translated above relates emptiness to a penetrative insight into the impermanent nature of each of the five aggregates of clinging. The importance of impermanence comes up again in the final part, targeting the one aggregate whose transient nature indeed needs to be fully recognized to ensure genuine progress toward awakening: consciousness. The continuous presence of the faculty of knowing or cognizing throughout all experiences can easily give the misleading impression that consciousness is somehow permanent. Yet, even consciousness is impermanent, arisen from conditions, and hence to be let go of as well.

Signlessness in turn finds its application in relation to the objects of the senses.[127] In this way, based on insight into the impermanent nature of the five aggregates, practice proceeds to the six senses by way of signlessness, in the sense that the signs that usually arise in relation to the objects of these senses should be abandoned. The discourse then takes up in particular the signs of lust, anger, and delusion. This highlights the key function of signless forms of practice, which is to overcome mental defilements. These impact perception through the basic process of taking up signs. Cultivating signlessness can furnish a basis for understanding and countering the only too easily overlooked impact of defilements on what is experienced.

The practice next turns toward the source on which defilements thrive: selfing. This takes the form of an inquiry: whence does this sense of "I" and "mine" arise? Just as the three root defilements, this sense of "I" and "mine" comes embedded in the taking up of signs when seeing, hearing, etc. In this way, the groundwork laid in emptiness leads to signlessness, which in turn finds its complement in a deepening appreciation of emptiness. The dynamics behind such deepening appreciation could be understood along the lines of a comment by Ñāṇananda (2015, 580) that when "there is no grasping at signs, there is no direction or expectation, in the absence of which, existence ceases to appear substantial."

12. A Gradual Meditation on Emptiness

A complementary perspective on the interrelationship between signlessness and emptiness emerges from the Smaller Discourse on Emptiness, extant in Pāli, Chinese, and Tibetan. The parallel versions depict a gradual meditative approach to emptiness that leads up to signless concentration (translated by Ñāṇamoli 1995/2005, 965). The starting point is a statement by the Buddha that he often dwelled in emptiness, and the ensuing instructions provide a practical approach for emulating him in this respect. This practical approach takes the situation in which the Buddha and his audience found themselves at that moment as its starting point, drawing attention to the monastic dwelling being empty of elephants and horses, etc.—in other words, empty of the hustle and bustle of ancient Indian city life.

Attention then proceeds to the perception of the forest, the perception of earth, and then the perceptions corresponding to the first three of the four immaterial spheres: infinite space, infinite consciousness, and nothingness, each of which should be contemplated as empty of the perceptions cultivated just previously. The Pāli version also takes up the fourth immaterial sphere, neither-perception-nor-nonperception, which comparative study shows with high probability to be a textual error.[128] The Chinese and Tibetan parallels instead proceed directly from nothingness to signlessness, which then forms the springboard for the breakthrough to awakening in all three versions. In terms of emptiness as a reference to an absence, such signlessness is empty of any sign.

The perceptual progression described in relation to each of the above perceptions can be illustrated with the example of the transition to signlessness, which in the Chinese version takes the following form:[129]

> Again, Ānanda, if monastics wish to dwell much in emptiness, those monastics should not be mindful of the perception of the sphere of infinite consciousness and not be mindful of the perception of the sphere of nothingness but should frequently be mindful of the unitary signless concentration of the mind.

> In this way they know: "[This is] empty of the perception of the sphere of infinite consciousness and empty of the perception of the sphere of nothingness. Yet, there is non-emptiness: just the unitary signless concentration of the mind."
>
> [They know:] "Whatever weariness there is because of the perception of the sphere of infinite consciousness, that is not there for me; whatever weariness there is because of the perception of the sphere of nothingness, that is also not there for me. There is only the weariness because of the unitary signless concentration of the mind."
>
> Whatever is not present herein, they for this reason see it as being empty; whatever remains present, they see as being truly present. Ānanda, this is reckoned to be dwelling in true emptiness, without distortion.

The instructions begin by emphasizing that the two previously developed perceptions (in the present case those of infinite consciousness and of nothingness) should be disregarded in order to devote oneself fully to the present step. The reference to "perception," found similarly in the parallel versions, is of considerable practical import, as it differs from the way the early discourses usually introduce the actual attainment of an immaterial sphere. The implication that can be drawn from this is that the practice described here does not require mastery of the immaterial spheres (which in turn appears to require mastery of the fourth absorption as a foundation). Instead, arousing a unitary mental condition based on the relevant perception appears to suffice for being able to put into practice the gradual approach to emptiness.

The meditative trajectory comes interwoven with an awareness of the type of weariness or disturbance that has been left behind through such meditative progression. This awareness has its counterpart in a clear recognition that some subtler degree of weariness or disturbance is still present, which is precisely the perception cultivated at present.

Such attending to the ultimately unsatisfactory nature of these rather sublime and subtle meditative perceptions is framed in terms of emptiness: present experience is empty of what has been left behind and not empty of what is still there. Once signlessness has been reached in this way, the final step to the breakthrough to awakening takes slightly different forms in the three parallels. Here is the Chinese version of this final step:[130]

> One reflects: "I am based on the signless concentration of the mind, which is based on being volitionally constructed and based on being intended. What is based on being volitionally constructed and based on being intended, I do not delight in that, do not seek that; I should not become established in that."

Whereas the Chinese version places importance on not delighting in such an experience, seeking it, and becoming established in it, the Tibetan parallel expresses the same in terms of not approving and not becoming attached to it:[131]

> One reflects: "Yet, the signless element is constructed and produced by the mind. It is not suitable to delight in what is constructed and produced by the mind, to approve of it, to become attached to it, or to remain attached to it."

Given the profundity of the meditative experience of signless concentration, cultivated as the final step in an already rather remarkable series of meditative experiences, the challenge of attachment (and of becoming "established" in relation to this meditative experience, to use the terminology from the Chinese parallel) is quite a pertinent concern. The Pāli version offers a practical tool for avoiding excessive delight and attachment:[132]

> One understands: "Even this signless concentration of the mind is constructed and produced by volition; whatever is constructed and produced by volition is impermanent and of a nature to cease."

Combining the indications provided in the parallel versions, signless concentration should be seen as impermanent, in order to avoid delight and attachment. In this way, it can fulfill its purpose in the present context of leading to liberating insight into emptiness. The three versions agree that their respective reflections can lead to the destruction of the influxes, corresponding to full awakening. In this way, the mind can be emptied of defilements, a mental condition the Pāli and Tibetan versions explicitly qualify as the supreme type of emptiness.[133]

When viewed from the meditative trajectory that leads up to this culmination point, a progressive refinement of emptiness experiences culminates in the irreversible and perpetual condition of the mind being empty of defilements with full awakening. This condition holds no matter what experiences may present themselves at any sense door. In this way, the gradual training in ever-subtler perceptions, leading up to signlessness, has a purpose that points beyond meditative perceptions, including those related to emptiness. Just like all other types of experience, even such profound meditative perceptions arise and eventually disappear. The key question is therefore to what extent any such meditative perception can become a tool to transform the mind, changing the way one relates to any experience, be it in profound meditation or daily life. Remaining empty of defilements is the key aspect underlying meditation on emptiness in early Buddhist thought and at the same time also serves as the orientation point for a cultivation of signless concentration.

13. Summary

The sign is the characteristic mark of something that enables its identification and recognition. The basic operational mechanism of perception relies in particular on those signs that correspond to features less liable to change, thereby almost inevitably introducing an assumption and repeated confirmation of permanency into the very fabric of cognition. The providing of signs for others to form certain associations and arrive at particular evaluations is a pervasive dimension of human behavior, impacting ways of behaving, dressing, speaking, etc. In a more general sense, the sign stands at the very root of conceptualization and linguistic usages.

The taking up of signs during the process of perception tends to combine sensory data with various evaluations and projections, which often happens without being noticed. As a result, subjective evaluations and biases are perceived as if these were intrinsic qualities of the object. A first step to counter this distorting tendency of signs, which can lead to a range of unwholesome reactions, can take the form of sense restraint: closely monitoring what happens at any sense door in order to detect swiftly when a trigger of unwholesome reactivity arises in the mind. Whenever this happens, one needs to let go of the sign that has triggered the reactivity and avoid savoring its secondary characteristics in order to guide the perceptual process back into wholesome terrain.

Early Buddhist analysis agrees with modern psychology that the world of experience is, to a considerable degree, a construction of the mind. The world arises in the six senses, an arising that tends to be influenced by the mirages created by perception, by the unceasing constructing activity of volitional constructions, and by the magical illusion of consciousness.

A central tool for becoming aware of the construction of the world of experience is mindfulness, which particularly in the role of a bare form of awareness can enable one to stay with what is seen, heard, etc., just as it is, before the onset of any elaboration of signs and of concomitant patterns of identification and reactivity.

The relevance of such training in bare awareness extends from insight into the construction of experience to the mundane challenge of dealing with pain. Even severe physical illness can be met with mindfulness in a way that protects one from being overwhelmed by physical suffering, thereby enabling the mind to stay healthy when the body is sick. A key to such ability revolves around countering the mind's tendency to take up signs in a self-referential manner, in particular the sign of "my pain." The potential that emerges in this way has found ample confirmation in the contemporary employment of mindfulness in the clinical setting to enable precisely a diminishing of the degree of suffering resulting from physical pain by way of adjusting one's mental attitude.

Cultivating signless concentration can also offer substantial help in eradicating unwholesome thoughts and undermining conceit. The reason for this potential appears to lie in a disclosure of the constructed nature of experience. Such disclosure reveals the degree of subjective fabrication involved in those signs that trigger unwholesome thoughts or serve as building blocks of conceit. Alongside recognizing such potential, it also needs to be noted that the mere ability to gain signless concentration is not in itself a reflection of having reached a level of awakening or even just an irreversible degree of inner transformation.

The practice of signless concentration does not appear to require previous mastery of the absorptions, although the ability to collect the mind will certainly be of much benefit. The basic task required to enter and remain in signless concentration is not paying attention to any signs, which thus necessitates a high degree of continuity of mindfulness. The type of mindfulness called for here can conveniently be built up with previous training in sense restraint and the practice of bare awareness. As the actual practice is about being mindful of an absence, its cultivation naturally relates to other mindfulness practices that are concerned with various forms of absence, such as the temporary absence of a defilement in the mind. A difference here is that with signless concentration such absence becomes thoroughly pervasive in the form of the absence of any sign whatsoever.

The rather subtle type of practice under discussion here appears to require a thorough diminishing, if not near absence, of volitional endeavor. Rather than holding on to a particular object, the stability of this type of "concentration"—a term here evidently not intending a circumscribed focus on a particular object—basically appears to result from letting go. In other words, the task would be for attention to remain free from any mental latching on to anything. Such attending to complete absence can find additional support in a subtle type of contentment with precisely such an object-less condition, and such contentment in turn fosters an absence of distractions or other types of agitation.

Further support for such dwelling in the absence of signs could be garnered from a reformulation of a meditative reflection, apparently related to the attainment of neither-perception-nor-nonperception, which takes this form: "It might not be, and it might not be for me. It will not be, and it will not be for me!" An appropriate target for such reflection would be any form of attachment to one or the other of the five aggregates of clinging. Another tool could be found in the promotion of nonidentification, in the sense of not allowing anything, even profound meditative attainments, to become building blocks of the ego, thereby making sure that one will "not be made of that." Progress in such nonidentification can culminate in consciousness no longer being established, when with the eradication of defilements the prospect of becoming established in some type of future rebirth has been transcended.

Signlessness also stands in a close relationship to emptiness, which in its early Buddhist usage comprehensively covers all phenomena, be it persons, things, or anything else. The peak of emptiness will be reached when the mind has been emptied of defilements. At this point, the tendency of the three root poisons to act as makers of signs has been overcome for good, together with conceit and self-referentiality as other dimensions often activated when the unawakened mind takes up signs.

Signless concentration also features in a gradual meditative entry into emptiness. In this context, it falls into place after a previous meditative progression through perceptions related to infinite space, infinite consciousness, and nothingness, which in a way serve to prepare for a complete letting go of signs. The mental condition resulting from such a complete letting go of signs can in turn be contemplated as impermanent and hence not worth delight and attachment, in order to proceed toward the breakthrough to the deathless.

In sum, the different approaches to a gradual stepping out of the construction of perceptual experience could be summarized as follows: building on sense restraint by way of forestalling unwholesome reactions toward anything cognized, through the cultivation of bare awareness in what is cognized through any of the senses, there will be just what is actually being cognized. With signless concentration, there will no longer be anything recognized, as the mind no longer takes up the signs for recognizing and processing what appears at any sense door. With the experience of the deathless or Nirvana, to be explored in the second part of my study, there will no longer be any relationship to cognizing through the senses at all.

II. The Deathless

THE SECOND PART of my exploration concerns various passages related to the realization of Nirvana. Based on the understanding of the early Buddhist perspective regarding the construction of experience that I have tried to develop in the first part of my study, a central point I intend to make in what follows is the idea that Nirvana stands for a complete stepping out of the construction of experience. My proposal is that the aim of fostering such a stepping out can help explain what the early texts say and, perhaps more importantly, do not say.

My survey begins with the term "deathless" itself, after which I turn to the breakthrough to the deathless, which the texts show to involve a unique type of perception. Then I examine the repercussions of such a breakthrough, in particular the quenching of the fire of defilements, and the nature of the final goal as involving a middle path position.

1. The Deathless

The "deathless" (*amata/amṛta*) is one of several epithets for Nirvana. A Pāli discourse and its Chinese parallel report the Buddha using this term when announcing his recently gained awakening to those five monastics who were to become his first disciples (translated by Ñāṇamoli 1995/2005, 264).[134] The employment of the term "deathless" in this announcement is in line with the report of the central motivation of his earlier quest, which according to the same sources had been to find a way out of the predicament of being subject to death (together with being subject to old age, defilements, etc.).

The term "deathless" also comes up in a prior meeting with a wanderer, in the course of which the recently awakened Buddha reportedly announced that he was on his way to beat the "drum of the deathless."[135] According to the Pāli version of what preceded this meeting, the Buddha had announced his decision to teach others by stating that the "doors to the deathless" are now flung open.[136] Another Pāli discourse reckons the Buddha to be a "giver of the deathless."[137] This designation reflects the general principle that one who teaches the Dharma is a giver of the deathless (translated by Bodhi 2000, 121).[138]

A significant departure from notions apparently in circulation in the ancient setting appears to be that the deathless stands for something to be gained while still alive. The texts show the Buddha attaining the deathless at the moment of the realization that made him a Buddha, rather than at the time of his passing away. An important dimension of such realization of the deathless is a transcendence of death in the sense of any fear of death, a transcendence that can indeed occur well before the actual event of death.[139] The same sense appears to stand in the background of another passage, which lists death among a set of ten things that the Buddha had transcended (translated by Bodhi 2012, 1440).[140] Such indications do not conflict with the well-known report of the Buddha's passing away, as their point is not to propose some sort of bodily immortality. Instead, the idea would be simply that the event of death has lost its sting for one who has fully realized the deathless.

At the same time, however, the realization of the deathless is considered to have repercussions on what happens after death. In fact, the early Buddhist scheme of levels of progress to full awakening stands in close relationship to potential rebirths, as already a stream-enterer is sure not to be reborn more than seven times at most, and an arahant/arhat has gone completely beyond any rebirth.[141] Nevertheless, the emphasis in the early texts is on the transformation caused by the breakthrough to the deathless while the practitioner is still alive. In my exploration of various passages relevant to Nirvana, I do not attempt to separate the one dimension from the other. It seems to me that these are best considered to be two sides of the same coin, with the repercussions in life being the more prominent concern of the early texts.

A thorough type of transcendence of the prospect of any type of rebirth in *saṃsāra* seems to be reflected in references to going beyond both this shore and the other. This notion comes up repeatedly in a set of Pāli verses that revolve around the same image of a snake shedding its old, worn-out skin (translated by Bodhi 2017, 157).[142] The imagery of the snake doing all it can to get rid of its worn-out skin conveniently encapsulates the early Buddhist perspective on the cycle of rebirth. Like an old skin carried along and perhaps even cherished for a long time that now has lost all its former attraction, the desire for any realm or type of existence is to be abandoned in the quest for the deathless.

Another verse offers a presentation that helps to avoid an undue emphasis on the contrast between this shore and the other shore. This takes the form of describing one for whom there is neither the far shore nor the near shore nor both (translated by Norman 1997/2004, 56).[143] Such poetic imagery can be taken to convey the notion of a total transcendence of all aspects of *saṃsāra*. This is indeed a central dimension of the deathless, a feature to which I will have occasion to come back repeatedly.

The complete realization of the deathless stands for full liberation (translated by Ñāṇamoli 1995/2005, 873)[144]—that is, the complete removal of all defilements from the mind (translated by Bodhi 2000, 1528).[145] Nevertheless, a realization of the deathless already takes place at levels of awakening that fall short of full liberation. This can be illustrated with an episode involving the conversion of Sāriputta/Śāriputra and Mahāmoggallāna/Mahāmaudgalyāyana, the two who were to become the chief disciples of the Buddha. According to the relevant narration, the former had just realized stream-entry after having heard an enigmatic statement on conditionality from a Buddhist monastic. When he approached his longtime friend and companion, Mahāmoggallāna/Mahāmaudgalyāyana realized that something must have happened and reportedly inquired if Sāriputta/Śāriputra had attained the deathless; the latter confirmed that this had indeed happened (translated by Horner 1951/1982, 54).[146] In this way, comparable to the case of the Buddha himself, these two chief disciples are on record for choosing the term "deathless" to convey to others their recently gained breakthrough to Nirvana.

A use of the term "deathless" that is not confined to full awakening can also be seen in a set of Pāli discourses without parallels, which name a range of lay practitioners who had come to know the deathless (translated by Bodhi 2012, 989).[147] Several of these are on record in other passages for having passed away at lower levels of realization. It follows that the position of the texts in question is that the direct experience of the deathless is not the sole reserve of those who are arahants/arhats but is relevant also to stream-entry, once-return, and nonreturn.[148] As explained by Bodhi (2012, 1772n1453), the "terms used to describe these lay followers are descriptive of *all noble ones* from stream-entry on up. They all . . . are seers of nibbāna, the deathless."

Although stream-enterers have thus already had a first realization of the deathless, it is only fully awakened ones who have gone completely beyond being afflicted by death. Regarding their resultant freedom from any fear of death, Karunadasa (1991, 56–57) reasons:

> Since the saint does not identify himself [or herself] with any of the *khandhas* [aggregates], the saint does not, in any way, participate in mortality . . . For at the so-called moment of death, what comes to an end is what does not belong to the saint . . . Strictly speaking the liberated saint does not die.

A similar sense appears to be relevant to a discourse passage according to which a fully realized one is not born, does not grow old, and does not pass away (translated by Ñāṇamoli 1995/2005, 1094).[149] Such an indication need not be seen as confined to the eradication of future rebirth and consequently of aging and death in a future existence. Instead, it can fruitfully be read, in keeping with the relevance of the deathless to those still alive, as implying a transcendence experienced right here and now. Quoting again Karunadasa (1991, 62), although "decay and death as physical facts cannot be overcome," an "experience of decay and death is there only when one identifies oneself with what is subject to decay and death." That is, an arahant/arhat is completely beyond old age and death from the moment of becoming a fully awakened one, due to no longer being in any way identified with the physical body (or the other aggregates). For this reason, those who have gone to the "death-free place"—another term for the deathless—have reached complete freedom from any type of grief:[150]

They go to the death-free place,
Having gone to which, they do not grieve.

The complete absence of any grief as a central implication of a realization of the deathless can perhaps best be illustrated with the fearless reply reportedly given by an arahant/arhat to bandits who were about to kill him. When asked why he did not show any sign of fear at the prospect of his imminent death, the arahant/arhat in question is on record for offering the following reply as part of his explanation:[151]

It does not occur to me
That "I was" or "I will be."
Constructions will come to end,
So what is there to lament?

2. The Breakthrough to Liberation

The actual breakthrough to the realization of the deathless should be envisioned as taking place at a distinct moment in time. This can be seen from a Pāli listing of three events worth being recollected in the life of a practicing monastic, which in this respect resemble three events in the life of a king (translated by Bodhi 2012, 206). In the case of the latter, these are the place of birth, of being crowned king, and of victory in battle. These three episodes in the life of a king compare to a monastic's going forth to practice the path, the vision of the four noble truths gained with stream-entry, and the attainment of arahantship.[152]

The early discourses distinguish five possible avenues for the breakthrough to awakening to take place (translated by Walshe 1987, 497).[153] These are covered under the heading of "spheres of liberation" (*vimuttāyatana/vimuktyāyatana*). Four of these relate to the teachings, namely by way of hearing them, communicating them to others, reciting them, and reflecting on them. The fifth is during actual meditation practice. In each of these alternative situations, an understanding can arise that results in joy and tranquility, leading to concentration (several versions of such descriptions add that this then leads on to knowledge in accordance with reality).

The mental qualities described in this way correspond to three out of the seven factors of awakening (*bojjhaṅga/bodhyaṅga*), which are mindfulness, investigation of *dharma*s, energy, joy, tranquility, concentration, and equipoise/equanimity. A Pāli discourse and its Chinese and Sanskrit parallels explicitly relate cultivating the whole set of seven awakening factors to the occasion of listening to a teaching (translated by Bodhi 2000, 1571),[154] which would correspond to the first of the five spheres of liberation. In such a situation, the foundational awakening factor of *mindfulness*, aroused while attending closely to what is being said, can lead on to the second awakening factor when the meaning of what has been heard is *investigated*. Pursuing such investigation with dedication arouses mental *energy*, in the sense of an application of the mind, which in turn leads on to the three qualities of *joy*, *tranquility*, and *concentration*, already mentioned above. These then culminate in *equipoise* or equanimity, a mental state of inner balance fully enriched by the other awakening factors and thereby gradually becoming ready for the plunge into the deathless.

To foster this plunge, the cultivation of the awakening factors should be related to a set of insight themes. The relevant formulation in a discourse extant in Chinese, found similarly in its Pāli parallel (translated by Bodhi 2000, 1586), describes the development of each awakening factor in the following way:[155] "Supported by seclusion, supported by dispassion, supported by cessation, leading to letting go."

Presented in brief, a way of understanding this series is to take the first three to stand for *seclusion* from what is unwholesome, *dispassion* as the fading away of craving, and an orientation toward the *cessation* of what is constructed (or what is *dukkha/duḥkha*).[156] Being supported by these three then leads to *letting go* in the sense of relinquishing, giving up, surrendering, and abandoning. Such letting go would have to comprise everything, without exception. For the plunge into the deathless to take place, the entire gamut of experience—based as it is on the central peg of construction in the form of an I-entity that is assumed to be at its center and somehow in control—would need to be relinquished, given up, surrendered, and abandoned.

The early discourses report with considerable frequency the occurrence of such letting go, resulting in the attainment of stream-entry, taking place while someone is listening to a discourse given by the Buddha. The frequency of such reports appears to be a result of the circumstances that led to such breakthroughs.[157] Should the same have happened while reflecting or reciting, or else while meditating, this would not have occasioned a discourse and for this reason would have stood considerably less of a chance of being recorded.

In addition, such descriptions also highlight how the Buddha's way of teaching had a special effect on the audience, which facilitated the breakthrough to stream-entry. That is, an arousal of the seven awakening factors, and then relating these to the insight themes, could apparently occur as a natural by-product of listening to the Buddha. This much seems to be implicit in a standard pericope used for such occasions, according to which the Buddha had become aware of the listener's mind being glad and receptive, free from the hindrances.[158] The description implies that the Buddha should be envisaged as monitoring the listener(s)' mind while giving a teaching and adjusting his presentation in such a way as to facilitate the breakthrough taking place.

The discourses depict the mind that has become ready and receptive in this way as being similar to a clean cloth that easily takes dye.[159] In the same way, the listener comes to see, understand, and attain the Dharma, crossing over doubt and uncertainty. The standard pericope in the early discourses refers to the actual attainment of stream-entry as the arising of the Dharma-eye. The relevant Pāli pericope relates the Dharma-eye to the understanding that all that is of a nature to arise is of a nature to cease (translated by Ñāṇamoli 1995/2005, 485). However, such a specification tends to be absent from parallel versions.[160] A counterpart to this particular pericope can nevertheless be found in a discourse extant in Chinese, which reads:[161]

> Whatever there is, it is of a nature to arise; all of it having ceased, one attains the arising of the eye of Dharma that is free from any defilement.

Regarding the other spheres of liberation, the placing of meditation as the last one in the list need not be taken to convey a form of ranking, somehow implying that dedication to meditative cultivation of the mind is not of central importance. To the contrary, previously undertaken meditation practice, in particular cultivating the awakening factors, would provide an important support for actualizing the potential of breaking through to the deathless. At the same time, however, for such a realization to happen the practitioner need not be seated in formal meditation right at that time. From the viewpoint of the actual breakthrough, what appears to be particularly necessary is the occurrence of something unexpected, a sudden insight or understanding, which triggers such profound letting go that the whole construction of experience comes to a momentary halt and the unconstructed can be realized.

In fact, the breakthrough to the unconditioned, or perhaps better the "deconditioning," is not the automatic result of the path. In relation to full awakening, a Pāli discourse explains that a practitioner of the higher training in morality, concentration (literally "the mind"), and wisdom does not have the power to determine that their mind be liberated today (or tomorrow or the day after).[162] Yet, as long as these three higher trainings are undertaken, a time will come when the mind will realize liberation from all defilements (translated by Bodhi 2012, 325). In the words of Collins (1998, 185), "the path is a necessary but not sufficient condition for attaining the goal."

In trying to make sense of such indications, it seems to me that a perspective based on the construction of experience can be of considerable help. The three higher trainings, which in the early discourses serve as a comprehensive referent to the different dimensions of progress on the path, are still within the realm of what is conditioned or constructed. They prepare the ground for a stepping out of constructing to happen, which indeed does require such groundwork (especially for those who are unable to avail themselves of the presence of a living Buddha who is giving a teaching). But the indispensability of these three higher trainings combines with the need for a total letting go so that the breakthrough to the deathless can take place.

Since the letting go needs to be total, it also involves letting go of the very means that have been employed up to that point. That is, it applies even to the three higher trainings. However much these have been useful, indeed indispensable, up to that point, they also need to be relinquished. This does not mean that the practitioner should now behave in ways that are immoral, distracted, and foolish. Instead, the point is only that any clinging to the three trainings, however subtle, any trace of identification with them, at this juncture becomes an obstacle to the total letting go required for a complete stepping out of the construction of experience. I will come back to this topic below, in relation to the notion of the breakthrough to Nirvana as truth (see p. 85).

Some Pāli verses refer to the breakthrough to Nirvana as a region or direction to which one has never gone (translated by Bodhi 2017, 318).[163] Another verse, extant in a range of parallel versions, refers to the condition of having come to know the destruction of constructions, whereby one becomes a knower of the unmade (translated by Norman 1997/2004, 56).[164] To reach a region to which one has never gone and to become a knower of the unmade of course requires leaving behind all that is familiar and known. This is more easily said than done. A poetic injunction, extant in a range of parallel versions, expresses what appears to be required once the indispensable groundwork in the three higher trainings (etc.) is in place. The Pāli version of this poetic injunction, which presumably expresses the matter in terms of the three periods of time, takes the following form:[165]

> Let go of what is before,
> Let go of what is afterward,
> Let go of what is in the middle,
> Transcend becoming.

Another piece of advice, extant in a different Pāli verse, brings out in particular the element of inner disengagement:[166]

> [What is] taken up or rejected:
> Let none of these be found in you!

The first of these two verses probably does not intend to encourage a complete and perpetual discarding of anything past, present, and future, which would make the practitioner unable to function in daily life. Nor does the recommendation to avoid taking up and rejecting involve an obliteration of the guiding principle of right view and of the need to maintain moral conduct. Instead, these poetic teachings are probably best read as pointers to the need for employing any means for progress on the path without clinging to it, being willing to let go completely whenever this should be required. To use a metaphor prominent in later tradition, it all seems to be about not mistaking the finger for the moon.[167]

A description that exemplifies how the breakthrough to the deathless could take place can be found in the following Pāli passage, which recurs with minor variations in Sanskrit and Chinese parallels. The relevant text occurs as the climax of an exposition on how perception can be trained, which leads to the following reflection and ensuing form of practice:[168]

> "What if I were neither to intend nor to construct?" So one neither intends nor constructs. For one who is not intending and not constructing, those very perceptions cease, other gross perceptions do not arise, and one experiences cessation.

In this way, the intending and constructing activity of the mind (that is, of the fourth aggregate in particular) comes to be subdued to such an extent that it becomes possible to step out of the process of perceiving, of connecting one perception with the next, as a result of which the experience of cessation becomes possible. This appears to happen right at the moment when the present perception comes to an end, if at that very moment—due to letting go of the intending and constructing activity of the mind—the deeply ingrained tendency to reach out toward the next perception is absent. In other words, the experience of cessation is located—if this word can be used at all—right at the outer edge of the ending of the present perception.

3. A Unique Perception

The need to go beyond known ways of intending and constructing experience comes up also in relation to a special form of meditation described in a Pāli discourse (translated by Bodhi 2012, 1561), which has several parallels. The discourse in question sets out on the contrast between a wild colt and a thoroughbred. A practitioner comparable to a wild colt is not free from the five hindrances (sensual desire, ill will, sloth-and-torpor, restlessness-and-worry, and doubt) and then meditates in dependence on various objects, such as the elements, the immaterial spheres, or what is experienced through the senses. In contrast, the way of practice for one comparable to a thoroughbred is based on the removal of the five hindrances. The actual practice then takes the following form in a Chinese version of the relevant passage:[169]

> One who meditates like this neither cultivates meditation in dependence on earth, nor cultivates meditation in dependence on water, fire, wind, space, consciousness, nothingness, neither-perception-nor-nonperception; neither cultivates meditation in dependence on this world, nor in dependence on that world, nor [in dependence on] the sun and the moon, nor [in dependence on] what is seen, heard, experienced, and cognized, nor [in dependence on] what is attained, nor [in dependence on] what is sought, nor [in dependence on] what is accordingly realized, nor [in dependence on] what is accordingly contemplated.

The Pāli parallel, which proceeds similarly, concludes by additionally emphasizing that such a practitioner nevertheless still meditates. The same is also evident from the beginning of the passage translated above: "One who meditates like this." Such a form of meditation—if it can indeed be called such—goes beyond the whole range of objects a meditator could possibly take up and thereby beyond all known avenues of meditating. The parallels explain that any perception related to generally recognized objects of meditation "has disappeared," which the practitioner has "subdued," or else such perceptions are being seen as "false, not having a reality."[170] According to the Pāli commentary, this type of meditation refers to the fruition attainment of an arahant/arhat and takes Nirvana as its object.[171] The implication of this commentarial gloss is that those who have fully awakened can take Nirvana as the "object" of their meditation practice.

Several Pāli discourses offer a similar presentation, with the difference that, instead of employing the verb "to meditate" (*jhāyati*), they speak of having such a perception (*saññā*). A relationship to meditation is nevertheless evident in the fact that the description of this quite extraordinary type of perception comes in reply to an inquiry about an "attainment of concentration" (*samādhipaṭilābha*) that does not involve the four elements, the four immaterial spheres, etc.

These discourses provide a significant additional indication, as they spell out what serves as the object or theme of such meditative perception. This takes the following form:[172]

> This is peaceful, this is sublime, namely: the calming of all constructions, the letting go of all supports, the extinguishing of craving, dispassion, cessation, Nirvana.

One of the Pāli passages under discussion offers the further explanation that the reference here is to the "highest track" (*aggapada*),[173] which the commentary confirms as referring to Nirvana.[174]

Although no parallels to these Pāli discourses are known, the same type of reflection is found as a discourse quotation in an exegetical work from a different reciter lineage, where it features as a mode of inclining the mind toward the deathless element.[175] The same function can be seen reflected in an otherwise unrelated Pāli discourse, which also introduces the above maxim as a way of inclining the mind toward the deathless element. This discourse further specifies that such inclining toward the deathless element can be expected to lead to nonreturn or full awakening (translated by Ñāṇamoli 1995/2005, 540 and Bodhi 2012, 1299).[176] Yet another and also unrelated Pāli discourse relates the same maxim, qualified again as an attainment of concentration, to overcoming conceit and gaining liberation of the mind and liberation by wisdom (translated by Bodhi 2012, 228).[177]

Clearly, the passage translated above must be intending a meditative experience, and a rather transformative one at that. Although this maxim can of course be employed as a means for conceptually recollecting Nirvana as peace, in the present setting it appears to be more about an inclining of the mind toward the deathless element, presumably undertaken by those who have already had a direct experience of Nirvana.

Returning to the Pāli instances concerned with the above maxim as a perception that is distinct from all other types of known perceptions, nearly all these instances explicitly set aside any perception related to what has been seen, heard, sensed, cognized, and pursued by the mind.[178] Listings of these activities usually function as a comprehensive coverage of the range of possible cognitions by way of the six senses. It follows that any form of mental reflection has been set aside, wherefore a perception in line with the above quotation could not intend a form of internally verbalized recollection. Instead, the actual perception, which despite differing from all other types of perception is still a "perception,"[179] must indeed be envisaged as taking Nirvana as its reference point, be this by inclining toward it or by actually experiencing it. That is, even though the maxim quoted above ("this is peaceful . . .") expresses what takes place in words, it must be the maxim's significance, the meaning conveyed in this way, that would form the "object" of this particular perception: Nirvana. Ñāṇananda (2015, 500) affirms that it "is Nibbāna, then, that one attends to while in that attainment," adding that "Nibbāna is not an experience as dry as a log of wood, but a state of serene awareness of its true significance. It is a transcendence of the world by realization of its cessation."

The same type of meditative experience features as a particular way of paying attention (*manasikaroti*) in another Pāli discourse, again preceded by noting that this involves not attending to any of those things that one may ordinarily attend to (translated by Bodhi 2012, 1560).[180] One more relevant Pāli discourse provides a complementary perspective, as here the basically same inclination of the mind toward the deathless, by leaving behind all the known objects of perception, takes instead the form: "the cessation of becoming is Nirvana."[181] The quick arising and vanishing of this type of perceptual notion finds illustration in the quick arising and passing away of the flames of a twig fire (translated by Bodhi 2012, 1345), an image conveying that this could not intend some form of sustained intellectual reflection or recollection. These two instances confirm the impression that the maxim quoted above is probably best understood to express in concepts an experience that goes far beyond the employment of concepts. Commenting on the perceptual notion that "the cessation of becoming is Nirvana," Ñāṇananda (1974/1985, 72–75) reasons:

> Here, then, is a consciousness of the very cessation of consciousness. Though well nigh a contradiction, it is yet a possibility because of the reflexive character of consciousness. Instead of consciousness of objects, here we have a consciousness which is without an object or support. Whereas, under normal circumstances, consciousness "mirrors" or manifests something, in this concentration it is "non-manifestative" . . . "Objects" play no part in this "perception" precisely for the reason that the "subject" is missing. This experience of the cessation of existence (*bhavanirodho*), which is none other than "Nibbāna here-and-now," is the outcome of the eradication of the conceit "I am."

The above descriptions have in common that they point to something that is completely different from any other experience, yet at the same time it is also an experience. For this very reason the texts employ verbs like "to meditate" and "to pay attention," and speak of a "perception" obtained as part of an "attainment of concentration." In other words, they appear to describe a conscious meditative experience, which does involve perception or paying attention, yet at the same time it is so completely other that it differs from all types of meditations, perceptions, or modes of paying attention known thus far. Although such descriptions do not imply that there is no perception, or that the practitioner does not meditate, or that there is no attention, they do point to a form of perceiving and meditatively attending that is completely unlike all previously known avenues of experience and for this reason cannot be adequately reckoned on a par with them.

Another passage extant in Pāli, which refers to what appears to be the actual meditative realization of the deathless with the term "sphere" (*āyatana*), explicitly encourages that this "should be experienced" (*veditabbe*).[182] The Chinese parallel uses similar terminology:[183]

> You should realize that sphere, where the eye ceases and which then is apart from a perception of forms, [where] the ear . . . the nose . . . the tongue . . . the body . . . the mind ceases and which then is apart from a perception of mental objects.

The Pāli commentary on the corresponding reference in the Pāli discourse (translated by Bodhi 2000, 1191) explains that the cessation of the six sense spheres stands for Nirvana.[184] Already the instruction attributed to the Buddha in the Pāli discourse and its Chinese counterpart makes it clear that this particular sphere of experience involves a cessation of all six senses that make up the whole possible range of perceptions, that is, eye, ear, nose, tongue, body, and mind. In addition to that, the Buddha's attendant Ānanda is on record for explicitly confirming that this description is about the "cessation of the six sense spheres."[185]

Still, this is explicitly designated a *sphere* which is to be *experienced*. It seems that, once again, the same basic point emerges, in that the texts appear to convey the idea of something utterly beyond the six sense spheres. This is the case to such an extent that these six sense spheres have to cease for this particular experience to be possible, yet the result is nevertheless not just a form of being unconscious but rather a sphere to be experienced. The message here appears to be a positioning of the encounter with the deathless as otherwise to such an extent that it cannot be fitted into the schemes used to analyze ordinary experience, whether these be the six sense spheres or the aggregate of perceptions. Nevertheless, it is being consciously perceived. It is a conscious experience that involves the cessation of the six sense spheres.

Understood in this way, the paradoxical injunction to experience the cessation of the six sense spheres—including the sphere of the mind—can serve as a directive and reference point for actual practice, pointing to the realization of an experience that involves the absence of anything previously experienced. In other words, such indications are best read as practice instructions.

With later exegesis and the attempt to build a coherent system of thought in which everything is neatly defined, however, this type of paradoxical presentation can become problematic. Operating from such a viewpoint of system building, once the presence of the mind that is implicit in the injunction to experience that sphere is analyzed into its various constituents,[186] the problem becomes how to account for the reference to a sphere that involves the cessation of all six sense spheres (and not just of the five physical senses). This appears to have led to positing the cessation of the six sense spheres as the object taken by the mind at the time of the breakthrough to the deathless, instead of being a description of the subject—that is, of the realization of the cessation of the subject—at that moment. In this way, the cessation of the six sense spheres becomes just the cessation of the six sense objects. Although this conveniently solves the doctrinal problem, it risks missing out on the potential of the paradoxical injunction to experience the sphere wherein all six spheres of experience cease. In other words, the need to step out of the subjective contribution to the construction of experience is no longer fully evident.

In a critical assessment of this development and the resultant tendency to posit Nirvana as something existing in its own right,[187] Ñāṇananda (2015, 18) argues that "there is no justification for a periphrastic usage like 'on reaching *Nibbāna*.' No glimpse of a distant object is necessary." To exemplify what he means by a periphrastic usage, he provides the following illustration: "When one says 'the river flows,' it does not mean that there is a river quite apart from the act of flowing. Likewise, the idiom 'it rains' should not be taken to imply that there is something that rains. It is only a turn of speech" (283). Such a turn of speech should not lead to the idea that "the rain rains, and the river flows," as in this way a "natural phenomenon becomes mystified and hypostasized" (284). Ñāṇananda (2015, 339) then offers the following comment on the notion of a cessation of the six sense spheres (or six "sense-bases"):

> The cessation of the six sense-bases does not mean that one does not see anything. What one sees then is voidness. It is an in-"sight" . . . *suñño loko*, "void is the world."

Understood in this way, the cessation of the six sense spheres refers to the most thorough experience of absence possible. This function appears to be comparable to the role of the expression "signless element," discussed above (see p. 32), as a referent to the absence of any sign. In fact, the cessation of the six sense spheres shares with the signless element the absence of any sign—and thus the absence of any taking up of an object—with the difference that it goes still further in matters of absence, as the sphere under discussion also involves the experience of the absence of the subject.

A thorough absence of the subject is evident in another passage, which in a way complements the above descriptions of the experience of Nirvana in life by taking up the condition of fully awakened ones after death, these two perspectives being two sides of the same coin, as briefly mentioned earlier. A Pāli discourse without known parallels reports the Buddha clarifying that of previous Buddhas there is no longer any of the six senses, including the mind, by which one might designate them (translated by Bodhi 2000, 1163).[188]

Returning to the experience of the cessation of the six sense spheres in life, the term "sphere" (*āyatana*), which can alternatively be translated as "base" or "domain," also features in descriptions of the aspiration to reach the final goal, where it functions as a referent to something realizable in the present. This finds expression in the wish to abide in that sphere in which awakened ones abide (translated by Ñāṇamoli 1995/2005, 1069).[189]

Another Pāli passage employs the same term in the following declaration, introduced as an inspired utterance reportedly made by the Buddha while giving a teaching on Nirvana:[190]

> Monastics, there is that sphere where there is no earth, no water, no fire, no wind, no sphere of infinite space, no sphere of infinite consciousness, no sphere of nothingness, no sphere of neither-perception-nor-nonperception, not this world, not a world beyond, and not both the moon and the sun. Monastics, I say that there is also no coming, no going, no staying, no passing away, and no re-arising; indeed, it is unestablished, unmovable, and unsupported. This itself is the end of *dukkha*.

Dhammadinnā (2021, 115) explains that such descriptions show "that the same experiential terminology encompasses the ordinary six-sense experience of the world and the immaterial spheres . . . and that which transcends them, namely Nirvāṇa." Understood in this way, the passages surveyed above seem to accomplish two things at the same time. On the one hand, they communicate the utter otherness of the realization of the deathless, which is not commensurate with any dimension of experience known thus far, be it ordinary sense experience or deep states of meditation. On the other hand, however, it is still an experience—in fact, it should be experienced—progress toward which is the central axis around which early Buddhist soteriology revolves. As expressed by Conze (1962, 71), Nirvana is "the *raison d'être* of Buddhism, and its ultimate justification," adding:

> This "Nirvana" is surely a very strange entity which differs greatly from anything that we have ever met before, and has nothing in common with objects about which assertion is possible. In order to do justice to it, one must withdraw from everything by which, of which or with which anything can be asserted.

In sum, what emerges from the passages surveyed above appears to be a form of meditation that is almost nonmeditation, at least when considered from the viewpoint of what is usually employed for meditative practice. It would involve a type of perception that is beyond all known types of perception. It seems to be an attainment of concentration that does not concentrate on anything that one might think could serve as an object of concentration and instead just inclines the mind toward the deathless. It would require a form of attention that, rather than constructing experience through the act of paying attention, instead attends to the calming of all constructions. Being a sphere of experience that involves the cessation of the six spheres of experience, it is completely other to an extent that defies imagination, conceptualization, and reasoning. All that is left to say would thus be that "it should be experienced."

4. Gone Beyond Conflict

There is still another passage to be covered regarding the unique nature of the perception related to the breakthrough to the deathless, found in the Discourse on Quarrels and Disputes (*Kalahavivādasutta*). Taking up the statement in question requires some preparatory exploration. For this reason, I proceed in a somewhat oblique manner by first turning to the topic of going beyond disputation with the world, based on another two discourses, and only then examining the context of the cryptic statement under discussion.

My first example related to the transcendence of disputations occurs in a discourse that reports the Buddha being asked in a somewhat challenging way to proclaim his view (translated by Ñāṇamoli 1995/2005, 201). The first part of his reply in a Chinese version of this discourse takes the following form:[191]

> What causes no disputation with the entire world, with its celestials and Māras, its Brahmās, its recluses, and its brahmins, from humans to celestials . . . that is my basic tenet, and I also teach in this way.

Commenting on the corresponding statement in the Pāli version, Ñāṇananda (2015, 245) reasons that "generally, in the world, if anyone proclaims a doctrine, it is natural that it will come into conflict with other doctrines." In the present case, however, "the Buddha's teaching is such that he does not come into conflict with others."

The foundation for this tenet of no disputation must be the realization the Buddha had gained with full awakening. In other words, this realization not only is beyond all other perceptions but also leads beyond competing with others in terms of debating one's respective views. This would be why, on being challenged to proclaim his view, according to the present episode the Buddha was able to reply by proclaiming the noncontentious implications of his realization rather than propounding any specific view.

The second relevant discourse takes the form of an exchange between the Buddha and Sakka/Śakra, the celestial king in the Heaven of the

Thirty-Three (translated by Walshe 1987, 328). Sakka/Śakra wants to know why celestials and human beings keep quarreling with each other. This leads on to a question-and-answer exchange that analyzes in detail the conditions responsible for quarrels and disputes, with the result that the celestial visitor attains stream-entry.[192] In this way, although falling short of removing the conditions for quarrels and dispute for good—which would require becoming an arahant/arhat—Sakka's/Śakra's realization of the deathless when attaining stream-entry would have offered him a direct experience of what leads beyond dispute.

The Discourse on Quarrels and Disputes also involves a question-and-answer exchange leading up to an enigmatic statement that offers a significant perspective on the topic of a perception that is beyond perceptions. The progression of the exchange shows quarrels and disputes to be rooted in affection, desire, and preferences, ultimately depending on contact. In the early Buddhist analysis in general, contact stands for the event of experience. The present discourse shows such contact to be in turn based on name-and-form, representative of the mental processing of experience by way of concepts—quite literally giving them a "name"—and the impact of materiality on such experience, "form."[193]

The next verse states that "contact depends on name-and-form" but then continues with the indication that "with the disappearance of form, contacts do not make contact."[194] Thus, even though name-and-form is identified as the condition for contact, the verse continues by mentioning only the disappearance of form as what leads beyond contact. Yet, with the disappearance of form, such as can take place with the immaterial spheres, contact still occurs. To go beyond contact requires the disappearance of name as well. In view of the resultant inconsistency of this verse, it seems reasonable to consider the reference to just form here to serve as a shorthand for name-and-form, following observations made by other scholars.[195] Given that the present discourse involves a question-and-answer exchange similar to that between the Buddha and Sakka/Śakra, it could have originally been in prose as well, in which case it would have been versified only on a subsequent occasion for ease of oral transmission and recitation. Such versification could have resulted in a need to shorten "name-and-form" to just "form" in order to fit the meter and at the same time stay as close as possible to the wording of the prose. Such shortening would presumably not have been experienced as problematic, as the present verse begins by giving the full term "name-and-form," wherefore it can reasonably be expected that an abbreviation in the concluding line to just "form" will be understood to intend the same.

Another problem to be examined ahead of turning to the enigmatic verse itself is the remainder of the exchange. This reports the listener stating that the Buddha had explained the matter he had been asked about, which implies that the verse under discussion completes the explanation of the conditioned arising of quarrels and disputes. From the viewpoint of the two discourses taken up above, it would be reasonable to expect that this verse should refer in some way to the deathless.[196] It is the full realization of the deathless that enabled the Buddha to proclaim his non-contentiousness rather than detailing a specific view. The same realization, at the level of stream-entry, features as the culmination point of the question-and-answer exchange with Sakka/Śakra regarding why celestials and human beings keep quarreling with each other.

With this much of preparatory exploration in place, the time has come to turn to the actual verse in question. A Chinese parallel of this verse could be translated as follows:[197]

> Not being percipient of a [normal] perception [or] an immaterial perception,
> Nor being impercipient [or] with a dysfunctional perception,
> All perceptions are abandoned, being without attachment [to them],
> Because perception is the root of proliferation and its consequent *dukkha/duḥkha*.

The first part of the verse, in the way translated above, appears to indicate that going beyond quarrels and disputes relates to an experience that is not a normal perception, not one related to the immaterial spheres, not being just unconscious, and also not having a dysfunctional perception. The corresponding Pāli verse could be translated in this way:[198]

Not being percipient of a [normal] perception and not percipient of a distorted perception,
Also not being impercipient and not percipient of the disappearance [of materiality],
For one endowed in this way [name-and-]form disappears,
As reckonings and proliferations originate from perception.

The Pāli verse, in the form translated above, would convey a sense similar to the above proposed rendering of the Chinese version, albeit in a different sequence. Here, after normal perceptions have been set aside, the reference to a "distorted" perception could be considered to be similar to the case of the "dysfunctional" perception mentioned last in the Chinese parallel. The term used in the Pāli poem recurs in a *Vinaya* passage to describe the confused behavior of a monk who had gotten drunk and, having been brought to the presence of the Buddha, had turned around to lie in such a way that his feet were pointing toward the latter.[199] In ancient India as well as in many parts of Asia up to today, pointing the feet at someone is a gesture of disrespect. From this perspective, the monk in question, who normally behaved with deep respect toward the Buddha, indeed had a distorted or even dysfunctional perception. The sense of perception being distorted emerges also in another passage, according to which those who misperceive what is impermanent, *dukkha/duḥkha*, unattractive, and not self to be the opposite have a deranged mind and distorted perceptions (translated by Bodhi 2012, 438).[200]

Being impercipient, mentioned in both versions as the third item in the series of negations, appears to refer to being unconscious. Regarding the Pāli version's last reference to not being "percipient of the disappearance [of materiality]," my supplementation follows Ñāṇaponika (1977, 331),[201] who reasons that this expression is probably an abbreviation of the expression "perception of the disappearance of materiality," found in another verse in the same collection.[202] This would then correspond to setting aside an "immaterial perception," mentioned as the second item in the Chinese version.

My supplementation of "name" in the next line is based on the abovementioned impression that references to just "form" in the later part of this poem appear to be due to metrical constraints. In fact, just the disappearance of form does not put an end to reckonings and proliferations, wherefore it falls short of providing a satisfactory answer, at least from an early Buddhist textual perspective, to the basic inquiry after the transcendence of quarrels and disputes.[203]

On the understanding that emerges in this way from the two versions, the four negations would point to the same perception that is beyond all perceptions, discussed earlier, namely the experience of the deathless through the cessation of the six sense spheres. The present instance would then provide the additional information that, besides being different from normal perceptions (including those related to the immaterial spheres), such a perception neither is in some form dysfunctional or distorted nor corresponds to a state of unconsciousness. It is a fully functional perception, yet it is thoroughly other than anything else.

Turning to the second part of the verse, a difference in wording appears to convey nevertheless the same sense; the indication in the Chinese version that "all perceptions are abandoned" could be taken to correspond to the Pāli version's intimation that "[name-and-]form disappear." This would then to some extent corroborate the suggestion, made above, that "name" should be supplemented in the Pāli version.

The Chinese version offers an additional indication by highlighting that such attainment requires being without attachment to perception. This is precisely the challenge, as the habit of relying on perception to make sense of the world is deeply ingrained and consequently upheld firmly as a supposedly indispensable part of one's existence. This can then prevent the letting go required for the cessation of perception, qua the cessation of name-and-form, to occur. The two versions proceed by providing support for navigating this challenge by pointing out that proliferation has perception as its root. The revelation of the inherent drawbacks of perception, made in this way, becomes even more evident in the Chinese version, which spells out the obvious: proliferation results in *dukkha/duḥkha*.

What emerges from the proposed understanding of this verse, as well as from those passages taken up earlier, is the complete otherness of the type of perception that comes with the realization of the deathless. This in turn is significant for appreciating different positions taken on the nature of Nirvana in later traditions. Simply said, the problem appears to be that the very unfamiliarity of this experience naturally calls up an attempt to relate it to something familiar in order to make sense of it. Regarding the arising of different positions in the Buddhist traditions, Pande (1957, 443) offers the following reasoning:

> From ancient times there has been a great diversity of interpretations concerning the nature of Nirvāṇa as taught by Buddha. Partly at least it has been due to the fact that in the light of the later developed philosophic thought the original texts appeared to be deficient in precision. The interpreter therefore concerned himself with determining the unexpressed implications of the texts, and in this he naturally took the assistance of his own philosophy about things. Since different interpreters had different philosophies, a diversity of interpretations was the inevitable consequence.

The basic problem that emerges in this way not only holds for those who rely on descriptions of Nirvana but can also affect those who have actually experienced it. That is, the actual breakthrough to the deathless can be perceived in different ways, in line with the mind attempting to make sense, in terms of the known, of what is so completely unknown. The very nature of the breakthrough to what is beyond construction implies that any attempt to convey such deconstruction can only take place within the limits of language that is based on what is constructed and therefore necessarily is inadequate, leaving room for alternative attempts to convey the same meaning.

In the case of a practitioner trained in analyzing objects, the total absence of any object would naturally be the most conspicuous feature. If another practitioner is more accustomed to aim meditative attention at the meditating subject, however, what would stand out prominently would be the fact that, in spite of the complete disappearance of all aspects of subjectivity known thus far, the experience is a conscious one and can be recollected. In this way, descriptions of the breakthrough to the deathless that employ quite different terms—either emphasizing the cessation aspect or else the knowing dimension—could in principle still be about the same stepping out of the construction of experience. That is, what in theory may appear as irreconcilable contrasts could still reflect the same basic realization.

The almost inevitable impact of subjectivity on descriptions of the realization of the deathless may be why in the early texts the emphasis appears to be more on the transformative repercussions of this breakthrough. The overall interest appears to be less descriptions of the actual event than the effect(s) of this on the practitioner in question.[204] In addition to the gradual eradication of defilements and fetters with different stages of progress to full awakening, a topic to which I will return below, a key element here could be—in keeping with the above exploration—the absence of contentiousness and dogmatic clinging to one's own view(s).

5. Arrival at Truth

With the above I have not yet exhausted the topic of going beyond conflict, another dimension of which concerns the early Buddhist notion of truth. A Pāli verse that directly relates the absence of disputations to the arrival at truth takes the following form:[205]

> There is one truth, indeed, there is no second,
> By understanding of which a person would not dispute [with others].

The Pāli commentarial tradition indicates that the reference to "one truth" intends the realization of Nirvana.[206] On this understanding, the above verse can be related to the passage taken up earlier, according to which the Buddha, on being challenged to proclaim his view, just replied by stating: "What causes no disputation with the entire world . . . that is my basic tenet."

In commenting on the above verse, Premasiri (1972, 29) reasons that "disagreement is resolved when that truth is known." In other words, the verse does not appear to be presenting a fundamentalist claim to truth, held so strongly as to allow no alternative. Instead, the point would rather be that the very building blocks of views are seen through. For one who has seen the escape from constructing, anything constructed, including any view, can no longer appear as real or solid as it may have seemed earlier. Hence, any felt need to go around and dispute with others has been deprived of much of its foundation and the acceptance of a view has been reduced just to the instrumental purpose of serving as an orientational reference point for progress on the path.

Indications found elsewhere among the early discourses concord with the impression that the breakthrough to the deathless was conceived as an arrival at what is true and real. A verse extant in Pāli expresses the matter in the following way:[207]

> Nirvana is of a nondeceptive nature,
> That noble ones have truly known;
> Through the breakthrough to truth,
> They have become stilled and cool.

This verse serves to provide a contrast to a pervasive tendency in the world to misconceive what is of a false nature as being true or real. The indication made in this way could be related to another verse, taken up in the first part of my study (see above p. 15), which states, in relation to the world, that "all this is unreal."

The point of these poetic indications would not be to promote some form of idealism. Instead, such passages can preferably be approached from the viewpoint of the construction of experience. Due to the influence of defilements, all unawakened experiences will inevitably be tinged by what is deceptive and of a false nature. In fact, the motto "all this is unreal" has precisely the function of serving the purpose of eradicating defilements. The actual existence of defilements in the mind is certainly not being put into question. But contesting the innate confidence in the accuracy of the way the world is normally perceived, by way of noting that "all this is unreal," can reveal the impact of the construction of experience.

This appears to be precisely what enables one to step out of what is false and arrive at what is true and real.

Another Pāli discourse offers the following proclamation about an arahant:[208]

> The liberation of such a one is unshakeable, being established in truth . . . this is indeed the supreme noble truth . . . namely Nirvana, which is of a nondeceptive nature.

Although the parallels extant in Chinese and Tibetan do not employ exactly the same expression, they convey in complementary ways that Nirvana corresponds to the arrival at truth.[209]

The reference to "the supreme noble truth," employed in the Pāli version, can be relied on to relate the proclamation that "there is one truth, indeed, there is no second" to the well-known teaching of *four* truths, which according to tradition was the central topic of the Buddha's first sermon.[210] The fourfold presentation as such appears to reflect the influence of an ancient Indian scheme of medical diagnosis.[211] The actual grounding in truth, however, would rely in particular on the third truth, the cessation of craving through the experience of the deathless. This is the one out of the four truths that can indeed be reckoned the "supreme noble truth," to borrow the terminology from the extract translated above, being the one on which the other three depend for reaching their consummation.

Needless to say, this is not meant to convey the impression that there is something incorrect in considering the event of awakening to involve a realization of the four truths, which the early discourses indeed do repeatedly.[212] The point is only to counter too literal an interpretation of such presentations, by keeping in mind that the truth-dimension of these four is grounded in an encounter with a reality devoid of conceptual or doctrinal content. In fact, "reality" is an alternative way of rendering the Sanskrit and Pāli term usually translated as "truth." Gethin (1998, 60) points out:

> The word *satya* (Pali *sacca*) can certainly mean truth, but it might equally be rendered as "real" or "actual thing". That is, we are not dealing here with propositional truths with which we must either agree or disagree, but with four "true things," or "realities" whose nature, we are told, the Buddha finally understood on the night of his awakening.

This clarification need not be taken to require a complete discarding of the notion of truth as something to be taken on trust.[213] In fact, most practitioners will probably not gain realization on hearing about the four truths for the first time. In such cases, one would have to take on trust the diagnostic scheme of the four truths, which in the form of right view is an indispensable guiding principle of the eightfold path and thus of vital importance. Nevertheless, such taking on trust for the purpose of progress to realization has only an instrumental purpose, as it is meant to lead on to an eventual personal verification.

The scheme of the four truths as right view can take a range of manifestations, from being taken up by the worldling who has just begun to embark on the practice all the way up to the arahant's profound insight. In view of this spectrum, it may be best to take the two nuances of "truth" and "reality" as equally valid. In other words, what may well start off as a mere belief or intellectual conviction regarding a *truth* proclaimed according to tradition by the Buddha can gradually transform into an actual *reality* for the practitioner.

Now, in terms of the event of awakening, at that time the "real"-ization, if I am allowed more wordplay, must be of a nonconceptual nature. All the six sense spheres and with them all known avenues of knowledge and experience must, for the time being, cease. At such a moment, it would hardly be possible to have a conceptual understanding or insight, such as the reflection: "Ah, this is *dukkha/duḥkha*," and then: "Oh, this is its arising," etc.

For reaching the breakthrough to the cessation of the six sense spheres, however, the four truths have a central role to play in the form of right view as the guiding principle of the practice of the path. Moreover, once this breakthrough has happened, the scheme of four truths offers a convenient way of conveying to others what has taken place. Nevertheless, the actual breakthrough itself would not involve a conceptualization of the four truths (or of any other teaching). In fact, holding on to concepts would risk preventing the breakthrough from taking place, as it would mean that the letting go is not complete. In sum, the proper place of insightful conceptualization in terms of the four truths appears to be before and after the actual realization of the one truth of cessation.

This relates to a topic already explored above (see p. 68), in that the three higher trainings are indispensable for progress but any holding on to them needs to be relinquished at the actual moment of realizing the deathless. The same must hold for all doctrinal teachings, including the four truths. Support for this suggestion can be garnered from a verse extant in Pāli and Chinese, according to which neither view, nor learning, nor the practice of virtue leads in itself to the purity of freedom from delusion, nor does the same take place in the absence of view, learning, and virtue (translated by Bodhi 2017, 301).[214] The verse continues with the indication that a key requirement is to let go of these and not grasp them.[215]

According to another Pāli discourse, one does not make an end of *dukkha/duḥkha* just by means of knowledge. The passage clarifies that to envisage that making an end of *dukkha/duḥkha* takes place by means of knowledge—or else by means of conduct or by means of both conduct and knowledge in combination—would imply that one can achieve realization while still being with something clung to or relied on, in other words, while still being within the realm of what is constructed. Presumably to avoid any misunderstanding, the passage continues by indicating that one bereft of conduct and knowledge will be completely unable to make an end of *dukkha/duḥkha*.[216] Summing up the situation, the Pāli discourse offers the following clarification:[217]

> Friend, one devoid of conduct does not know and see as it really is. One endowed with conduct knows and sees as it really is. Knowing and seeing as it really is, one becomes an end-maker [of *dukkha/duḥkha*].

That is, although neither conduct nor knowledge causes awakening, conduct provides the foundation for knowledge and knowledge in turn the required preparation for awakening to take place.

The same point comes to the fore in another Pāli discourse and its two Chinese parallels.[218] The relevant discussion clarifies that none out of a set of seven types of purification, ranging from morality to knowledge and vision, can be identified with final Nirvana (translated by Ñāṇamoli 1995/2005, 243). Nevertheless, each of these seven purifications leads on to the next, and the last in turn leads on to the realization of final Nirvana.[219]

The situation finds illustration in a relay of seven chariots used by the local king to travel from one town to another. Each of the chariots leads on to the next, and the last leads him up to the entrance of the palace. In this way, the relay of seven chariots enables him to arrive quickly and attend to the matter that required his presence. The chariots are just instrumental to the purpose of reaching the palace, and none of them is the final goal. In fact, when entering the palace to attend to that matter, the king will have to leave behind even the last chariot that brought him to the palace doors. If he were to refuse to get off that chariot, he would not be able to enter the palace. In the same way, any knowledge and vision as the outcome of previous practices can indeed lead up to the threshold of the deathless, but at this point one has to get off, so to say: one has to go beyond even that knowledge and vision in order to realize the supreme truth.

The perspective conveyed by these passages has not always been fully appreciated in later times. A telling example from the Pāli commentarial tradition is Buddhaghosa's adoption of the scheme of seven purifications as the basic scaffolding for his Path of Purification (*Visuddhimagga*), in the course of which he identifies the seventh stage of purification with the path-moments of the four levels of awakening.[220] To include even the path-moment of arahantship under the seventh stage of purification is difficult to reconcile with another discourse, in which the seven purifications recur as part of a listing of nine, with "liberation" as the last purification (translated Walshe 1987, 519).[221] It follows that after the seventh purification another two stages were considered necessary for complete arrival at liberation.

In terms of the simile illustrating the function of the set of seven purifications, mentioned above, it is impossible to drive with the last chariot into the palace. However useful the chariot was earlier when on the road, one needs to get off and walk the last bit on one's own feet to go inside the building. Similarly, the breakthrough to liberation can only happen when all of these seven purifications, after they have performed the needed preparatory work, are completely relinquished.

As noted by Ñāṇananda (2015, 49) in a different context: "There are some who fondly hope to get a vision of their lists of concepts when they realize *Nibbāna*." Yet, as he points out, penetrating to the final goal goes beyond all concepts. Such penetration is in a way the last hurdle, when even the most useful concepts and profound insights need to be relinquished in order to "real"-ize the one truth of Nirvana. Ñāṇananda (2015, 296) illustrates the situation by comparing concepts to a scaffolding employed in building work:

> We should make use of the conceptual scaffolding only for the purpose of putting up the building. As the building comes up, the scaffolding has to leave. It has to be dismantled. If one simply clings onto the scaffolding, the building would never come up.

Understood in this way, it is the complete stepping out of all constructions, and therewith necessarily out of all conceptualizations—including core doctrinal teachings like the four noble truths—that stands in the background of the early Buddhist notion of truth and provides it with its epistemic grounding. As succinctly expressed by Dhammadinnā (2021, 102), "Nirvāṇa informs the entire early Buddhist approach to truth and valid pathways to knowledge."

Grounding truth in the realization of the deathless, in the sense of stepping out of the construction of experience in toto, appears to be also relevant to a tendency in a few discourses to pursue a line of investigation by way of positing counterparts. For example, what is pleasant has its counterpart in what is unpleasant, and so on.[222] When this type of inquiry reaches Nirvana, however, the procedure comes to a halt. Anyone attempting to push things further, by inquiring after the counterpart to Nirvana, will incur criticism for attempting to do what is not possible (translated by Ñāṇamoli 1995/2005, 403).[223]

Cousins (1983, 107 and 106) reasons that since Nirvana is beyond time or space, "it cannot be related to that which is temporal or spatial—not even by the relation of negation!" For the same reason, no "place or time can be nearer to or further from the unconditioned."

A poetic expression of the relationship between the path and the goal can be found in a Pāli discourse (translated by Walshe 1987, 302), whose Sanskrit parallel takes the following form:[224]

> Just as the water of the Ganges and the water of the Yamuna, flowing into each other, indeed flow into the ocean, in the same way . . . Nirvana and the path going toward Nirvana flow into each other.

The reference here is to two rivers in India that merge into each other (in the area of modern Allahabad) before reaching the ocean. In fact, the Pāli version does not even mention their subsequent flowing into the ocean, thereby conveying the main point with additional clarity. For a considerable part of their trajectory, the Ganges and Yamuna are two distinct rivers. Yet, at the place of their conjunction they become one and coalesce.

The implications of the poetic image of the two rivers coalescing offers a welcome corrective to a potential temptation to set *saṃsāra* and Nirvana too far apart. Without losing the basic distinction between the path as something conditioned and the goal as unconditioned, the image of the two rivers coalescing prevents positing these two as totally apart from each other. At the same time, it also does not go so far as to conflate them. It is not necessary to go to the other extreme of flatly equating *saṃsāra* and Nirvana in order to avoid a binary opposition between the two. The above simile does a better job in this respect, as it does not overlook the fact that, for a considerable part of its trajectory, the path is as distant from the goal as these two rivers are from each other before reaching their merging point. Yet, progress to that merging point reveals what the path—as the conditioned means for arrival at the unconditioned—has in common with the goal. From that viewpoint, the water can just be allowed to run its natural course by eventually coalescing and becoming one.

6. Beyond Views

The early Buddhist notion of truth stands in a close interrelationship with going beyond views. A well-known analysis of views in the Discourse on Brahmā's Net (*Brahmajālasutta*) focuses on the contrast between seeing the truth and the construction of views (translated by Walshe 1987, 89). Contrary to a popular assessment, the concerns of the discourse are not to provide a catalogue of views as such.[225] The Pāli version surveys sixty-two "grounds" (*vatthu*) for views, rather than sixty-two views, and the concerns of this survey are epistemic in nature. The purpose is to reveal how certain experiences, often related to meditation practices, result in the construction of views. Yet, seeing through the construction of experience leads beyond such views. A Chinese version of the discourse expresses such transcendence of views in the following manner:[226]

> If a monastic knows as it really is the arising of the six [spheres of] contact, their cessation, their advantage, their disadvantage, and the escape from them, then this is supreme and leads out of all those views.

The cessation of the six sense spheres, equaling the cessation of the corresponding types of contact, is at the same time also a cessation of the constructing of views. Once this much has become a matter of personal experience, it undermines holding on to views dogmatically, ready to debate with anyone who dares to disagree. It appears to be precisely for this reason that a full realization of the deathless leads to the absence of disputation with the entire world, to employ the phrase quoted earlier (see above p. 79).

The same basic stance comes up again in another analysis of views extant in Pāli and Tibetan. The relevant passage occurs repeatedly as the concluding assessment of various types of views, which are qualified as gross and constructed. In contrast to these, the Buddha has realized the cessation of constructions and therefore transcended all such views (translated by Ñāṇamoli 1995/2005, 840).[227]

Yet another discourse relevant to the present topic is addressed to the wanderer Vacchagotta/Vatsagotra, who in the early discourses features as a person quite obsessed with views, presumably influenced by a tendency in the ancient Indian setting to consider the adopting of a view as purificatory in itself.[228] In reply to Vacchagotta's/Vatsagotra's insistence to affirm one or the other out of a particular set of views, the Buddha is on record for clarifying that, through his vision, he had gone beyond views (translated by Ñāṇamoli 1995/2005, 592). In the parallel versions this reply involves a play on what is basically the same word, by presenting *vision* as that which leads beyond *views*. The Tibetan version presents the matter in the following manner (referring to the Buddha as the "Thus Gone One"):[229]

> The Thus Gone One has relinquished all types of view. Although the Thus Gone One has relinquished all types of view, he has a certain point of view. What is that?

The Pāli version expresses the difference to be made here by distinguishing between "resorting to views" (*diṭṭhigata*), which has been left behind, and what has been "seen" (*diṭṭha*). Whereas in the parallel versions that which has been seen takes the form of a vision of the four noble truths, in the Pāli version it concerns seeing the arising and passing away of the five aggregates of clinging. Although adopting different formulations, the parallels can be taken to agree on the realization of the deathless—corresponding to full insight into the third noble truth and the realization of the cessation of the five aggregates of clinging—as the type of vision that leads beyond views. This thereby points to the type of stepping out of the construction of experience that leads beyond resorting to views, yet without thereby discounting the view, or more accurately the vision, that results from that very stepping out.

The problem of flatly rejecting any view without allowing for an alternative comes up in an exchange with another wanderer, who reportedly introduced himself as one who did not approve of anything; some versions indicate that this meant not approving of any view or any teaching.[230] The Buddha is on record for querying, somewhat tongue-in-cheek, if the wanderer at least approved of the position taken by himself (translated by Ñāṇamoli 1995/2005, 603). This inquiry goes to show that one way or another, it is not possible to escape completely from having a viewpoint. The claim "I do not hold any view" is in turn also a view.

The background provided by these passages enables a better appreciation of references to views in the Chapter on Eights (*Aṭṭhakavagga*). Some of these indicate that the accomplished sage "has shaken off all views right here" and hence "does not even fall back on any view at all," being "a wise one who is released from resorting to views."[231]

Such references are best read in the light of the passages explored above; in fact, the last reference to "resorting to views" (*diṭṭhigata*) employs the same terminology as the clarification addressed to Vacchagotta/Vatsagotra. It would hardly do justice to the Chapter on Eights if its poems were to be read without taking into account similar material found elsewhere among the early discourses. Be it the verses assembled in this chapter or any other particular passage occurring in another collection, a proper understanding of early Buddhist thought requires what Park (2012, 78 and 74) has aptly called a "systematic reading." This calls for an "honest effort to understand the whole context of a text or its doctrinal system." Such a systematic reading "provides a consistent understanding of the text, consistent not merely within itself but within a wider textual context."

The recommendation to adopt a systematic reading of such references in the Chapter on Eights, in the sense of contextualizing them with the help of other relevant passages found elsewhere among the early discourses, runs counter to a popular tendency of positing this collection as supposedly reflecting an early stage of Buddhist thought that differs substantially from the remainder of the early texts. In a critical reply to such a procedure,[232] Norman (2003, 513) points out that it is hardly surprising if a collection of just sixteen individual poems does not cover each and every doctrinal item found elsewhere. In fact, the Chapter on Going Beyond (*Pārāyanavagga*), which has a similar claim to antiquity, contains references to some of the doctrinal teachings not covered in the Chapter on Eights. Rather than presuming that the Chapter on Eights represents a pre-canonical Buddhism of sorts, "it is essential to consider the Aṭṭhakavagga in the context of what we know about the history of Buddhism from other canonical sources, and the cultural background which led to the origin of Buddhism" (517). In sum, there is "no reason whatsoever for believing that the form of Buddhism taught in the [Aṭṭhaka]vagga represents the whole of Buddhism at the time of its composition, and that everything not included in it must be a later addition" (519).

Although de-contextualization can lead to surprising results, it risks not doing proper justice to the texts and can end up merely catering to personal preferences (which in the case of such readings of the Chapter on Eights can easily be influenced by postmodern sensitivities). If the aim is to gain a proper understanding of the attitude toward views in the Chapter on Eights, then material found outside of it cannot be ignored. A starting point for such exploration could be the discourse passage mentioned above which reveals that the claim "I do not hold any view" is in turn also a view. It follows that, at least from an early Buddhist perspective, to promote "no view" is not fully coherent. The task is rather to promote a lack of attachment to views. As succinctly clarified by Smith (2015, 174): "non-attachment to views is not the same as having no views."

Another relevant instruction is the famous simile of the raft (translated by Ñāṇamoli 1995/2005, 228).[233] The warning sounded by the original delivery of this simile is that one should be willing to let go of a raft once it has fulfilled its purpose of enabling the crossing of a water current. The raft is needed, as otherwise one would be unable to cross over. Yet, once the other shore has been reached, it is of no use to keep carrying the raft along. The delivery of the simile of the raft then leads on to the powerful instruction to the listening disciples that they should be ready to leave even the teachings behind, not to speak of leaving behind what is contrary to them.[234] This instruction is just as powerful as the verses on views in the Chapter on Eights.

The importance accorded to the raft simile can be seen from the fact that, in addition to its original occurrence, another discourse reports the Buddha quoting this very simile (translated by Ñāṇamoli 1995/2005, 352).[235] The Buddha quoting his own simile of the raft occurs at the end of a teaching to establish the listening monastics in a correct understanding of conditionality. The teaching was reportedly occasioned by the affirmation of a serious misunderstanding by a monastic disciple, in the form of making a claim implying the notion of a permanent consciousness. After having made sure that this misunderstanding has been fully removed, the teaching closes in the following manner in the Chinese version:[236]

> If, having understood it in this way and seen it in this way, you were to consider that "in this way this view of mine is pure" and attach to it, cherish it, be defensive about it, and be unwilling to abandon it, would you have understood what I have for a long time taught you about the Dharma resembling a raft?

In this way, right after having had to clarify a serious misunderstanding and ensuring that his disciples had a proper grasp of the all-important principle of conditionality, the Buddha is on record for immediately turning to any possible grasping at the very understanding or view he had just inculcated (the Pāli version explicitly uses the term "view" here). This conveniently embodies the attitude that is also relevant to some of the verses in the Chapter on Eights. The raft simile clearly conveys the need to have the correct view. In fact, the monastic—whose obstinate adherence to a serious misunderstanding reportedly caused the whole teaching—met with a strong rebuke by the Buddha. In other words, the raft has an important purpose, and throwing it away before having used it for crossing over would be self-defeating. At the same time, however, the correct understanding of the matter should remain just a raft, rather than becoming something to latch on to with attachment.

Absence of attachment is precisely a concern of right view in the form of the four truths scheme, which offers a diagnostic tool to spot the role of craving as the chief cause of *dukkha/duḥkha*. Such craving can only too easily arise in relation to one's own views and then result in attachment and dogmatic adherence. For this reason, the challenge remains to allow the role of view as an orientation point to perform its function without causing any attachment. As a Pāli verse puts it, based on a play on derivatives of the same root (*dṛś*) underlying the terms "vision" and "views," one should be "endowed with vision, without going into a view."[237]

7. Altogether Beyond

The procedure of contextualization and systematic reading proposed above can similarly be applied to study other and somewhat tantalizing references in the Chapter on Eights. One of the verses already mentioned above is a case in point. Besides commending shaking off all views, it also indicates that for a sagely person "there is nothing taken up or rejected."[238] Similar references recur elsewhere,[239] in addition to which the sage is described as one who is "not attached to passion and not attached to dispassion"; in fact, such an accomplished person "neither attaches nor detaches."[240]

The advantage of reading such references in the light of other relevant passages can be illustrated with the example of a description of an arahant/arhat, found in the following manner in a Pāli discourse:[241]

> One neither builds up nor dismantles, [but] abides having dismantled, one neither abandons nor grasps, [but] abides having abandoned, one neither disbands nor binds, [but] abides having disbanded, one neither extinguishes nor kindles, [but] abides having extinguished.

Although the parallels to this Pāli passage do not provide an explicit indication that one abides in having accomplished the activities mentioned, the presentation translated above conveys the same basic message made in a succinct form in the standard description of an arahant/arhat in different reciter traditions. The parallel versions agree in indicating that such a person "has done what is to be done."[242] Another standard indication found in different reciter traditions is the designation of someone proceeding through the different levels of progress to awakening as a "trainee" (*sekha/śaikṣa*), whereas an arahant/arhat is a "non-trainee."[243]

In the ancient Indian setting, these were important indications to make, in that an arahant/arhat has completed the task well before passing away. The deathless has been realized while still alive. One accomplished in this way has no need to dismantle, to abandon, to disband, or to extinguish, because that has already been done. The same would in turn hold for rejecting, becoming dispassionate, and not attaching, mentioned in the verses quoted above from the Chapter on Eights. The sage has no need for these, since that much has already been accomplished. The situation differs for one who has not yet done what is to be done. In such a case, there is indeed a need for dispassion and for abandoning, etc.

An analogy could perhaps be developed with the help of the idea of a path that leads to a mountaintop.[244] First of all, the top of the mountain is not caused by the path leading to it. Still, following the path can lead to the top of the mountain. In the same way, although the deathless is not caused by the path, following the proper path can lead to the breakthrough to the deathless. Moreover, seeing that someone who has successfully reached the mountaintop is just standing or sitting there, enjoying the scenery, should not be taken to imply that the standing and sitting postures are the only acceptable means for getting to the mountaintop. There is a need to keep walking upward, as long as the mountaintop has not been reached.

During such progress, at times one may stand or even sit down and rest before moving on. So the standing and sitting postures have a place even when going up the mountain. But the ascent to the mountaintop should not be confined to these postures, as that would be self-defeating. In the same way, although for a non-trainee who has done what needed to be done there is no longer any need to develop dispassion and letting go, these are important means for eventually being able to sit on the mountaintop of full liberation.

Finally, as a way of rounding off this illustration by relating it to the simile of the Ganges and the Yamuna rivers flowing into each other: when viewed from the bottom of the mountain, the path and the mountaintop are far apart. Yet, eventually the path and the mountaintop will converge, as the final part of the path is on the mountaintop.

The need to distinguish between the accomplishments of an arahant/arhat and the qualities required by someone who is still training to become a fully liberated one is also evident with another verse in the Chapter on Eights, which in addition to referring to the absence of attachment also qualifies such a person as being without faith or confidence (translated by Bodhi 2017, 303).[245] A verse in a different textual collection similarly describes the highest person as being one without faith or confidence (translated by Norman 1997/2004, 14).[246] This does not imply a rejection of the need for faith or confidence (*saddhā/śraddhā*) to embark on and pursue the path. The point is rather that the realization of the deathless is of such a transformative type that it results in an unshakeable inner certitude; at that point there is no longer any need to arouse faith or confidence for what has become a matter of direct and personal realization.

The basic principle here finds expression in another otherwise unrelated passage, according to which only those who have not had personal realization of a particular matter will have to place their faith or confidence in others (translated by Bodhi 2000, 1690).[247] This stands in contrast to the inner certitude, already gained by a stream-enterer, from having realized the deathless. In this respect, a stream-enterer is considered comparable to a gate post firmly planted in the ground, which cannot be shaken by any wind (translated by Bodhi 2017, 194).[248]

Not only faith or confidence but even moral observances are in a way to be given up, in the sense of not holding on to them with attachment. A verse in the Chapter on Going Beyond states that those who have abandoned moral observances and also everything else, having penetrated craving with understanding and being without influxes, are reckoned to have crossed over the flood (translated by Bodhi 2017, 337).[249] An otherwise unrelated discourse passage takes up the topic of the complete cessation of wholesome moral conduct (*kusalā sīlā*). The Pāli version's exploration of this topic (translated by Ñāṇamoli 1995/2005, 651), which adds to the relevant reference a pointer to liberation of the mind and liberation by wisdom, indicates that one is virtuous without identifying with such virtue, literally without "being made of virtue" (*sīlamaya*).[250] The Chinese parallel, which presents the matter without an explicit reference to liberation, proceeds in this way:[251]

> Where is wholesome conduct eradicated without remainder, where is it destroyed without remainder? When a learned noble disciple practices virtue without being attached to virtue, this is wholesome conduct being eradicated without remainder, destroyed without remainder.

The reference in both versions to being virtuous or to practicing virtue makes it clear that the tantalizing reference to the cessation or eradication of wholesome conduct, even to its destruction, is not meant to endorse misbehavior. The need for a foundation in morality is not in question. The target of the exposition appears to be much rather attachment to conduct, identification with it.

Such references to the need to go altogether beyond can be appreciated from the viewpoint of fostering progress toward stepping out of the construction of experience. Although moral conduct and faith or confidence are important means for progress, there is an overarching need to step out of patterns of identification. Otherwise, the very supports for progress could turn into obstructions for the letting go required for the breakthrough to the deathless to take place.

Understood in this way, the central message that emerges with the intriguing verses from the Chapter on Eights, briefly surveyed above, can be understood to carry similar implications as a short instruction reportedly given to the celestial king Sakka/Śakra, which in the Pāli version takes the following form:[252] "All phenomena are not worth adhering to!"

The Pāli version continues by depicting how this type of injunction can lead to contemplating any feeling tones (*vedanā*) from the viewpoint of impermanence, dispassion, cessation, and letting go (translated by Ñāṇamoli 1995/2005, 344). Building on impermanence, the other three are key insights that activate the awakening factors (see above p. 66). As a result of such contemplation, there is no clinging to anything and no agitation. This in turn provides the groundwork required for the breakthrough to Nirvana to occur.

A parallel extant in Chinese similarly follows its version of this injunction with contemplation of impermanence, leading to the absence of attachment and agitation, and to the realization of Nirvana. This Chinese version expresses the actual injunction in this way:[253] "Understand: all phenomena are empty and insubstantial, nothing indeed to be attached to!"

8. Nonproliferation

The nature of the breakthrough to the realization of Nirvana can be explored further with the help of a Pāli discourse and its Chinese parallel, which set out by recording that Sāriputta/Śāriputra was queried if there is still something left when the six spheres of contact cease (translated by Bodhi 2012, 539). The reply reportedly given by Sāriputta/Śāriputra refuses to assert this option. The inquiry continues with the alternative question of whether nothing remains when the six spheres of contact cease, followed by exploring an additional two alternatives envisaged in ancient Indian thought: that there could remain at the same time something and nothing or else that there could be neither something nor nothing. Sāriputta/Śāriputra dismisses each of these alternatives. Since these four alternatives exhaust the possible replies that, according to ancient Indian thought, could be given on any particular matter, the discussion naturally continues with a request to explain the position he had taken. According to the Chinese version, he offered the following clarification.[254]

> This is indeed baseless talk: "When the six spheres of contact have been eradicated, faded away, ceased, appeased, and disappeared, is there a remainder?" This is indeed baseless talk: "Is there no remainder?" This is indeed baseless talk: "Is there a remainder and no remainder?" This is indeed baseless talk: "Is there neither a remainder nor no remainder?" If one says: "When the six spheres of contact have been eradicated, faded away, ceased, appeased, and disappeared, one is apart from all that is baseless and false and attains Nirvana," then this is indeed what the Buddha taught.

According to the Pāli version, Sāriputta/Śāriputra explained that by taking up any of these four positions one conceptually proliferates what is not proliferative (*appapañcaṃ papañceti*). The Pāli explanation continues by clarifying that the range of the six spheres of contact corresponds to the range of conceptual proliferation; with their cessation, proliferation ceases as well.

From the viewpoint of the parallel versions of this discourse, these four alternatives are simply baseless talk or a conceptual proliferation (a term that in its early Buddhist usage invariably carries negative connotations). In short, each misses the point. Notably, this holds also for the position that there is nothing left when the six spheres of contact cease. Affirming flatly that there is nothing left is just as misguided as the affirmation that there is something left.

A pointer to the limitations of language can also be seen in a Pāli verse featuring an exchange between the Buddha and a brahmin youth in search of the final goal. The exchange leads to the topic of the destiny of one who has reached the final goal:[255]

> Like a flame flung away by the force of wind,
> Goes out and is beyond reckoning,
> So the sage, freed from the category of name,
> Goes out and is beyond reckoning.

The brahmin youth Upasīva insists on being given more information. Apparently attempting to fit this description into the model of either eternal survival or annihilation, Upasīva's next inquiry is whether such going out should be understood to entail that there is nothing or else that there is eternal absence of affliction. This leads to the following clarification in reply:[256]

> There is no measuring of one gone to the end;
> That by which one might speak [of the sage] no longer exists [for the sage].
> All things being removed,
> All pathways of language are removed as well.

The realization of that which is not proliferative sets a limit to what can be expressed by language. The sage gone beyond the domain of name—in the sense of the mental operations responsible for giving names to things and experiences—can no longer be reckoned in terms of such naming. The basic point is similar to the indication that it is baseless talk or a proliferation of what is not proliferative to try to define the nature of the stepping out of the construction of experience. The very attempt to do so undermines the need to wean the mind gradually from its habit to construct; it thereby runs counter to what is required for progressing to the final goal.

Concepts are not problematized in toto, as they have an important role to play for moving toward what is not proliferative, comparable to the employment of a raft to cross a river (see above p. 96).[257] However, reliance on concepts should not result in trying to force the final goal of stepping out of construction and nonproliferation into the limited mold of verbal construction and conceptual proliferation.

The need to beware of proliferation comes up in a complementary way in relation to a teaching that lists eight thoughts of a great person. The relevant Pāli discourse and one of its Chinese parallels report that Anuruddha/Aniruddha was reflecting on key requirements for progress on the path, which led him to the realization that the Buddha's teaching is for one who has few desires, is content, resorts to seclusion, is energetic, mindful, concentrated, and wise (translated by Bodhi 2012, 1160). The Buddha reportedly added an eighth quality: delight in nonproliferation.[258] The Pāli discourse and most of its parallels conclude by reporting that Anuruddha/Aniruddha took this advice to heart and, after a period of diligent practice, became an arahant/arhat. A verse extant only in Pāli explains the basic principle as follows:[259]

> One who, abandoning conceptual proliferation,
> Delights in the track of nonproliferation,
> Such a one achieves Nirvana,
> The supreme security from bondage.

From the viewpoint of the realization of Nirvana as a stepping out of the construction of experience and therewith of course out of any conceptual proliferation, the track of nonproliferation would indeed be crucial in order to be able to arrive at the deathless, the supreme security from bondage. In other words, the refusal to declare what is or is not left, once the six spheres of contact cease, just as the unwillingness to concretize the after-death condition of the sage, is not merely a form of sophistry or equivocation. Instead, it seems unavoidable as long as the speaker is sincerely trying to convey the matter in a way that enables others to cross the flood themselves.

9. The Quenching of Fire

The lofty perspectives emerging from the various passages surveyed above can in a way be considered to converge on the down-to-earth matter of freedom from defilements, which is perhaps the most central implication of full awakening in early Buddhist soteriology. This implication finds reflection in a succinct definition of Nirvana, which speaks simply of the eradication of the three root defilements (translated by Bodhi 2000, 1294). The Chinese version presents the matter as follows:[260]

> The perpetual eradication of lustful desires, the perpetual eradication of anger, the perpetual eradication of delusion, and the perpetual eradication of any defilements: this is called Nirvana.

The definition of arahantship/arhatship is in turn the successful eradication of these three root poisons.[261] Later exegesis takes up this second definition, regarding the arahant/arhat, to argue that the equation of Nirvana with the destruction of the defilements should not be read in a reductionist manner, as if Nirvana were only such destruction. Such a reading fails to work for arahantship/arhatship, even though this is defined in the same manner (translated by Ñāṇamoli 1956/1991, 515).[262] In other words, although the eradication of the three root poisons is indeed characteristic of arahants/arhats, much more can be said about their qualities. One such additional quality, which is particularly noteworthy as it does not conform to some polemic depictions of arahants/arhats in later texts, is their compassion.[263]

In practical terms, the eradication of all defilements means that, from an early Buddhist viewpoint, an arahant/arhat is held to be incapable of deliberately killing a sentient being, of taking what is not given by way of theft, of engaging in sexual intercourse, and of intentionally speaking a falsehood (translated by Walshe 1987, 435).[264]

The imperturbable nature of the mind of an arahant/arhat can be illustrated with the help of an image that already came up in relation to a stream-enterer's firm faith or confidence, which the texts compare to a firm gate post (see above p. 100). In the case of an arahant/arhat, however, such firmness goes further, as it applies to equanimity in relation to anything experienced. The relevant passage proclaims that the mind of a fully awakened one cannot be perturbed by whatever happens at any sense door, just as a mountain or a column firmly planted in the ground will not be shaken by wind from the four directions.[265]

A Pāli discourse draws out the implications of the ethical perfection reached with full awakening by indicating that, with the three root defilements eradicated, one will no longer form intentions for what is harmful to others or oneself. This corresponds to the basic idea underlying the early Buddhist conception of compassion, which is the motivation to avoid or at least diminish any harm afflicting others and oneself.[266] The same discourse continues by highlighting that in this way Nirvana can be considered something directly visible right here and now (translated by Bodhi 2012, 253).[267] Another Pāli discourse draws attention to the fact that arahants/arhats, who do not torment others or themselves, dwell in happiness and can even be reckoned to have become divine themselves (translated by Ñāṇamoli 1995/2005, 453).[268] This again resonates with compassion, which is one of the divine abodes (*brahmavihāra*).

In contrast, the agitation caused in the mind by the three root defilements of lust, anger, and delusion finds illustration in the image of three types of fire (translated by Walshe 1987, 484).[269] In other words, the root defilements set the mind on fire. According to what traditionally is regarded as the third sermon given by the Buddha, such setting on fire can affect every aspect of experience through the six senses (translated by Bodhi 2000, 1143).[270]

The imagery of the fire of defilements that emerges in these passages can in turn conveniently be related to the basic underlying sense of the term *nibbāna/nirvāṇa* as the quenching of a fire.[271] Discussions of the Buddhist conception of Nirvana at times refer to passages in the *Upaniṣads* as conveying the sense that, even though a fire has gone out, it is nevertheless in some way still latent.[272] This notion could be relevant to the verse spoken reportedly by the Buddha to the brahmin Upasīva, discussed above (see p. 103),[273] as the latter's attempt to ascertain the matter further may be read as reflecting the influence of such an idea of latent existence. However, such a sense would not be applicable to the fires of the three root defilements. These are considered to have become extinct for good in an arahant/arhat and to be incapable of manifesting again. The same holds for another employment of the image of a fire going out, found in descriptions of the passing away of an arahant/arhat. This relates in particular to all feeling tones becoming cool. The Chinese version of one such passage presents the matter like this:[274]

> Experiencing the final feeling tones in life, one then knows to be experiencing the final feeling tones in life. One knows that, with the breaking up of the body and the ending of life, the life span having come to be completed, all that is being felt will be extinguished and cease, becoming cool . . .
>
> It is like, for example, a lamp that burns in dependence on oil and in dependence on a wick. If nobody adds further oil and also does not supply the wick, what was there previously, having come to an end, will not continue further, with nothing more to be experienced.

The sense of some latency that still remains, in line with the apparent implications of the imagery of extinguished fire in some *Upaniṣads*, is not applicable here. The feeling tones described are those experienced during life. With the passing away of an arahant/arhat, these will indeed become cool in the sense of coming to an end, rather than continuing to exist in some latent form.

Another usage of the same imagery appears to be related to the nature of the actual breakthrough to the deathless. In such cases as well, the idea of some form of latent continuity would not be relevant. An example is the following statement: "Liberation of the mind was like the Nirvana of a lamp."

The instance just quoted is preceded by an injunction to examine the teachings and see their meaning with wisdom.[275] Another such instance speaks of the cessation of consciousness and of liberation by the destruction of craving (translated by Bodhi 2012, 322).[276] Although these instances could in principle be read in the light of another such reference related to the Buddha's passing away (translated by Walshe 1987, 271),[277] it seems to me fair to propose that they could also convey a sense of the actual experience, perhaps serving as a double entendre.

In fact, as already mentioned, a distinct characteristic of the early Buddhist approach to liberation is that the deathless is considered within reach while one is still alive, rather than only occurring when passing away. For this reason, it seems safe to assume that a reference to "liberation of the mind" would intend the moment someone becomes an arahant/arhat, rather than their passing away. The realization of full awakening has of course repercussions on such passing away as well. In the case of the Buddha, this reportedly took place in a way that fully reflected his superbly liberated mind. Still, the actual liberation of his mind had already been attained earlier, namely in the night of his awakening.[278] This sense holds indubitably for yet another relevant instance, which describes the actual breakthrough to the deathless by the nun Paṭācārā at precisely the moment when she pulled out the wick of her lamp:[279]

> Then I took a pin and drew out the wick.
> Liberation of the mind was like the Nirvana of the lamp.

The preceding verses convey that she had earlier not yet reached the final goal and on this particular day had aroused a strong perception of impermanence on watching the flow of water. Having reached a concentrated mind, she decided to enter her hut. As it had presumably become dark by then, she needed a lamp to check the place where she was going to sit. To do so is natural in the Indian setting, as one needs to check if insects or other small creatures have settled in that place. Presumably seated and ready to continue meditating, she drew out the wick and the Nirvana of the lamp apparently coincided with the Nirvana of her mind.

The assumption that such a nuance could also underlie the other references would then imply that the imagery of the extinction of the lamp can convey the actual experience *and* its repercussions. To some extent, these are in fact two sides of the same coin. The very experience of totally stepping out of the construction of experience is what deprives the fire of the defilements of their fuel, by way of undermining and eventually rendering inoperative those unwholesome perceptions that tend to trigger defiled reactivity. When viewed from the perspective of the harmful repercussions of defilements, the emphasis of the basic image of a fire being quenched would then be on conveying that the fires of defilements no longer burn oneself and others. That is, an image that on the surface may appear merely negative can, on closer inspection, be understood to carry quite positive connotations. In a later part of my exploration, I will return to the need to balance negative and positive connotations (see below p. 120).

An image descriptive of an arahant's/arhat's knowledge of having gained freedom of the mind takes the form of describing a person who stands on the bank of a pond and sees clearly the animals inside of the pond (translated by Walshe 1987, 108).[280] The image conveys that fully awakened ones are endowed with similar clarity regarding the liberation of their minds from defilements. The positive image of watching various animals in a pond complements the image of the extinct fire, supporting the impression that it would probably not do justice to the implications of the latter if it were to be read in an entirely negative light.

The transformative repercussions of a breakthrough to the deathless already apply to stream-entry. In line with a standard type of description, a Pāli discourse indicates that with the arising of the Dharma-eye the first three fetters are abandoned:[281]

> When the dustless and stainless Dharma-eye arises in a noble disciple, with the arising of vision . . . three fetters of the noble disciple are eradicated: the view of a [reified sense] of identity,

> doubt, and dogmatic clinging to conduct and observances [as in themselves liberating].

The imagery of an eye, employed here, appears to convey the inner clarity that comes with a genuine breakthrough to stream-entry. Even though the fires of the root defilements will only be completely extinguished with full awakening, already the first encounter with the deathless results in a substantial transformation of the mind by way of eradicating three of its fetters. In order to appreciate the shift of perspective and inner change that, according to the texts, takes place in this way, the construction of experience can again be of considerable help.

The parallel versions of the enigmatic verse in the Discourse on Quarrels and Disputes, discussed above as presenting a perception different from all other kinds of perception (see p. 80), end by noting that "proliferations originate from perception" (Chinese) or else that "perception is the root of proliferation" (Pāli). Another verse in the same collection offers the following assessment:[282] "There are no bonds for one who is unattached to perception."

Clearly, the way perception operates is central for the problem of mental bondage and the arising of proliferation. This in turn can conveniently be related to an aspect of the sign, explored in the first part of my study, namely that sensual lust, ill will, and delusion are makers of signs (see above p. 8). Through the operation of the corresponding signs, the root defilements are, in a way, woven into the manner in which the unawakened mind experiences the world. The problem is that the influence of the three root defilements on the construction of the world of experience usually goes unnoticed. From the subjective point of view of a mind that is still subject to defilements, things out there are sensually alluring, irritating, or bewildering.

This situation can change through awareness of the constructed nature of experience. It seems reasonable to assume that one who has had a breakthrough to the unconstructed will no longer be able to take the constructed as seriously as earlier. This could in turn be related to another passage, taken up in the first part of my study (see above p. 15), which relates the insight that "all this is unreal" to freedom from defilements. In other words, it would be precisely the diminishing belief in those signs that are triggers of defilements as "real," as a result of having experienced the unconstructed, that undermines their ability to carry the mind away.

A complementary perspective on the gradual diminishing of the tendency for the mind to be carried away emerges in a detailed analysis of the way the same objects are perceived by a worldling, a "trainee" (*sekha/śaikṣa*), and an arahant/arhat. Whereas the worldling is caught up in various misconceptions and reifications, the trainee avoids these and the arahant/arhat is completely free from them. The illustration of these different modes of perceiving takes up a similar range of possible objects as the passages surveyed earlier that describe a way of meditating, of paying attention, and of perceiving that is substantially different from average perception (see above p. 71). A significant difference is that in the present case the difference in how things are perceived applies even to Nirvana itself (translated by Ñāṇamoli 1995/2005, 87).[283] Here, too, the worldling tends to misconceive and reify Nirvana. Since the trainee, in spite of having already had a personal experience of it, still has to make an effort to avoid reification, it is only with the profound insight of an arahant that Nirvana has been completely understood and will no longer be reified in any way.

In this way, successive encounters with the deathless during one's progress to awakening change the way perceptual appraisal operates. One who has had even a first such encounter, involving a perception that differs completely from all other perceptions, would no longer be able to operate based on the assumption that those ordinary perceptions are all that there is. In the case of a stream-enterer, this applies in particular to the notion of a self. Even just a momentary stepping out of the construction of experience would make it a matter of direct personal experience that all self-referentiality is based on a construct, not on an actually existing entity. The central peg of unawakened constructing activities—namely the assumption that self-referentiality is grounded in something that really exists—would no longer fit into its place as well as it did before.

Once the stream-enterer has had an experience completely without even a trace of this sense of self-referentiality, which otherwise features as a constant given of ordinary experience, any view that reifies the self becomes meaningless. The resultant inner conviction appears to be such that fundamental doubts no longer arise and the role of conduct and observances is properly understood. Needless to say, overcoming the last of these three fetters does not imply an abandoning of morality as such. To the contrary, virtuous conduct becomes ever more natural and even inevitable the more one progresses on the path to awakening. The eradication of the abovementioned fetter only implies that one correctly understands the role of conduct and observances.

The same basic pattern would hold for continued progress toward full awakening. Due to the impact of the successive levels of such progress, perception would become ever more transformed, until eventually the three root defilements are no longer able to make signs, in the sense of influencing perception. In this way, the second breakthrough to the deathless can lead to a diminishing of sensual desire and anger with once-return, the third to their complete eradication with nonreturn, and eventually the fourth will result in the eradication of all defilements with full awakening.

Alongside this standard pattern of progress by attaining stream-entry, once return, nonreturn, and then becoming an arahant/arhat, the texts also show exceptionally gifted persons like the Buddha himself or Bāhiya (discussed above p. 17), directly reaching full awakening. In such cases, then, the breakthrough to the unconstructed must have been so penetrative as to result in a complete eradication of all defilements and fetters at once.

Whether full awakening is reached gradually or at once, in terms of some of the references from the Chapter on Eights, discussed above (see p. 95), the accomplished sage would indeed be beyond taking up or rejecting, beyond passion and dispassion, beyond attachment and nonattachment. There would no longer be any need to counter or restrain, since the way perception now operates no longer gives defilements, passion, and attachment any scope to arise in the first place. Their breeding ground has been rendered infertile by permanently disabling the functionality of the signs required for the construction of sensually alluring, irritating, or deluding perceptions. Not only have defilements apparently been rendered inoperative but selfing must also have gone into abeyance. This seems to have happened to such an extent that the one who has fully realized the deathless has gone beyond even the fear of death.

The way the process of perception changes with progress to full awakening finds illustration in a simile concerning a dead cow and its hide (translated by Ñāṇamoli 1995/2005, 1123). Suppose a butcher were to cut all the ligaments that connect the hide to the flesh of the cow and then cover it again with the hide. Even though it may at first sight resemble the state of affairs before the ligaments were cut, the flesh is no longer connected to the hide. In the same way, the ligaments of attachment between the flesh (= the senses) and the hide (= sense objects) should be cut with the sword of wisdom.[284] Another discourse employs the example of two oxen that are yoked to each other (translated by Bodhi 2000, 1230). The bondage is due not to one ox (= the senses) or the other ox (= sense objects) but due to the yoke (= desire and lust). The same discourse concludes by stating quite emphatically that the Buddha still has each of the sense organs and experiences their corresponding objects, yet he is free from reacting to them with desire and lust.[285] As noted by Karunadasa (1994, 3), "what comes to an end when Nibbana is attained is . . . a wrong interpretation of the world," in the sense of perceiving things in the world in a way that activates defilements.

Placed in a wider context of the average mode of progress on the path, then, practices such as sense restraint, bare awareness, and signless concentration, together with regular contemplation of impermanence, can provide the "gradual" training of perception that then has its "sudden" complement in the transformative breakthrough to the unconstructed. These two dimensions of transforming perception—gradually and suddenly—in conjunction lead to complete freedom of the mind from defilements. In fact, even just cultivating sense restraint well can provide a basis for stepping out of the world created by the six spheres of contact:[286]

> With [sense] doors guarded and well restrained
> Having abandoned the six spheres of contact,

> Having vomited out the root of misery,
> The eradication of the influxes has been attained by me.

10. Freedom from Ignorance

Freedom from fear and defilements equals freedom from ignorance, which is the root cause of *dukkha/duḥkha* in the standard presentation of dependent arising. A discourse of particular relevance for my exploration presents dependent arising as apart from the two extremes of existence and nonexistence (translated by Bodhi 2000, 544). The Chinese version of the relevant section proceeds as follows:[287]

> Rightly seeing and knowing the arising of the world as it really is, there is no supposing that the world does not exist. Rightly seeing and knowing the ceasing of the world as it really is, there is no supposing that the world exists.
>
> This is called being on the middle path taught apart from these two extremes; that is, because this is, that is; because of the arising of this, that arises; that is, conditioned by ignorance there are volitional constructions . . . up to . . . the whole great mass of *dukkha/duḥkha* arises. Because of the cessation of ignorance, volitional constructions cease . . . up to . . . the whole great mass of *dukkha/duḥkha* ceases.

The above passage is one of several instances of introducing the standard presentation of dependent arising by way of twelve links (given in the Chinese version in abbreviation) by formulating the basic principle of specific conditionality that stands in the background of the twelve links (as well as of other presentations that at times involve less than the full set of twelve). The basic principle of dependent arising seems to be precisely such specific conditionality, which the above passage expresses in terms of "because this is, that is; because of the arising of this, that arises." This has its complement in a similar formulation for the cessation mode of dependent arising, abbreviated in the above passage, which would then take the form: "because this is not, that is not;

because of the ceasing of this, that ceases." The standard set of twelve links, regularly employed to exemplify the workings of this basic principle, appears to stand in dialogue with an ancient Indian creation myth (see also below p. 149).[288]

Since the original of the extract translated above does not explicitly list the intervening links, its presentation in a way throws into relief the relationship between volitional constructions under the influence of ignorance and the great mass of *dukkha/duḥkha*, which will only cease with the cessation of ignorant constructions. From this perspective, reactivity by way of craving and clinging, described in the part of the twelve-link formula presented only in abbreviation in the above passage, is ultimately the outcome of ignorant modes of constructing.

Now, at the time of the actual breakthrough to the deathless, the twelve links cease altogether. In other words, none of them could be performing its usual causal operation. Nevertheless, after the experience is over, the stream-enterer still has some level of ignorance and will occasionally react with craving and clinging. Although these reactions are no longer able to go completely overboard and lead to the performance of serious misdeeds—which would at least in principle have been possible earlier—all of the twelve links are operative. Ignorance has only been diminished and not yet been completely eradicated.

Once ignorance has been completely eradicated in the case of an arahant/arhat, there would be no more craving and clinging, and hence no more arising of *dukkha/duḥkha*. This is probably best understood to refer to the type of *dukkha/duḥkha* that results from mental reactivity influenced by ignorance. An arahant/arhat can still experience physical pain. In fact, the Buddha himself is on record for explicitly stating on occasions that he had back pain and wanted to ease himself by lying down, asking a disciple to give a teaching in his stead.[289] What has been gained with the eradication of ignorance would be immunity not from physical pain but from ignorant reactions to physical pain (and also to any other manifestation of the inevitable ups and downs of life).[290]

From the viewpoint of dependent arising, several of the intermediate links not mentioned in the above abbreviation, from consciousness to feeling tones, must still be operating in the case of an arahant/arhat or a

Buddha. What has been removed for good would be the reactivity to feeling tones by way of craving and clinging. This reactivity in turn depends on ignorant constructions and no longer can take place when these have been overcome.

But even with ignorance completely eradicated, some degree of construction of experience would still be required in order to function in the world. In fact, a Pāli discourse and its parallels explicitly distinguish between the aggregates as such and the aggregates affected by clinging (translated by Bodhi 2000, 886).[291] In other words, all of the five aggregates are still there with an arahant/arhat.[292] The crucial difference appears to be that with full awakening gained, there would no longer be even a trace of clinging in relation to these five aggregates.[293] With clinging gone for good, any identification with these five aggregates would also be gone for good.

Having gone beyond any identification with the five aggregates, the arahant/arhat in turn can also no longer be identified by way of these five aggregates. Hence, the different positions apparently held in the ancient Indian setting regarding the after-death condition of a fully realized person, referred to in such contexts with the term Tathāgata, do not apply. In short, the reason why the Buddha is on record for not taking up any of these positions appears to be that they involve premises he was not willing to accept.[294]

The situation is comparable to a fire that has become extinct, in which case it will not be possible to point out a direction in which the fire has gone (translated by Ñāṇamoli 1995/2005, 593). Ñāṇananda (1971/1986, 112) reasons that "the attempt to locate a fire that has 'gone out' is a ludicrous category-mistake caused by the enslavement to linguistic conventions." Lin (2022, 155) explains: "The word 'fire' in the phrase 'an extinguished fire' fails to refer to anything within the domain of experience. Similarly, saying that the *tathāgata* 'is reborn,' 'is not reborn,' 'is both reborn and not reborn,' and 'is neither reborn nor not reborn' are all meaningless," since all such propositions are based on taking the term Tathāgata to refer to a self. Yet, the notion of a self fails to refer to anything within the domain of experience of a Tathāgata (in the Buddhist use of the term). This holds even while such a Tathāgata is still alive, preventing any predication about the destiny of such a nonexistent self after death.

A Chinese parallel to the Pāli version of the simile of the extinct fire that cannot be traced in any direction draws out the implications of this illustration in the following manner:[295]

> [A Tathāgata] has known that bodily form has been abandoned, has known that feeling tone, perception, volitional constructions, and consciousness have been abandoned, abandoned at their root, like cutting off the head of a palm tree that will not grow any further branches and in the future will never arise again. It is thus not as if [a Tathāgata] were to reach the eastern direction, the southern, the western, or the northern direction; [instead, a Tathāgata] is extremely profound, vast, immeasurable, beyond reckoning, having forever ceased.

The parallel versions agree that the image of the extinguished fire illustrates the Tathāgata's abandoning of clinging to the five aggregates, which is further exemplified with an additional simile that describes cutting off the head of a palm tree (which results in its inability to continue living). This prevents interpreting the fire simile as conveying the sense of some form of latent continuity.[296]

At the same time, however, the above passage employs the qualifications "extremely profound, vast, immeasurable, beyond reckoning, having forever ceased." The Pāli version compares the profundity of a Tathāgata, similarly described as immeasurable and beyond being fathomed, to the nature of the ocean (not mentioned in another two parallels).

Fully appreciating the above description requires keeping both dimensions in mind: the extinct fire and the beheaded palm tree as well as the profundity and the transcendence of reckoning. The simile of the ocean recurs in a Pāli discourse featuring a local king perplexed by the fact that the Buddha and his disciples were unwilling to affirm any of the different positions regarding the after-death condition of a Tathāgata. The setting is thus the same as in the passage above, as the fire simile also features in an explanation of why these different positions are all set aside without the Buddha affirming any of them. The nun Khemā/Kṣemā reportedly clarified the matter to the king in this way:[297]

> [Khemā/Kṣemā said:] "Do you have an accountant or calculator or mathematician who can count the water in the great ocean: 'there are so many gallons of water,' or 'there are so many hundreds of gallons of water,' or 'there are so many thousands of gallons of water,' or 'there are so many hundreds of thousands of gallons of water'?"
>
> [The king replied:] "No, revered lady. Why is that? Great is the ocean, revered lady, deep, immeasurable, difficult to fathom."
>
> [Khemā/Kṣemā said:] "In the same way, Great King, that bodily form by which, [in an attempt at] defining, one may define a Tathāgata, that bodily form has been abandoned by a Tathāgata, cut off at the root, made like a palm-tree stump, made something that does not become, being of a nature not to arise again in the future. Great King, a Tathāgata is freed from being reckoned in terms of bodily form, being deep, immeasurable, and difficult to fathom, just like the great ocean.
>
> 'A Tathāgata exists after death' does not apply, 'a Tathāgata does not exist after death' also does not apply, 'a Tathāgata exists and does not exist after death' also does not apply, 'a Tathāgata neither exists nor does not exist after death' also does not apply."

The same exposition then applies to the other four aggregates of feeling tone, perception, volitional constructions, and consciousness.

The explanation offered by Khemā/Kṣemā proceeds in line with a basic pattern also evident in other such instances, in that the concern of the questioner with the future destiny of a realized one is redirected to the present. The point is that the nature of a Tathāgata while still alive needs first to be clearly understood. The problem arises not just in relation to what happens after death; as right here and now a Tathāgata has already gone beyond reckoning. The same holds all the more for what happens after death. Trying to fathom the matter in terms of the constructed—existence, nonexistence, both, neither—is like trying to count the quantity of water in the ocean: a futile endeavor.[298]

At the same time, the ocean simile conveys connotations that complement the fire simile. Tilakaratne (1993, 78–79) comments that "if the arahant's end is such a simple phenomenon like that of fire, why at all is the latter's life compared to the unfathomable ocean? We usually do not make such enigmatic and grandiloquent statements about the extinguished fire." Ñāṇananda (2015, 447–50 and 487) employs the motif of a vortex to explain the ocean simile in the following manner:

> If, for instance, a vortex in the ocean comes to cease, can one ask where the vortex has gone? It will be like asking where the extinguished fire has gone. One might say that the vortex has "joined" the ocean. But that, too, would not be a proper statement to make. From the very outset what in fact was there was the great ocean, so one cannot say that the vortex has gone somewhere, nor can one say that it is not gone . . . The vortex has now become the great ocean itself. That is the significance of the comparison of the emancipated one to the great ocean . . .
>
> In reality, the vortex is merely a certain pervert state of the ocean itself. That perversion is now no more. It has ceased. It is because of that perversion that there was a manifestation of suffering. The cessation of suffering could therefore be compared to the cessation of the vortex, leaving only the great ocean as it is . . .
>
> It is where a vortex ceases that the great ocean prevails unhindered. To give up the limitations of a vortex, is to inherit the limitless ocean . . . With the cessation of a vortex, the attention of one who has been looking at it turns towards the depth, immeasurability and boundlessness of the great ocean. This line of reflection might even enable one to get a glimpse of an unworldly beauty in this philosophy of the void.

Khemā's/Kṣemā's illustration shares with the reply given to Upasīva (see above p. 103) the indication that the realized sage is beyond reckoning. The reply to Upasīva clarifies that the possibility of measuring is no longer there because all pathways of language have been transcended. Khemā's/Kṣemā's explanation instead turns to the nature of the realized sage, whose relinquishing of clinging to the five aggregates has led beyond being reckoned or measured. The principle behind this indication is that, from the viewpoint of early Buddhist thought, as long as one has an underlying tendency to defiled states, by that very tendency one can be reckoned and measured (translated by Bodhi 2000, 877).[299] Conversely, one who has eradicated all underlying tendencies has thereby gone beyond reckoning and being measured.

Such going beyond comes up in a poetic manner in relation to the Buddha himself, reportedly being his reply to an attempt to lure him with sensual pleasures. After pointing out that no craving at all could be found in him, the remainder of the verse offers the following clarification:[300]

> By what track could you lead
> One who is trackless,
> That awakened one,
> Whose range is unlimited?

11. Annihilation and Happiness

The text translated at the outset of the previous section presents dependent arising and ceasing as apart from the two extremes of reifying existence or nonexistence. The passage applies this to the existence and nonexistence of the world. Given the understanding of the world as equaling what is experienced through the six senses, discussed in the first part of my exploration (see above p. 12), perhaps this passage could be relied on for developing a similar approach for understanding the cessation of the world of the six senses, that is, the deathless. Such an approach could then take the form of proposing that interpretations which affirm either total annihilation or else some form of eternal existence risk missing the middle path position.

Notably, craving for nonexistence is one of the three types of craving recognized in the Pāli discourses as the chief causes responsible for the arising of *dukkha/duḥkha*,[301] rather than being a cause for its cessation. Conze (1962, 67) reasons that, under the influence of such craving, one may "misconceive Nirvana as a kind of death followed by mere nothingness, and fail to see the difference between a desire for the extinction of craving and a craving for extinction."

In commenting on the final Nirvana of the Buddha or of an arahant/arhat, Sharf (2014, 135) reasons that in the "early texts this nirvāṇa looks much the same as death looks to a modern atheist who does not believe in an afterlife: it is simple annihilation." Now, the materialist type of annihilation features as one out of seven alternative annihilationist views, described in the Discourse on Brahmā's Net and its parallels (translated by Walshe 1987, 84). The relevant view takes the following form in a Chinese version:[302]

> The self is the body, with its four elements and six sense spheres . . . which is indeed impermanent and will certainly fall apart, and this is correctly reckoned becoming completely annihilated.

The inclusion of this materialist view in the analysis provided in the Discourse on Brahmā's Net and its parallels implies that such views were already known among Buddhists in the ancient Indian setting. Yet, the Buddha is on record for quite explicitly rejecting the allegation that he teaches any form of annihilation (translated by Ñāṇamoli 1995/2005, 234). The Chinese version of the relevant passage proceeds as follows:[303]

> Recluses and brahmins misrepresent me by falsely saying what is untrue: "The recluse Gotama proclaims what leads to annihilation; he proclaims the cutting off and destruction of truly existent sentient beings." Yet, I make no statements about what herein does not exist. I do state that here and now the Tathāgata is free of sorrow.

The Pāli parallel proceeds differently, as here the similarly worded report about being misrepresented with what is false and untrue leads to the Buddha declaring that he just teaches *dukkha/duḥkha* and its cessation. The part preceding the above quote also differs, as the Pāli version asserts that (the support of the consciousness of) a Tathāgata is beyond being tracked here and now, whereas the Chinese version affirms that a Tathāgata has become cool, free from heat, and not otherwise.[304]

Alongside such differences, the agreement between the two parallels on the rather strongly worded rejection of the allegation to be proclaiming annihilation is noteworthy.[305] In fact, the Pāli and Chinese terminology rendered as "to mispresent" could alternatively be translated as "to slander." The statement as a whole occurs in the context of a teaching addressed to monastic disciples, following a detailed exposition of the untenability of views proclaiming a self, which leads to the description of a fully awakened one. In a different setting, when confronted by outsiders with the accusation of being an annihilationist, the Buddha is on record for replying, apparently somewhat tongue-in-cheek, that he indeed teaches annihilation, namely the annihilation of what is unwholesome (translated by Bodhi 2012, 1132).[306]

In the present case, the strong rejection of the allegation of promoting annihilation comes in both versions coupled with an indication that such annihilation concerns what is supposed to be an actually existing being. In both reciter traditions, the one responsible for transmitting the above-translated Chinese discourse and the one responsible for handing on the Pāli parallel, this phrase is not unique to the present instance. In the former reciter tradition, it recurs in another description of the Buddha being wrongly accused of annihilationism; in two Pāli discourses, it features in descriptions of annihilationist views held by non-Buddhists.[307] In its usage in Pāli discourses, this phrase thus serves as a general qualifier of annihilationist views and is not specific to the case of the Buddha being accused of teaching annihilationism.

Suppose the early Buddhist position on the nature of a Buddha or an arahant/arhat were indeed that at their death just a blank nothingness occurs. In the setting of the above statement, addressed to his own disciples, it would have better reflected such a position if the text were to convey that the Buddha indeed teaches such annihilation (in line with the humorous remark he is on record for making to non-Buddhists) and that the misunderstanding of others is simply their belief that this implies the annihilation of a truly existing self.

The same reasoning would also be relevant when evaluating the explanation reportedly given by the Buddha to Upasīva, discussed earlier (p. 103). The reply to Upasīva's inquiry, which is clearly about the after-death condition of a fully awakened sage, indicates that "there is no measuring of one gone out" and that "all pathways of language are removed," conveying that the condition of the sage gone out is beyond the reach of language. Now, the materialist type of annihilation is certainly not beyond the reach of language, as the passage quoted above clearly shows. Just leaving out the reference to the self at its outset would lead to this formulation: "The body, with its four elements and six sense spheres . . . is indeed impermanent and will certainly fall apart, and this is correctly reckoned becoming completely annihilated." There seem to be no constraints of language preventing an identification of the falling apart of the body, the four elements, and the six sense spheres as amounting to complete annihilation.

Since Upasīva's query concerned either annihilation or an eternal condition, it seems that he should be envisaged as operating under the assumption that there is a self. Hence, there may have been an additional need to clarify that there is no self in the first place to be extinguished or perpetuated. But that is also not beyond the reach of language, as the teachings on the characteristic of not self, found among the early discourses, show.[308] Thus, the reply to Upasīva does not fit the assumption that Nirvana is a mere nothingness but much rather conveys an utter transcendence that is completely beyond the reach of language and measurements.

In addition to the realization of Nirvana being distinct from mere annihilation, another relevant consideration concerns the recurrent affirmation that Nirvana is a supreme form of happiness (translated by Ñāṇamoli 1995/2005, 613).[309] According to a Pāli discourse without known parallel, to see Nirvana as happiness is even a necessary condition for being able to realize awakening (translated by Bodhi 2012, 983).[310]

An emphasis on wholesome forms of joy and happiness is indeed fairly pervasive in early Buddhist texts. An example is a depiction of the gradual path of training in a Pāli discourse, which involves an ongoing refinement of happiness (translated by Ñāṇamoli 1995/2005, 450).[311] This refinement proceeds through the happiness of blamelessness due to ethical conduct, the immaculate happiness of sense restraint, and the successive levels of happiness experienced during progress through the absorptions until, by becoming an arahant/arhat, one lives in happiness. The joy of cultivating insight could be added to this depiction, described in a verse found elsewhere, which proclaims that "there is delight beyond human [delights] on rightly seeing the teachings with insight."[312]

An emphasis on happiness comes up also in a circumstantial report. A king is on record for describing the inspiration he gained from seeing the happy demeanor of the Buddha's monastic disciples (translated by Ñāṇamoli 1995/2005, 730).[313] The verses of monastic disciples confirm this impression with recurrent assertions of their living in happiness. Here are a few selected examples:[314]

> "one who seeks happiness gains happiness,"
> "happiness has been reached through happiness,"
> "happiness has been gained through happiness,"
> "very happy indeed is Nirvana,"
> "the wise obtain happiness,"
> "happily I shall delight in the happiness of liberation,"
> "happily I lie down [or] stand; happily I live my life,"
> "I meditate happily, [thinking:] 'Oh happiness,'"
> "there is nothing superior to the happiness of Nirvana."

Even the ascetically inclined Mahākassapa/Mahākāśyapa features as the speaker of a series of verses that express his enjoyment of the beauty of nature, with the repeated exclamation "those rocks delight me."[315]

The Buddha himself is no exception to this, being on record for indicating that he even sleeps happily (translated by Bodhi 2012, 232).[316] When getting no food, he is on record for proclaiming that he nevertheless lives in happiness, just feeding on meditative joy (translated by Bodhi 2000,

207).[317] In a debate with ascetics, the Buddha reportedly claimed to be superior in access to happiness even compared to the king of the country, as he was able to sit in pure happiness for seven days without interruption (translated by Ñāṇamoli 1995/2005, 189).[318]

A type of Nirvana that is just a blank form of nothing does not seem to fit particularly well the qualification of being the foremost happiness and thus even happier than the other types of happiness described in the passages surveyed above. Just the ending of suffering could reasonably be considered a form of happiness from the viewpoint of someone sorely afflicted and sick, living in constant pain. But the same is a considerably less convincing proposition in the case of those who, to all appearances, live in happiness.[319]

The idea of a blank nothing would fit the condition of being unconscious. The early discourses recognize such unconsciousness as a goal apparently aspired to by some contemporary practitioners (translated by Ñāṇamoli 1995/2005, 840),[320] leading to rebirth in the celestial realm of unconscious beings. According to later exegesis, for such unconscious beings the mind and mental activities have completely ceased.[321] These exegetical explanations concord with indications found in the early discourses, according to which these unconscious beings are devoid of any form of experiencing (translated by Bodhi 2012, 1281).[322] In fact, such beings are characterized as passing away as soon as a perception arises for them (translated by Walshe 1987, 382).[323] This confirms the impression that, as long as they exist in that realm, these beings should indeed be imagined as entirely unconscious and thus bereft of, for example, any feeling tone or perception.

Yet, such unconsciousness, to all appearances involving a complete cessation of the mind and experience through any of the six senses, is not reckoned a form of happiness in the early discourses; in fact, it is not even accorded a positive evaluation comparable to that accorded to the immaterial spheres, for example.[324] Had the early Buddhist conception of supreme happiness been just about the absence of anything felt, perceived, or cognized, then a condition of being completely unconscious would have deserved being reckoned at least a form of happiness (though perhaps a lesser one due to failing to lead beyond the prospect of rebirth).

Such considerations provide a helpful background when attempting to appreciate the early Buddhist notion of the supreme happiness of Nirvana as going beyond pleasant feeling tones (translated by Ñāṇamoli 1995/2005, 505).[325] In a way this is obvious, since once the six sense spheres cease, and with them the six corresponding types of contact, there cannot be any feeling tone. This condition would apply equally to the experience of Nirvana while alive and to Nirvana entered by the arahant at death. Both equally go beyond pleasurable feeling tones.

Another Pāli discourse specifies that with Nirvana it is precisely the absence of feeling tones that is a source of happiness (translated by Bodhi 2012, 1292).[326] This indication can be considered in the light of descriptions of the condition of unconscious beings. The implication would probably not be to celebrate the mere absence of feeling tones as happiness in itself. Instead, the point seems to be to highlight that the presence of any feeling tone, even pertaining to the most refined happiness, would imply that Nirvana has not been realized, since what is constructed still continues. In fact, it is precisely with the ending of feeling tones that Nirvana is attained (translated by Bodhi 2000, 1260).[327] In other words, for a cessation of feeling tones to deserve being reckoned happiness, at least from an early Buddhist perspective, it needs to be related to Nirvana. It would be such a relationship that endows the ending of feeling tones with the quality of happiness.

An uncoupling of the notion of happiness from pleasant feeling tones is in fact not unique to the case of Nirvana. The same already takes place when the fourth absorption and the immaterial spheres are considered states of happiness (translated by Ñāṇamoli 1995/2005, 504).[328] This holds even though at this stage the joy and happiness characteristic of the previous three absorptions have been left behind and the actual experience is one of equanimity and neutral feeling tones. Still, these are reckoned states of happiness. The conception of Nirvana as a type of happiness that is not felt goes a step further in the same direction. This suggestion finds support in a Pāli passage that qualifies the happiness of the three absorptions as unworldly (in contrast to the worldly happiness of sensuality), whereas the happiness accessible to arahants/arhats on surveying the freedom of their minds from the root defilements is, quite literally, even more unworldly than (the previously mentioned) unworldly happiness (translated by Bodhi 2000, 1284).[329]

Besides being a natural culmination in this early Buddhist scheme of increasingly subtle and refined types of happiness, the notion of Nirvana as a form of happiness appears to have been a natural one in the ancient Indian setting. Examples are views that according to the early discourses were held by some non-Buddhist practitioners, who are on record for identifying sensual pleasures or the happiness of absorption as the attainment of Nirvana here and now (translated by Walshe 1987, 85).[330] Another discourse features a wanderer who even took just bodily health to deserve being called Nirvana (translated by Ñāṇamoli 1995/2005, 614).[331] These notions of Nirvana carry distinctly positive connotations.

Such usage is not as far-fetched as it may seem at first sight, even for the case of identifying bodily health as Nirvana. Rhys Davids and Stede (1921/1993, 362) note, as an alternative to the sense of the "going out of a lamp or fire," the following meaning for the Pāli term *nibbāna*: "Health, the sense of bodily well-being (probably, at first, the passing away of feverishness, restlessness)." The nuance of allaying a fever brings out an indubitably positive nuance that nevertheless is closely related to the basic idea of a fire going out.[332] As pointed out by Pasanno and Amaro (2009, 40), India is "a land of blazing heat, and in such environments 'coolness' can easily gather to it an aura of intrinsic goodness and attractiveness," whereas in "the northern regions where the English language originated, 'warmth' takes on a similar nuance of desirability; the source of oppression and danger is not the merciless sun but the chill bitterness of winter." In the same vein, Gómez (2004, 600) comments on the fire imagery:

> In this context extinction means relief, calm, rest, and not the annihilation of being. In an Indian setting, fire is mostly hot and uncomfortable, or it is associated with a raging destructive forest conflagration during the dry months before the monsoon; it is not a symbol of life, but a symbol of painful desire.

The indications provided in the early discourses regarding positive connotations of the term Nirvana in ancient Indian thought in general can be complemented with references in the *Mahābhārata* to Nirvana as the supreme happiness.[333] The same work even uses the term Nirvana when describing the going out of a lamp,[334] thereby providing another parallelism. Commenting on the Buddhist and Brahminical employment of the term Nirvana, Senart (1903, 102) concludes that their common point of departure was clearly not the meaning of destruction.[335]

In this way, the Buddhist identification of Nirvana as the supreme happiness appears to have been in line with positive connotations commonly associated with this term in ancient India, differing from these insofar as the conception of Nirvana as a supreme happiness transcends even felt experience. In line with the quite literally extra-ordinary nature of the perception of the deathless, explored above, the corresponding happiness appears to be similarly extra-ordinary. On pursuing the indications provided in the texts in relation to such perception, perhaps the same could be applied here, in the sense that such happiness is related neither to a normal perception nor to a somehow distorted or dysfunctional perception, nor does it involve an immaterial perception, nor does it result from just being unconscious. Hence, what remains to be said about this supreme summit of happiness would then be that "it should be experienced."

12. A Middle Path Position

Besides forming the peak of a gradual refinement of happiness, Nirvana can carry quite positive connotations, which are evident in a range of epithets and images. As noted by Fink (2015, 26), "positive epithets—the 'supreme noble peace,' the 'far shore,' and so on—surely indicate that it is something more than 'a blank state of nothingness.'" At the same time, however, such epithets and images should also not be reified, which would be the other extreme to be avoided.

A Pāli listing of epithets of Nirvana agrees with its Chinese counterpart in mentioning, for example, a "shelter" and an "island."[336] The last epithet can be explored further with the help of a versified exchange extant in Pāli. This sets out with the request that the Buddha disclose an island that is beyond the flood of old age and death. The reply to that request then reportedly took the following form:[337]

> Having nothing, taking up nothing:
> This is the unsurpassable island.
> I call it "Nirvana,"
> The destruction of old age and death.

Although the reply does employ the term "island," in line with the key term in the inquiry, at the same time it leaves no room for reification, as the island becomes having nothing and taking up nothing. Ñāṇananda (2015, 27) comments: "When we are told that *Nibbāna* is an island, we tend to imagine some sort of existence in a beautiful island." The above verse "gives a good corrective to that kind of imagining." Nevertheless, the idea of an island is not only placed into perspective with the reference to having nothing—the reference to having nothing is also placed into perspective by being reckoned an island. Had this been a totally inappropriate idea, the Buddha could have been shown to reject the term and use something else instead. That is, a balanced appraisal of this verse exchange could acknowledge both dimensions of the identification of having nothing (and taking up nothing) as being an island. In fact, the idea of an island need not invariably be taken to carry a reified sense of some form of a substantial existence but could also be read in a metaphorical way as simply conveying that Nirvana is quite apart from the rest of the world, just as from the viewpoint of the ancient Indian audience an island surrounded by the ocean would have been seen as quite apart from the Indian subcontinent.

The nineteenth-century philosopher Arthur Schopenhauer reasons—in a general comment unrelated to this particular verse—that when Nirvana is defined as nothing, this only entails that *saṃsāra* does not contain even one element that could be used to define or construct Nirvana.[338] In other words, a reference to "nothing" or "no-thing" can be taken to convey the absolute otherness of Nirvana. Understood in this way, the idea of an island to be found in having nothing can be seen to combine two complementary perspectives, even two sides of the same coin. Neither will yield an adequate assessment if taken just on its own.

The same holds for an inspired utterance attributed to the Buddha and extant in Pāli, which has sometimes been taken to convey an affirmation of Nirvana as the "unborn," a term then read to convey quite affirmative connotations.[339] However, following a detailed discussion of this passage by Norman (1994),[340] the inspired utterance in question could instead be translated in the following manner:[341]

> Monastics, there is that where there is no birth, where nothing has come into existence, where nothing is made, where nothing is constructed. Monastics, if there were not that where there is no birth, where nothing has come into existence, where nothing is made, where nothing is constructed, an escape from what is born, what has come into existence, what is made, and what is constructed would not be discernible here. But since there is that where there is no birth, monastics, where nothing has come into existence, where nothing is made, where nothing is constructed, therefore an escape from what is born, what has come into existence, what is made, and what is constructed is discernible.

Ñāṇananda (1974/1985, 78–79n2) explains the import of the passage to be as follows:

> In a psychological sense, a design could be "unmade" or "dissolved" by shifting one's attention to its components. Even so, "what is born" (*jātaṃ*), "become" (*bhūtaṃ*), "made" (*kataṃ*) and "compounded" (*saṃkhataṃ*) is transformed into a "not-born," "not-become," "not-made" and "not-compounded" state by a penetrative insight into its causes and conditions . . . The above epithets of Nibbāna are therefore psychological, and not metaphysical, in their import.

In a critical reply to the tendency to take this passage as postulating a metaphysical unborn, Brahmāli (2009, 57) points out that "all this passage does is to affirm the possibility of ending *saṃsāra*."[342] At the same time, however, the passage does provide quite an emphatic affirmation of that possibility. Its highlight on something completely apart from birth and constructions is comparable to the description of a sphere apart from all other experiences, taken up above (see p. 77), which in fact occurs in close proximity to the above passage in the same Pāli discourse collection.

The passage translated above recurs as well in another Pāli collection, followed by a set of verses that are also extant in Sanskrit. These commend not delighting in what is born and then contrast such misdirected delight with the happiness to be gained upon finding an escape from what is born. The Pāli version presents this as follows:[343]

> The peaceful escape from that,
> Which is beyond the reach of reasoning and stable,
> Without birth and without an arising,
> Being a sorrowless and stainless track,
> The cessation of states of *dukkha/duḥkha*,
> The stilling of constructions: [this is] happiness.

The escape described in this way is again quite affirmative: stable, free of sorrow, and a source of happiness. The same type of transcendence finds expression in another inspired utterance, related to the story of Bāhiya. According to the preceding narrative, he became an arahant/arhat on the spot after receiving a succinct instruction on bare awareness (see above p. 18). The relevant part of the verse in Pāli, which has a similarly worded counterpart in Sanskrit, proceeds in this way:[344]

> Where water, earth,
> Fire, and wind no footing find,
> There stars do not glow
> And the sun does not shed light;
> There the moon does not shine;
> [Yet,] there is no darkness.

This poetic description would not be about positing some other source of light in addition to the stars, the moon, and the sun. Instead, it seems to convey the idea of going beyond the contrast between any light, whatever its source, and darkness. In one way or another, all such descriptions can be seen to converge on attempting to convey the utter otherness of the deathless or Nirvana.

The notion of the four elements not finding a footing recurs in another verse, which refers to a form of consciousness that is not manifesting (*anidassana/anidarśana*). However, a comparative study shows that the part of the Pāli verse that has this reference is not reliable.[345] Once this part is set aside, the rest of the poem is unproblematic, as it relates the absence of any foothold for the four elements to the cessation of name-and-form (translated by Walshe 1987, 180).[346] The same relationship recurs elsewhere as a reply to an inquiry regarding where the streams turn back (translated by Bodhi 2000, 103).[347]

Another relevant reference speaks of the "stream of consciousness" that is unestablished, be it in this world or another world (translated by Walshe 1987, 420).[348] This expression conveniently shows that the term "consciousness" just stands for an impermanent process; it is a stream and not an entity. In fact, the early discourses are quite explicit in stating that it is impossible to find any consciousness that is permanent (translated by Bodhi 2000, 956).[349] The same holds just as well for the consciousness of a fully awakened one. The reason preventing the positing of some form of consciousness beyond the death of a liberated one is simply that doing so would imply that complete freedom from *dukkha/duḥkha* has not yet been reached. The case of consciousness is in this respect comparable to the situation of feeling tones. Since their continued presence would imply that the experience is not yet Nirvana, at least in the way the term is used in early Buddhism, it follows that the happiness of Nirvana is grounded in the absence of feeling tones. In the same way, the continued presence of the aggregate of consciousness would imply that the letting go has not yet been thorough enough. A Pāli verse puts the matter succinctly:[350]

> Whatever *dukkha/duḥkha* manifests,
> It all depends on consciousness;

With the cessation of consciousness,
There is no [more] manifestation of *dukkha/duḥkha*.

This clear-cut assessment of the nature of consciousness could be complemented with an inspired utterance that takes as its occasion the passing away of an arahant/arhat in the presence of the Buddha, reportedly motivating the latter to utter the following poem:[351]

The body disintegrated, perception ceased,
All feeling tones became cool,
Constructions were stilled
And consciousness came to an end.

This poem expresses the situation in quite definite terms. Nevertheless, this is not the end of the matter. The relevant prose narration occurs twice in the same Pāli collection. One instance concerns the actual passing away of the arahant/arhat in question, whereas the other takes the form of the Buddha reporting this event to his disciples on a subsequent occasion. These two consecutive discourses come with different verses, both attributed to the Buddha. The other verse describes a splinter that flies off from a smith's hammer striking heated iron and then continues with the following indication:[352]

Similarly, of those completely liberated,
Who have transcended the flood of bondage to sensuality,
Of those who have attained unshakeable happiness,
There is no designating their destiny.

This verse, which has a range of parallels conveying similarly positive connotations,[353] complements the presentation in the previous verse regarding the cessation of the aggregates. When read in conjunction with the present verse, it seems that there is more to it than just the extinction of the five aggregates.

In relation to the central imagery of Nirvana as a fire that has gone out, Collins (1998, 213 and 220–21) offers the following comment:

> This is not an answer on the level of systematic thought; but it is a discursive moment which brings into being the Unsaid, the Unconditioned, and preserves nirvana as a contradiction-stilling enigma . . . what can be said about nirvana as a concept ends in a silence. The dynamic of the quenching of a fire . . . and of the associated idea of "cooling" depicts with perfect clarity a movement from activity and suffering to rest and peace, while deliberately withholding focus on the aftermath. The image does not solve the aporia, it states it.

According to Collins (1998, 283), a study of relevant passages shows that the early "texts do indeed speak of nirvana, up to a point, but also that the process of speaking about it leads up to silence, a silence within discourse which creates meaning as such."[354] Oldenberg (1881/1961, 265) sums up the position of the early texts as follows:[355]

> There is a path leading out of the world of what is constructed into unfathomable infinity. Does it lead to highest being? Does it lead to nothingness? The Buddhist creed keeps as if on a knife's edge between these two. The longing of the heart's aspiration for eternity does not have nothing, yet, thinking does not have a something that it could hold onto. The thought of infinity and eternity could not have receded further from the creed than here where, a gentle flutter, about to plunge into nothingness, it threatens to vanish from sight.

The gentle flutter that almost vanishes from sight can be better appreciated from the viewpoint of the construction of experience. The aporia or paradox serves its purpose precisely because it forces the mind to abandon well-known patterns of constructing experience. Thinking needs to be prevented from finding something to hold on to; hence only a gentle flutter is possible. Anything more than that, by trying to concretize or identify, is baseless talk or an instance of proliferating what should not be proliferated (see above p. 102). The reason is simply that engaging in such proliferations will prevent the complete stepping out of proliferation required for the encounter with the deathless. The final part of another verse extant in Pāli reports the Buddha offering the following assessment:[356]

> Apart from letting go of everything,
> I see no safety for sentient beings.

Two parallels in Chinese and Sanskrit speak of "liberation" instead of "safety";[357] both terms can be read as complementary pointers to the final goal. The breakthrough to the deathless would require letting go of everything without exception. Any explicit indication that could be construed as pointing to something one could hold on to—such as a particular type of consciousness apart from the five aggregates or a specific type of nondescript realm of existence—will probably prevent the very occurrence of the breakthrough. This appears to be why the island needs to be immediately qualified as nothing or why the affirmation of the deathless as a reality to be experienced is framed in terms of all those known dimensions of experience that are not there. To do so is simply necessary to facilitate the progress of individual practitioners to the actual realization of Nirvana, whereby they will then know for themselves. As pointed out by Cousins (1983, 97):

> Much can be said in praise of nibbāna to encourage the seeker, especially if it is in the form of simile or metaphor. Such we find frequently. But there must be nothing so concrete as to encourage attachment.

The problem of potentially encouraging attachment through descriptions that are just a bit too affirmative can be illustrated by comparing a Pāli discourse and its Chinese parallel, which distinguish between two Nirvana elements.[358] The distinction as such appears to differentiate between arahants/arhats while alive and after passing away. Narada (1987, 69) comments that the two Nirvana elements "are not two kinds of *Nibbana*, but the one single *Nibbana* receiving its name according to experience of it before and after death." Harvey (1995, 197) explains that "*nibbāna* in life and beyond death are not different *nibbāna*s, but the same state," occurring at different times.[359]

On this interpretation, the first of the two Nirvana elements is about leaving behind clinging to the aggregates, the second about leaving behind the aggregates as well. That is, the distinction drawn in this way points to two stages in the same process, of which the second will necessarily take place when the first has occurred and cannot happen without it. In terms of the fire simile, even though the flames have been quenched, some embers may still remain.[360] These can continue to smolder for a while before they become cool as well.

The passage illustrative of a slightly too-affirmative description occurs in the Chinese version's description of the second Nirvana element, which proceeds as follows:[361]

> What is called the Nirvana element without a residue? That is, monastics who have become arahants, have eradicated all the influxes, have established the holy life, have done what had to be done, have shed the heavy burden, have realized their own aim, have eradicated the fetter of becoming, have rightly understood, have been well liberated, and have gained penetrative knowledge. In the present, because there are no more impulsions and no more longings, which have all forever been extinguished, all that is being felt comes to be finally at peace, ultimately becomes cool, disappears, and no longer manifests.
>
> Only purity is still there in the absence of what is of the substance of conceptual proliferation. Purity like this in the absence of what is of the substance of conceptual proliferation cannot be reckoned as "it exists," cannot be reckoned as "it does not exist," cannot be reckoned as "that exists as well as does not exist," and cannot be reckoned as "that neither exists nor does not exist." It can only be called what cannot be designated, the ultimate, Nirvana. This is called the Nirvana element without a residue.

The Pāli version only has a counterpart to the first of the above two paragraphs and thus refrains from providing any indication about the after-death condition of an arahant/arhat, apart from noting that all that is felt will become cool. The Chinese version goes further by describing a form of purity that is free from conceptual proliferation but which at the same time cannot be reckoned as existing, or not, or both, or neither.

The Pāli and Chinese versions of the discourse collection in which this passage occurs follow a pattern of repeating in verse the teaching just given in prose. Yet, the second of the above two paragraphs has no counterpart in this verse repetition in the Chinese version. Together with its absence from the Pāli version, this makes it fairly probable that this part is a later addition, presumably reflecting an attempt to concretize what the early texts in general avoid concretizing.

The concretization offered in this way speaks of purity without conceptual proliferation. As if to forestall the natural attempt to relate that purity to something that experiences it or is endowed with it, there comes then the indication that none of the alternatives of the tetralemma on existence and nonexistence apply. So far so good, but the problem here is not just the question of how to understand that the existence of purity can be affirmed while at the same time denying all four modes of predication regarding existence. A perhaps more serious problem is that such a statement can easily stimulate a search for the presence of such purity, free from conceptual proliferation, in some form now in subjective experience. That is, it can lead to attempts to identify what continues even beyond. Latching on to that in the belief that it offers a promise of some form of continuity beyond death, even with full awakening, could prevent awakening happening in the first place.

One of the approaches to inclining the mind toward the deathless, discussed above (see p. 73), involves the perception that Nirvana is the cessation of "becoming" or "existence" (*bhava*). This conveniently encapsulates the basic principle that any holding on to some form of becoming or existence is diametrically opposed to the inclination toward Nirvana. In other words, any desire to become like this or like that, and any hope for an existence in this way or another way, stand a good chance of preventing the letting go required for the actual breakthrough to the deathless to occur.

The notion of the cessation of becoming or existence also exemplifies the advantages of employing negative terms or imagery. Compared to positive indications, such expressions do not stand a similar chance of being latched on to. A reference to the cessation of becoming or to the cooling down of all feeling tones points to something beyond what is present and thereby discourages clinging to any aspect of what is present. A reference to purity or any other similarly positive notion does not achieve that. In other words, in order to facilitate the breakthrough to the deathless, there is a need to avoid pointing the finger away from the moon. There is a need to avoid handing out a raft that does not float and which, on being put to water, will sink rather than support the crossing of the flood.

From this viewpoint, either negative expressions or else silence appear to be indeed the best way to proceed. This would be in line with a statement by the philosopher Ludwig Wittgenstein—obviously made in a different context—according to which "what can be said at all, that can clearly be said, but what cannot be spoken about, about that one must keep silent."[362] Applied to the passage translated above on the second Nirvana element, it would follow that the Pāli version does provide a preferable presentation, as it says what can be said but refrains from speaking about what one should keep silent about:[363]

> And what, monastics, is the Nirvana element without a residue? Here, monastics, a monastic is an arahant/arhat, with the influxes eradicated, who has fulfilled [the holy life], has done what had to be done, laid down the burden, has reached their own aim, has eradicated the fetter of becoming, and has been completely liberated through final knowledge. Monastics, of such a one right here all that is felt, not being delighted in, will become cool. Monastics, this is called the Nirvana element without a residue.

13. Summary

The textual sources show the Buddha employing the term "deathless" in his first reported references to his own realization of awakening. In its early Buddhist usage, the deathless as one of the epithets of Nirvana stands for the complete transcendence of mental affliction by mortality, be it related to one's own death or that of others. Such a form of deathlessness is considered attainable while still alive, the first realization of which already happens with stream-entry.

The discourses describe several alternative occasions for the actual breakthrough to the deathless, which is considered to occur at a specific point in time. It could happen while hearing a teaching, reflecting on the teaching or reciting it, giving a teaching oneself, or else when meditating. Any of these occasions can, based on an arousal of the awakening factors, culminate in a thorough letting go that enables a stepping out of the construction of experience. Due to the need for such letting go to be thoroughly comprehensive, the very tools, which have led up to the level of inner maturity where the breakthrough can take place at all, also need to be relinquished at that point. With the momentum gained through the previous training in ethics, concentration, and wisdom, there is a need to proceed further by staying free from any trace of clinging to, or identification with, these very trainings.

The unconditioned is not the product of conditions; it cannot be willed to happen. Nevertheless, it can occur if the appropriate preparations are in place, in particular if the practitioner is willing and able to let go completely, without any reservations or even a trace of holding back. The opportunity to do so appears to emerge right at the outer edge of the ending of the present moment, just before the next moment becomes the present one.

The actual breakthrough to the realization of the deathless is designated as a sphere of experience that involves the cessation of the six spheres of experience. It is also presented as a perception, a form of paying attention, and a way of meditating, each of which are different from all the other known modalities of perceiving, paying attention, and meditating. Such descriptions converge on conveying that the experience of Nirvana or the deathless is completely other than anything else imaginable, yet it is at the same time clearly seen as neither an unconscious experience nor a condition of having some sort of distorted perception.

The event of stepping out of the construction of experience can also be considered to be an arrival at truth. Any early Buddhist truth-claim—

including the doctrinal teaching of the four noble truths—appears to be grounded in the experience of the deathless, which by necessity is non-conceptual. Even knowledge and vision need to be left behind in order for the breakthrough to take place, comparable to the need to leave behind a chariot, used for a journey, to enter the building that is the final destiny of the journey. Nirvana by its very nature is in every respect beyond. The conditioned path and the unconditioned goal eventually coalesce, comparable to two individual rivers that at some point merge with each other.

The cessation of the six sense spheres appears to result in a vision that leads beyond dogmatic adherence to views. Although liberated sages still have a viewpoint, precisely informed by direct knowledge of the deathless, they are considered to have shaken off resorting to views. In the end, even the liberating teachings are but a raft for the purpose of crossing over. Hence, faith or confidence as well as moral observances are in a way left behind when the final goal is reached. Such leaving behind does not imply faithlessness or immorality but much rather concerns patterns of identification. The liberated one's behavior is moral through and through, a natural and even inevitable result of awakening. Yet, there is no identification with such morality, in the understanding that nothing whatsoever is worth being attached to.

Inquiring whether something or nothing is left when the six spheres of experience cease is baseless and proliferates what is not proliferative. The teachings are for the sake of crossing the flood; that is, they point beyond themselves. Concepts have their place in progress to the goal but can become an obstruction if they are employed in a way that does not align with the need to step out of the constructing activity of the mind. For this reason, the final goal is best envisaged as completely beyond the reach of reasoning and reckoning.

Although beyond the reach of reasoning and reckoning, the event of full awakening is considered to have very clear and directly evident repercussions: the fires of defilements in the mind have been quenched forever, and their ability to act as makers of signs during the process of perception has been nullified. Already at stream-entry such stepping out of constructed reality is associated with an eradication of three fetters; in particular the notion of a self as a substantial and enduring entity has been revealed to be merely an ignorant construction. The imagery of quenching in relation to the flame of a lamp also appears to convey the actual experience of awakening, when all constructions cease in a way similar to a lamp going out.

Ignorant constructions provide the starting point for the dependent arising of *dukkha/duḥkha*. Some of the conditions covered in the standard twelve-link presentation of dependent arising will continue operating even in the case of an arahant (such as consciousness and name-and-form, for example), although they no longer contribute to the conditioned genesis of *dukkha/duḥkha*. All conditions cease for good when an arahant/arhat passes away, similar to a fire that has gone out and which cannot be said to have gone in any particular direction. What happens at that time is beyond being framed in terms of existence, nonexistence, both, or neither. In fact, even while alive a Tathāgata has already gone beyond reckoning, similar to the water of the ocean that is beyond being measured.

In evaluating the implications of a full realization of the deathless, it can be helpful to keep in mind the report of the Buddha's strong rejection of the allegation that he teaches annihilation. A mere annihilation would also not really warrant being characterized as beyond reckoning. Another relevant point is the recurrent evaluation of Nirvana as a supreme happiness. At least in the case of those who are fully liberated and consequently able to live in happiness even in adverse circumstances, the happiness of Nirvana could hardly be reckoned still superior if it were to stand just for a blank nothing. In fact, the attainment of unconsciousness and its corresponding realm do not meet with a positive evaluation in early Buddhist thought and are not considered to be forms of happiness. The predominantly positive connotations of Nirvana as a supreme source of happiness are in line with a progressive refinement of happiness in early Buddhist thought; they also concur with the connotations the term apparently carried in the ancient Indian setting in general. In what appears to be a distinct departure from such usage, the Buddhist notion of Nirvana involves a unique conception of a form of happiness that transcends all felt experience.

The impression that equating Nirvana with a blank nothing does not fully capture the situation receives further support from some of its epithets and related images. These point consistently to something more than just a nothing, at the same time, however, attempting to restrain the opposite tendency toward reification. Nirvana is an island, yet that island is having nothing and taking up nothing. There is that where there is no birth, although to reify it as an unborn would be going too far. Light and darkness are both absent, all five aggregates cease, including consciousness, yet the destiny of those who have attained that much is beyond being designated.

When evaluated from the perspective of stepping out of the construction of experience, the absence of concrete positive indications about the after-death destiny of an arahant/arhat becomes quite understandable, because any such indication risks stimulating the type of craving and clinging that would prevent the breakthrough to the deathless taking place at all.

Conclusion

THE EARLY DISCOURSES that have been the main source material of my exploration in the preceding pages present themselves as records of individual teachings given to a variety of audiences on a broad range of topics. In view of the wealth of variegated material they offer, my presentation in this study only covers one particular strand of early Buddhist thought, namely the nature of perception and the possibility of training it in order to forestall its potentially detrimental repercussions. Even that strand I have not covered exhaustively, as my main focus has been on material relevant to the construction of experience in an attempt to make sense of textual descriptions related to the overarching goal of early Buddhist soteriology: the deathless, or Nirvana.

The challenges involved with this particular type of textual sources have been expressed by Bodhi (2003, 47) in the following manner:

> Not only are the texts themselves composed in a clipped laconic style that mocks our thirst for conceptual completeness, but their meaning often seems to rest upon a deep underlying groundwork of interconnected ideas that is nowhere stated baldly in a way that might guide interpretation. Instead of resorting to direct expression, the *nikāyas* embed the basic principles of doctrine in a multitude of short, often elusive discourses that draw upon and allude to the underlying system without spelling it out. To determine the principles one has to extract them piecemeal, by considering in juxtaposition a wide assortment of texts.

The situation that emerges from the above assessment makes it perhaps more understandable why the early Buddhist perspective on the construction of experience has up to now not received as much attention as I believe it deserves. My exploration in the preceding pages hopefully has shown the significance of the sign and signlessness in relation to the construction of experience, which in turn can serve as a convenient reference point for attempting to understand the implications of descriptions of the deathless or Nirvana.

In addition to the rather cryptic style of the early discourses, another factor probably contributing to a lack of attention to the construction of experience appears to be a tendency in later tradition to opt for constructing (pun intended) ever more detailed descriptions. As a natural result of the attempt to clarify and transmit the teachings after the Buddha's demise, this tendency can at times obfuscate the basic need of refraining from constructing and stepping out of constructs.

In the preceding pages I presented my exploration of the construction of experience, as reflected in the early discourses, in two main parts ending with summaries of the main points covered. There is thus no need for another summary in the present concluding section. Instead of repeating what has already been said, in what follows I attempt to sketch, albeit briefly, how the perspective on the construction of experience can be applied to some of the key doctrinal teachings of early Buddhism, set in contrast to relevant developments in later traditions. My sketch has as its reference point a textual account of progress to awakening. The case I have chosen is the instruction given, according to a discourse extant in Chinese, by the Buddha to his son, Rāhula, reportedly leading to the latter becoming an arahant.

The relevant Pāli and Chinese discourses differ substantially in their respective coverage. The Pāli version, which occurs twice in the Pāli discourse collections (translated by Ñāṇamoli 1995/2005, 1126 and by Bodhi 2000, 1195, respectively), reports in much detail the actual instruction that led to Rāhula's breakthrough. Its Chinese parallel gives this only in brief and instead depicts in detail the preceding events that helped mature Rāhula gradually until he was ready to be given the teaching that led to him becoming an arahant.

According to this Chinese account, Rāhula had requested a teaching in brief from the Buddha in order to withdraw into seclusion for intensive practice. This is a standard type of request in the early discourses, usually eliciting a succinct instruction by the Buddha, equipped with which the monastic then embarks on solitary practice aimed at full awakening. In the present case, however, the Buddha reportedly realized that Rāhula was not yet ready for such solitary practice, telling his son that he should rather give teachings to others on the five aggregates of clinging. When Rāhula had done this and again approached the Buddha in the hope of now going for secluded and intensive practice, the latter again realized that the time for that had not yet come and told him to give teachings on the six sense spheres. The same happened once more, this time leading to the injunction that Rāhula should give teachings on causality. The next time Rāhula returned with the same request as earlier, he was told that he should now reflect on the doctrines that he had been teaching to others and contemplate them while in seclusion.

The discourse continues by reporting that Rāhula came back to report the realization he had gained from such reflection and contemplation in the following form:[364]

> Blessed One, in a quiet and secluded place I considered and pondered the teachings I earlier had heard, the teachings I had earlier expounded, contemplating their meaning. I understood that all these teachings entirely proceed toward [the realization of] Nirvana, flow toward [the realization of] Nirvana, and are ultimately established on [the realization of] Nirvana.

According to the Chinese discourse, hearing the above made the Buddha realize that Rāhula's mind had sufficiently matured and he was now ready to receive the succinct teaching that he had all along been asking for. The passage translated above conveys the crucial realization that key doctrines—the five aggregates of clinging, the six sense spheres, and causality—all converge on the realization of Nirvana. Their purpose is to lead to a breakthrough to Nirvana, and they are oriented toward this end.

Seeing all teachings as intended to lead to freedom has a counterpart in several of the passages taken up in the second part of my study, according to which different doctrinal teachings, including the four truths, are means to an end. Their purpose is to serve as a raft for crossing over to the far shore. Even though the realization of the deathless itself does not involve concepts, teachings like the five aggregates of clinging, the six sense spheres, and causality have an important role as vehicles for progress on the path to that realization. It is such realization that serves as their main orientation point. Just as the ocean has the single taste of salt throughout, so do the teachings have the single taste of liberation (translated by Bodhi 2012, 1144).[365]

As briefly mentioned above, the instrumental function of central doctrinal teachings is not necessarily always evident with later traditions, due to an apparent tendency to elaborate and concretize. An example is the fourth of the five aggregates. Whereas in the early texts this stands predominantly for volitional constructions, distinct from the usage of the same Pāli or Sanskrit term to refer in general to what is conditioned,[366] with later tradition this aggregate becomes an umbrella category for subsuming anything mental that is not already covered by the other three mental aggregates.[367] Notably, later exegesis relies on the passage describing the constructing impact of the fourth aggregate on all five aggregates, discussed above (see p. 15), to authenticate this expanded meaning of the fourth aggregate.[368]

It is remarkable that precisely the passage on the role of the fourth aggregate in constructing is employed in support of this development. This conveys the impression that the implications of this passage were no longer fully appreciated. Moreover, this move then assigns mindfulness, which particularly in its role of bare awareness can be of significant support in disclosing the construction of experience, to the aggregate responsible for such construction. This comes in combination with a substantial reconceptualization of the nature of mindfulness, by way of de-emphasizing its receptive dimensions that are so central for becoming aware of, and stepping out of, the construction of experience.[369] In view of these developments—as outcomes of an attempt to provide a comprehensive coverage with the five aggregates employed as convenient headers for such purposes—it is quite understandable if the significance of the construction of experience has not remained fully evident.

Yet, the original purpose of the teaching on the five aggregates of clinging does not seem to have been providing a comprehensive inventory of all the different terms used in the texts to describe aspects of an individual's body and mind. Instead, it presents an analytical grid to capture patterns of identification.[370] As pointed out by Hamilton (2000, 29):

> The *khandhas* [aggregates] are not a comprehensive analysis of what a human being is comprised of . . . Rather, they are the factors of human experience (or, better, the experiencing factors) that one needs to understand in order to achieve the goal of Buddhist teachings.

The early discourses do indicate that each aggregate taken singly is meant to comprise all instances of the same type, be these past, present, or future, far or near, etc. Perhaps this type of indication led to the assumption that the entire set must also be meant to offer a completely comprehensive description of subjective experience. Yet, drawing such a conclusion is unwarranted. Take the example of five species of animals: even though the name provided for each case is intended to comprise all individual animals of that species, it does not follow that all existing animals should now be allocated to one or the other of these five species.

In the case of the analysis into five aggregates, the key point of this teaching seems to be to reveal chief patterns of clinging, with the purpose of facilitating progress toward the cessation of clinging. An example illustrating this key point occurs as part of the instruction on the five aggregates of clinging that reportedly led to Ānanda's stream-entry (translated by Bodhi 2000, 928). The relevant part clarifies that self-referentiality, in the form of the conceit "I am,"[371] occurs when there is clinging and not without it, just as seeing one's own face in a mirror occurs when one holds the mirror up—literally clings to it—and not without holding it up.[372] Ñāṇananda (2015, 217) comments: "It is when one looks into a mirror that one suddenly becomes self-conscious. Whether one has a liking or a dislike for what one sees, one gets the notion 'this is me.'"

Without intending to discount alternative interpretations, one understanding of the implications of this simile in relation to the five aggregates could be that it reveals a tendency to keep conceitedly posing in terms of how "I am" compared to others—that is, "I am" better, "I am" equal, or "I am" worse—in respect of bodily appearance or ability (= bodily form), access to enjoyment (= feeling tone), knowledgeability and comprehension (= perception), exercise of power and control (= volitional constructions), and having enviable experiences (= consciousness). Realizing what is taking place reveals an urgent need to let go of this type of clinging—that is, to drop the mirror. For that purpose, it does not matter what material the mirror is made of or what color or kind of ornamentation it has. The task is simply to put it down. Such putting down would fulfill the central purpose of the teaching on the five aggregates of clinging. That is, the emphasis is less on the *five aggregates* individually than on one's *clinging* to them and how to bring about its cessation.

The second doctrinal item that, according to the report quoted above, Rāhula had been teaching and reflecting on concerns the six sense spheres, which have been a prominent theme in the preceding pages of my exploration. A telling example of the tendency toward proliferation related to this teaching can already be found in a Pāli discourse, in a part that is clearly a later addition of commentarial or proto-abhidharmic style. The relevant passage occurs in the exposition on the four noble truths in the Greater Discourse on the Establishments of Mindfulness (*Mahāsatipaṭṭhāna-sutta*). The exposition of the third noble truth presents altogether sixty different ways in which craving can cease (translated by Walshe 1987, 347).[373] In this way, the single event of the cessation of craving becomes quite a complex matter. Particularly noteworthy is that this detailed breakdown features as a mindfulness practice in what comes under the header of being "the direct path" to the realization of Nirvana.[374]

Yet, the key for such realization lies in seeing through the six sense spheres. An example would be the instruction to Bāhiya, discussed in the first part of my study (see above p. 17), which requires staying with bare cognition in order not to be thereby, not to be therein, and not to be here, beyond, or between the two. Since the same instruction is reportedly also given to another monastic, who in spite of appearing somewhat confused and speculative was able to rely on it to gain awakening, it seems fair to consider it to be of general relevance.

One way of trying to make practical sense of the instruction could be to assume that, based on being established in bare awareness, by letting go of one's involvement with the content of experience and instead attending to its process character, ideally also to its constructed nature, one will not be thereby (*na tena*). Based on that, by letting go of the sense "I am" as some sort of epicenter that is in charge of experience, one will not be therein (*na tattha*). By then letting go of any reference point whatsoever, one will be neither here, nor beyond, nor between the two. Such a successive deepening of letting go would be sufficient for actualizing the potential of liberating insight in regard to the six sense spheres, without any need to get involved with further details.

The third teaching relevant to maturing Rāhula's mind was causality. The early Buddhist conception of causality tends to be associated in particular with a recurrent presentation of dependent arising by way of twelve links. In the ancient Indian setting, this presentation appears to have stood in dialogue with a Vedic creation myth,[375] presumably creating a sense of familiarity and at the same time conveying an important message by communicating that the glorious act of creation leads up to *dukkha/duḥkha* as the final and disconcerting result. For someone unfamiliar with this myth, however, the series of twelve links can be somewhat bewildering, since the conditional relationships between its links are rather complex.

Birth as a condition for old age and death involves a temporal succession, and it presents a necessary relationship in both directions. One who has been born will grow older and sooner or later have to die, and those who face old age and death must at some earlier time have been born. Feeling tone as a condition for craving is also about a temporal succession, as craving is a reaction to the type of feeling tone experienced, but it is no longer an inevitable consequence of it. Even with the root condition of ignorance still in place, not every single feeling tone will invariably lead to a reaction of craving. The potential of nonreactivity to feeling tones is particularly evident in the contemporary clinical employment of mindfulness, which does not require progress to the complete eradication of ignorance in order to work. The condition for feeling tone in turn is contact, and at this point a temporal succession is no longer as evident as earlier. Feeling tone is not so much a reaction to contact, as contact is rather itself felt. The same holds for consciousness and name-and-form, which occur simultaneously. In fact, they stand in a relationship of reciprocal conditioning to each other. The same is not the case, however, for other links. Besides, even though name already includes contact and feeling tone, these are mentioned again subsequently as individual links.

The complexity evident in this way just with a bare listing of the twelve links, especially if these are considered without recourse to the apparent Vedic precedent, further increases with traditional exegesis, which views this presentation as covering three successive lifetimes.[376] My point here is not to convey the impression that this mode of exegesis is somehow wrong. The early Buddhist conception of causality covers the present as well as the past and the future and therefore necessarily also the process of rebirth. At the same time, however, the series of twelve links are not just about explaining the process of rebirth, for which purpose the reciprocal conditioning between consciousness and name-and-form is already amply sufficient.[377]

The complexity of the presentation by way of three lives increases even more when further analysis is applied to the conditional relationship between each pair of links, for which Theravāda exegesis relies on a set of twenty-four conditional relationships (translated by Ñāṇamoli 1956/1991, 542).[378] With the resultant proliferation, the need to see through the operation of causality is no longer fully evident, as the overall tendency is to foster closely looking at a mass of details.

An example of the potential of seeing through causality to lead to liberating insight would be the case of Sāriputta/Śāriputra and Mahāmoggallāna/Mahāmaudgalyāyana, already mentioned above (see p. 63). Both are on record for having realized the breakthrough to the deathless on hearing a brief summary of the Buddha's teaching. According to this summary, the Buddha taught the cause responsible for the arising of things and their cessation (translated by Horner 1951/1982, 54).[379] This short instruction does not mention any of the twelve links. Nevertheless, according to a range of sources it was sufficient for both

Sāriputta/Śāriputra and Mahāmoggallāna/Mahāmaudgalyāyana, who up to that point had no acquaintance at all with Buddhist doctrine, to gain stream-entry on hearing just this short stanza. Notably, even though it lacks any reference to the twelve links, let alone a detailed analysis of each, this short teaching does lead up to the topic of cessation.[380] This appears to be the crux of the matter.

According to the traditional report, the Buddha's own pre-awakening investigation of causality had its starting point in the recognition of the affliction caused by old age and death, leading on to an inquiry regarding what causes these (translated by Bodhi 2000, 537 and 601).[381] Other discourses attribute the same line of reasoning to previous Buddhas (translated by Bodhi 2000, 536),[382] thereby presenting it as the standard approach for developing the Buddhist perspective on causality. The concern underlying this inquiry is how to bring about the cessation of old age and death. This is fully in line with the report of what motivated the Buddha-to-be to go forth, discussed above (see p. 61). In other words, the whole teaching on dependent arising is in the end about the deathless. Hence, the key aspect is in a way dependent cessation rather than dependent arising. Just as with the analytical schemes of the five aggregates of clinging and the six sense spheres, each of these three teachings offers a pointer to cessation.

This suggestion is not meant to dismiss detailed analytical approaches as such. These are frequently found in the early discourses. The teaching to Rāhula is a case in point, as in the subsequent section, to be taken up below, he reportedly received instructions on impermanence based on a detailed analysis of each sense door. At the same time, however, with the increase in details evident in the examples surveyed above, the converging point of the above three teachings on cessation is no longer evident. There is a danger that the main task of stepping out of the construction of experience becomes obfuscated due to excessive constructing activity in matters of Buddhist doctrine. It is a little as if, rather than putting together just a raft, one were to build a proper ship and then become so occupied with the building work that one almost forgets about crossing over.

The task of crossing over, with its converging point of cessation or letting go, finds an apt expression in the report of Rāhula's realization that "all these teachings entirely proceed toward [the realization of] Nirvana, flow toward [the realization of] Nirvana, and are ultimately established on [the realization of] Nirvana." The Chinese account of Rāhula's progress to awakening continues after this insight in the following manner:[383]

> Then the Blessed One, observing that Rāhula's liberation of the mind and his knowledge were mature, that he was ready to receive the higher Dharma, told Rāhula: "Rāhula, everything is impermanent."

The discourse continues by mentioning that the Buddha taught Rāhula about the impermanence of the eye, forms, eye-consciousness, and eye contact, followed by an indication given by the reciters of the discourse that the rest should be supplemented from another discourse. This probably refers to a discourse found earlier in the same collection which offers a detailed teaching on impermanence.[384] The Pāli parallel also reports that the Buddha realized that Rāhula's mind was sufficiently mature to gain liberation and then instructed him on the impermanent nature of the senses (translated by Ñāṇamoli 1995/2005, 1126 and Bodhi 2000, 1195).[385] This instruction continues by explicitly relating impermanence to the other two characteristics of *dukkha/duḥkha* and not self. According to the Pāli version, Rāhula gained full awakening while hearing these instructions, whereas in the Chinese parallel he reached it after further practice in seclusion.

Alongside such differences, the two parallels agree that the instruction leading to Rāhula's awakening was about the impermanent nature of all aspects of sense experience. Similar to the other teachings surveyed above, the conception of impermanence also underwent some change in later Buddhist traditions. Whereas impermanence in its early Buddhist form just implies that everything changes, this perspective became radicalized in later times in the form of the doctrine of momentariness, according to which everything ceases all the time, right after having arisen.[386]

Yet, the middle-path solution to the two extremes of "it exists" and "it does not exist," mentioned above (see p. 114), is not to opt for a rapid alternation between the two but much rather calls for a shift toward seeing everything as processes. Besides creating difficulties for seeing continuity, such as that of karma over several lifetimes or even just of memory over longer periods of time in a single life, another problem with the theory of momentariness—particularly relevant to my present exploration—is that it tends to banalize cessation. If the complete cessation of the six sense spheres, for example, occurs anyway in every moment of ordinary experience, the idea of the breakthrough to Nirvana as the complete cessation of the six sense spheres no longer carries much significance.[387]

The repercussions of the theory of momentariness complement the tendencies evident in the broadening of the scope of the fourth aggregate, the increasingly detailed analyses of each sense door, and the concern with various aspects of the presentation of dependent arising by way of twelve links. In view of such developments, it would be quite understandable if the construction of experience—or more precisely the cessation of the construction of experience—has become a less prominent feature in discussions about Nirvana and its realization. As the textual account of Rāhula's awakening conveys, doctrinal teachings like the five aggregates of clinging, the six sense spheres, and causality can offer an important contribution toward preparing the mind for the event of realization. But to fulfill this role, their function of providing merely a raft for crossing over needs to be kept at the forefront of attention. The converging point of these early Buddhist teachings appears to be cessation as something that "should be experienced," to quote from one of the passages on the unique type of perception related to the deathless (see above p. 74).

Based on the preparatory ground laid by an insight into the converging point of doctrinal teachings on Nirvana, in the reports of Rāhula's awakening the contemplation of impermanence falls into place. As mentioned in the first part of my exploration, contemplating the impermanent nature of whatever occurs in the present moment stands in a close relationship to signlessness. The very taking up of signs naturally strengthens a tendency of the mind to look out for what is less amenable to change, as such features facilitate recognition. Although the resultant tendency to ignore or overlook the fact of impermanence is something built into the very way perception appraises the world, it can be countered through contemplating impermanence. Such contemplation can correct the potentially misleading input resulting from taking up signs, whose "sign-"ificance fades away when everything is seen as constantly changing.[388] This can then eventually issue in the realization of the signless and deathless liberation of the mind:[389]

> Whose pasture is emptiness
> And signless concentration
> Their track is hard to trace,
> Like that of birds in the sky.

Abbreviations

Abhidh-k	*Abhidharmakośabhāṣya*
AN	*Aṅguttaranikāya*
Ap-a	*Apadānaṭṭhakathā*
B^e	Burmese edition
CBETA	Chinese Buddhist Electronic Text Association
Cp	*Cariyāpiṭaka*
C^e	Ceylonese edition
D	Derge edition
DĀ	*Dīrghāgama* (T 1)
Dhp	*Dhammapada*
Dhp-a	*Dhammapadaṭṭhakathā*
Dhs	*Dhammasaṅgaṇī*
DN	*Dīghanikāya*
E^e	Pali Text Society edition
EĀ	*Ekottarikāgama* (T 125)
EĀ^2	*Ekottarikāgama* (T 150A)
It	*Itivuttaka*
MĀ	*Madhyamāgama* (T 26)
Mil	*Milindapañha*
MN	*Majjhimanikāya*
Mp	*Manorathapūraṇī*

Nidd I	*Mahāniddesa*
Nidd II	*Cullaniddesa*
Paṭis	*Paṭisambhidāmagga*
Paṭis-a	*Paṭisambhidāmaggaṭṭhakathā*
P	Peking edition
Ps	*Papañcasūdanī*
SĀ	*Saṃyuktāgama* (T 99)
SĀ[2]	*Saṃyuktāgama* (T 100)
S[e]	Siamese edition
SHT	Sanskrithandschriften aus den Turfanfunden
SN	*Saṃyuttanikāya*
Sn	*Suttanipāta*
Sp	*Samantapāsādikā*
Spk	*Sāratthappakāsinī*
Sv	*Sumaṅgalavilāsinī*
T	Taishō edition (CBETA)
Th	*Theragāthā*
Th-a	*Theragāthāṭṭhakathā*
Thī	*Therīgāthā*
Ud	*Udāna*
Up	*Abhidharmakośopāyikāṭīkā*
Uv	*Udānavarga*
Vibh-a	*Sammohavinodanī*
Vin	*Vinaya*
Vism	*Visuddhimagga*

Notes

1. Griffiths 1983, 56 explains: "By 'early Buddhism' we mean, broadly speaking, pre-Aśokan Indian Buddhism."
2. Throughout this study, on numerous occasions I will be using the term "experience." This is meant to express the cluster of meanings conveyed by the noun *āyatana* (as a "sphere" of experience) and by verbs related to the roots *spṛś* and *vid* (including, e.g., Pāli *samphusati, paṭisaṃvedeti*), in particular when these are used in relation to meditative forms of experiencing; see also the discussion in Dhammadinnā 2021, 111–21.
3. The expression "early discourses" serves as a shorthand for "early Buddhist discourses," which refers to the four main Pāli *Nikāya*s, together with Dhp, It, Sn, and Ud from the fifth, and their parallels in other reciter traditions, which for the most part have been preserved in Chinese, Gāndhārī, Sanskrit, and Tibetan.
4. For a monograph study surveying the reception of the idea of Nirvana in the West see Welbon 1968.
5. See, e.g., Pande 1957, 443–510, and on the perspectives in various Buddhist traditions see also, e.g., Stcherbatsky 1968/1989, 26–58, Schmithausen 1969b, 161–70, and Hwang 2006, 50–105. Another relevant topic would be inscriptional references to Nirvana, for which see Collett 2019. A topic I am also not able to cover is the attainment of the cessation of perception and feeling tone, the classic study of which is Griffiths 1986/1991.
6. Adopting this approach implies that, whenever I quote a statement from a particular publication, this does not entail that I am necessarily in agreement with other positions taken in that publication or even with all of the conclusions the respective author may have drawn based on the part quoted by me.
7. References to Pāli discourses in the notes follow the standard procedure of adopting the PTS numbering. Bodhi 2000 and 2012 at times depart from this procedure, as a result of which the numbering given by him occasionally differs.
8. The term *nimitta* corresponds to 相 in Chinese (which the texts often confuse with 想, "perception") and *mtshan ma* in Tibetan. On the role of the *nimitta* see in more detail Anālayo 2003a.
9. Von Helmholtz 1878/1927, 10: "Ein Zeichen aber braucht gar keine Art der Ähnlichkeit mit dem zu haben, dessen Zeichen es ist. Die Beziehung zwischen beiden beschränkt sich darauf, daß das gleiche Objekt, unter gleichen Umständen zur Einwirkung kommend, das gleiche Zeichen hervorruft, und daß also ungleiche Zeichen immer ungleicher Einwirkung entsprechen."
10. Von Helmholtz 1878/1927, 11: "Wenn also unsere Sinnesempfindungen in ihrer

Qualität auch nur Zeichen sind, deren besondere Art ganz von unserer Organisation abhängt, so sind sie doch nicht als leerer Schein zu verwerfen, sonder sie sind eben Zeichen von Etwas, sei es etwas Bestehendem oder Geschehendem."

11. MN 82 at MN II 62,10: *hatthānañ ca pādānañ ca sarassa ca nimittaṃ aggahesi*, MĀ 132 at T 1.26.624c10: 取其二相, 識其音聲及其手足, with additional features mentioned in Waldschmidt 1980, 371: *(hastapādataś ca) mukhataś ca svara[g](uptitaś ca)*... *saṃjānāti* (see also Matsumura 1985, 51) and the Tibetan counterpart D 1 *kha* 104a1 or P 1030 *ge* 96a2: *lag pa dang rkang pa dang bzhin dang sna dang smra dngags dag gi mtshan ma shin tu legs par bzung nas*. Another two parallels, T 1.68.870a11 and T 1.69.873a12, do not explicitly mention the role of the *nimitta* in the act of recognition. My discussion of this episode is not meant to imply certainty about actual events happening in ancient India; instead, I simply take this as a narrative for the purpose of illustrating the functioning of the sign in recognition.
12. Paṭis II 58,19: *aniccato manasikaronto adhimokkhabahulo animittavimokkhaṃ paṭilabhati.*
13. On the training of perception see also Anālayo 2003b, 226–29.
14. See also Vism 659,6: *saṅkhāranimittassa avijahanato na nippariyāyena animittaṃ.*
15. MN 54 at MN I 360,2: *te hi te, gahapati, ākārā te liṅgā te nimittā yathā taṃ gahapatissā ti* and MĀ 203 at T 1.26.773a16: 汝有相標幟如居士 (adopting the 元 and 明 variant reading 標 instead of 幖).
16. MĀ 111 at T 1.26.600a1: 隨其想便說. 是謂知想有報, parallel to AN 6.63 at AN III 413,21: *yathā yathā naṃ sañjānāti, tathā tathā voharati: evaṃ saññī ahosin ti. ayaṃ vuccati, bhikkhave, saññānaṃ vipāko.* The formulation in a parallel extant as an individual translation, T 1.57.852c5, is cryptic and does not seem to provide a clear-cut parallel to this statement.
17. SN 46.2 at SN V 64,18 relates unwise attention (*ayoniso manasikāra*) paid to the sign of attractiveness or beauty (*subhanimitta*) to the arising of sensual desire, whereas the same type of unwise attention paid to the sign of aversion (*paṭighanimitta*) arouses ill will. The same basic correlation can be found in its parallel SĀ 715 at T 2.99.192a29, although the reference to the sign of attraction appears to have suffered from a translation or transmission error, as the text speaks of the "sign of touch" (觸相), which fails to make sense in this context, since a tangible will not necessarily trigger sensual lust. The counterpart to the *paṭighanimitta*, however, is appropriately presented by 障礙相, conveying basically the same sense.
18. SN 41.7 at SN IV 297,24: *rāgo kho, bhante, nimittakaraṇo, doso nimittakaraṇo, moho nimittakaraṇo* and SĀ 567 at T 2.99.150a7: 貪者是有相, 恚, 癡者是有相.
19. SN 41.7 at SN IV 297,29: *akuppā cetovimutti suññā rāgena suññā dosena suññā mohena* and SĀ 567 at T 2.99.150a10: 於貪空, 於恚, 癡空, which thus does not explicitly mention the unsurpassable liberation of the mind.
20. MN 152 at MN III 298,13 and SĀ 282 at T 2.99.78a28.
21. MĀ 144 at T 1.26.652b12: 若眼見色, 然不受相, 亦不味色 . . . 守護眼根, 心中不生貪伺, 憂慼, 惡不善法, parallel to MN 107 at MN III 2,14: *mā nimittaggāhī hohi mā anubyañjanaggāhī . . . cakkhundriyaṃ asaṃvutaṃ viharantaṃ abhijjhādomonassā pāpakā akusalā dhammā anvāssaveyyuṃ.*
22. SN 35.116 at SN IV 93,6: *nāhaṃ, bhikkhave, gamanena lokassa antaṃ ñāteyyaṃ* (E^e: *ñātayyaṃ*) *daṭṭheyyaṃ* (E^e: *daṭṭhayyaṃ*, S^e: *diṭṭheyyaṃ*) *patteyyan* (E^e: *pattayyan*) *ti*

vadāmi. na ca panāhaṃ, bhikkhave, appatvā (E[e]: *apatvā*) *lokassa antaṃ dukkhassa antakiriyaṃ vadāmī ti* and SĀ 234 at T 2.99.56c13: 我不說有人行到世界邊者, 我亦不說不行到世界邊而究竟苦邊者. Parts of this statement have been preserved in Sanskrit fragments, Bechert and Wille 1989, 120, SHT VI 1404V2: *n-ā[haṃ] gama[n]e[na lo]kasy-āṃtam-anuprāptavyaṃ va[d]āmi*. See also SN 3.26 at SN I 62,23, AN 4.45 at AN II 49,1, SĀ 1307 at T 2.99.359a14, SĀ² 306 at T 2.100.477b29, and EĀ 43.1 at T 2.125.756b23.

23. SN 35.116 at SN IV 95,27: *yena kho, āvuso, lokasmiṃ lokasaññī hoti lokamānī, ayam vuccati ariyassa vinaye loko*, with a less straightforward counterpart in SĀ 234 at T 2.99.56c28: 若世間, 世間名, 世間覺, 世間言辭, 世間語說, 此等皆入世間數; see also Dhammadinnā 2021, 111–12.
24. SN 1.70 at SN I 41,4: *chasu* (C[e]: *chassu*) *loko samuppanno* (see also Sn 169) and SĀ 1008 at T 2.99.264a12: 世六法等起; another parallel, SĀ² 235 at T 2.100.459b1, conveys a different sense, perhaps the result of an error in transmission or translation.
25. SN 35.23 at SN IV 15,13: *cakkhuñ* (E[e]: *cakkhuṃ*) *c' eva rūpā ca, sotañ ca saddā ca, ghānañ ca gandhā ca, jivhā ca* (*ca* not in E[e]) *rasā ca, kāyo ca phoṭṭhabbā ca, mano ca dhammā ca: idaṃ vuccati, bhikkhave, sabbaṃ*, with parallels in SĀ 319 at T 2.99.91a27: 一切者, 謂十二入處 and Up 9011 at D 4094 *nyu* 81b5 or P 5595 *thu* 127b6: *thams cad yod do zhes bya ba ni skye mched bcu gnyis kyi bar gyi chos rnams yin no zhes bya ba la*.
26. SN 35.68 at SN IV 39,29: *yattha kho, samiddhi, atthi cakkhu* (E[e]: *cakkhum*), *atthi rūpā, atthi cakkhuviññāṇaṃ, atthi cakkhuviññāṇaviññātabbā dhammā, atthi tattha loko vā lokapaññatti vā* (followed by applying the same to the other senses) and its parallel SĀ 230 at T 2.99.56a27: 謂眼, 色, 眼識, 眼觸, 眼觸因緣生受, 內覺, 若苦, 若樂, 不苦不樂 . . . 是名世間 (here, too, the same applies to the other senses). SĀ 230 is thus more detailed, as instead of referring to things to be cognized by the respective consciousness it lists the respective contact and the three types of feeling tones experienced based on that contact.
27. SN 1.62 at SN I 39,10: *cittena nīyati* (the new PTS edition by Somaratna reads *nīyatī*) *loko*, with a parallel in SĀ 1009 at T 2.99.264a26: 心持世間去 (the corresponding line differs in another parallel, SĀ² 236 at T 2.100.459b14), and AN 4.186 AN II 177,33: *cittena . . . loko nīyati*, with parallels in MĀ 172 at T 1.26.709a23: 心將世間去 and T 1.82.901c7: 以意故世間牽.
28. Dhp 1: *manopubbaṅgamā dhammā*, with Indic language parallels in the Gāndhārī *Dharmapada* 201, Brough 1962/2001, 151: *maṇopuvagama dhama*, the Patna *Dharmapada* 1, Cone 1989, 104: *manopūrvvaṃgamā dhammā*, and the Sanskrit *Udānavarga* 31.23, Bernhard 1965, 415: *manaḥpūrvaṅgamā dharmā* (on the edition by Bernhard 1965 see the observations in Schmithausen 1970). Here and elsewhere, I have decided to forgo extending a survey of parallels to a particular *Dhammapada* verse to Chinese and Tibetan parallels as well. Already as it is, my annotation is quite extensive; for my present purposes, the perspectives provided by the Indic language parallels should be sufficient.
29. Dhp 1: *manomayā*; for a more detailed discussion of this verse see Palihawadana 1984, Skilling 2007, and Agostini 2010. Ñāṇananda 2016, 393–94 relates the term to the role of attention (*manasikāra*): "'*manomayā*'—the mind-objects are 'mind-made.' That is why there is that word with its peculiar etymology: '*manasikāra*' (lit. doing-within-the-mind), i.e. attention . . . from the etymology of the term '*manasi-kāra*,' one

can understand that the mind-object itself is mind-made. That is why we say '*mano-mayā*.'"

30. SN 22.100 at SN III 152,1: *nāhaṃ, bhikkhave, aññaṃ ekanikāyaṃ pi samanupassāmi evaṃ cittaṃ yathayidaṃ, bhikkhave, tiracchānagatā pāṇā. te pi kho, bhikkhave, tiracchānagatā pāṇā citten' eva cittitā* (E^e: *cittatā*, S^e: *cintitā*) and SĀ 267 at T 2.99.69c13: 我不見一色種種如斑色鳥, 心復過是. 所以者何? 彼畜生心種種故, 色種種; the reference in SĀ 267 to just a bird, rather than animals in general, appears to be the result of a misunderstanding (the reference occurs also a bit earlier than in its counterpart in SN 22.100).
31. Spk II 327,26: *kammacitten' eva cittitā*.
32. SN 22.95 at SN III 141,18, SĀ 265 at T 2.99.68c17, T 2.105.501a22, T 2.106.501c29, and Up 4084 at D 4094 *ju* 239b3 or P 5595 *tu* 273b5.
33. Sn 9: *sabbaṃ vitatham idan ti ñatvā* (C^e: *ñatva*) *loke, so bhikkhu jahāti orapāraṃ*, with Indic language parallels in in the Gāndhārī *Dharmapada* 87, Brough 1962/2001, 131: *sarvu vidadham ida di ñatva . . . ku, so bhikkhu jahadi orapara*, see also Lenz 2003, 67: *save vita[ma]sea ti ña[tva] (*loghe)*, the Patna *Dharmapada* 412, Cone 1989, 214: *sabbam idaṃ vitadhaṃ ti moṣadhaṃmaṃ, so bhikkhu jahāti orapāraṃ*, and the Sanskrit *Udānavarga* 32.55, Bernhard 1965, 447: *jñātvā vitatham imaṃ hi sarvalokam, sa tu bhikṣur idaṃ jahāty apāraṃ*.
34. Sn 10: *sabbaṃ vitatham idan ti vītalobho*, Sn 11: *sabbaṃ vitatham idan ti vītarāgo*, Sn 12: *sabbaṃ vitatham idan ti vītadoso*, Sn 13: *sabbaṃ vitatham idan ti vītamoho*.
35. SN 22.79 at SN III 87,8: *saṅkhatam abhisaṅkharontī ti kho, bhikkhave, tasmā saṅkhārā ti vuccanti* (B^e: *vuccati*). *kiñca saṅkhatam abhisaṅkharonti? rūpaṃ rūpattāya saṅkhatam abhisaṅkharonti, vedanaṃ vedanattāya saṅkhatam abhisaṅkharonti, saññaṃ saññattāya saṅkhatam abhisaṅkharonti, saṅkhāre saṅkhārattāya saṅkhatam abhisaṅkharonti, viññāṇaṃ viññāṇattāya* (E^e: *viññāṇatthāya*) *saṅkhatam abhisaṅkharonti; saṅkhatam abhisaṅkharontī ti kho, bhikkhave, tasmā saṅkhārā ti vuccanti* (B^e: *vuccati*), with more succinct formulations in the parallels SĀ 46 at T 2.99.11c7: 於色爲作, 於受, 想, 行, 識爲作; 是故爲作相是行受陰 and Up 1014 at D 4094 *ju* 16b3 or P 5595 *tu* 18a7: *gzugs 'dus byas mngon par 'du byed pa dang tshor ba dang 'du shes dang 'du byed dang rnam par shes pa 'dus byas mngon par 'du byed de. dge slong dag, 'dus byas mngon par 'du byed cing 'dus byas mngon par 'du byed pa de'i phyir 'du byed nye bar len pa'i phung po zhes bya'o*. Although, unlike its parallels, SN 22.79 does not explicitly specify that its presentation intends the fourth aggregate, the same is implicit from the context.
36. For a survey of different renderings see Anālayo 2006b, 732.
37. What follows is based on extracts from Anālayo 2018a. The summary of the storyline given here (and other similar instances elsewhere) is not intended to present definite historical facts, instead of which the idea is only to report the narrative setting of the instruction. Throughout, my intention is not to claim that any of the episodes taken up in this study accurately reflect factual events; instead, my presentation is simply meant to report the viewpoint of the relevant texts.
38. Ud 1.10 at Ud 8,4: *tasmātiha te, bāhiya, evaṃ sikkhitabbaṃ: diṭṭhe diṭṭhamattaṃ bhavissati, sute sutamattaṃ bhavissati, mute mutamattaṃ bhavissati, viññāte viññātamattaṃ bhavissatī ti. evañ hi* (C^e: *evaṃ hi*) *te, bāhiya, sikkhitabbaṃ. yato kho te, bāhiya, diṭṭhe diṭṭhamattaṃ bhavissati, sute sutamattaṃ bhavissati, mute mutamattaṃ bhavissati, viññāte viññātamattaṃ bhavissati, tato tvaṃ, bāhiya, na tena; yato tvaṃ,*

bāhiya, na tena, tato tvaṃ, bāhiya, na tattha; yato tvaṃ, bāhiya, na tattha, tato tvaṃ, bāhiya, nev' idha na huraṃ na ubhayam antarena (C^e and S^e: *ubhayam antare*). *es' ev' anto dukkhassā ti* (the part between the first and the third *tato tvaṃ* in the above passage is faulty in E^e and S^e and has been restored based on B^e and C^e, whose reading is in line with the corresponding passage in SN 35.95 at SN IV 73,11 in all editions, including E^e and S^e).

39. I take the term *muta* to stand representative for smelling, tasting, and touch sensations (see, e.g., the comment on Sn 1086 in Nidd II 165,15: *diṭṭhan ti cakkhunā diṭṭhaṃ, sutan ti sotena sutaṃ, mutan ti ghānena ghāyitaṃ jivhāya sāyitaṃ kāyena phuṭṭhaṃ, viññātan ti manasā viññātaṃ*). A passage that would support the understanding expressed in this commentarial gloss can be found in MN 1 at MN I 3,15, which describes at first just perceiving what is *diṭṭha, suta, muta,* and *viññāta* and subsequent to such perceiving then engaging with each of these in various ways that involve the activity of *maññati*. In this context, *muta* must be standing for something more elementary than full-fledged thought. Another example is a listing of ignoble declarations, *anariyavohāra*; see, e.g., DN 33 at DN III 232,10. These take the form of misrepresenting what one has experienced by way of *diṭṭha, suta, muta,* and *viññāta*. The context requires a comprehensive listing of potential sources of experience, which would result from taking *muta* to stand for smelling, tasting, and touch sensations. A rendering of *muta* as "sensed" would also make sense of the phrasing *amute mutavāditā* and *mute amutavāditā* in a more straightforward manner compared to employing the translation "thought." The applicability of the meaning "sensed" rather than "thought" for *muta* in the context of Ud 1.10 finds confirmation in the detailed exposition of the same instruction in SN 35.95 at SN IV 74,22, as this proceeds from the objects of the eyes (= *diṭṭhe diṭṭhamattaṃ*) and ears (= *sute sutamattaṃ*) to the objects of the nose, tongue, and body, which here are clearly meant to explain the *mute mutamattaṃ* part of the instruction, followed lastly by the objects of the mind (= *viññāte viññātamattaṃ*). On this reading, then, the instruction regarding what is seen, heard, *muta*, and cognized covers the whole range of experience through the six senses, referred to in the order in which these are usually listed in the early discourses.

40. MN 63 at MN I 427,6, MĀ 221 at T 1.26.804b11, T 1.94.917c2, and T 25.1509.170a9.

41. SĀ 312 at T 2.99.90a26: 見色不取相, 其心隨正念, 不染惡心愛, 亦不生繫著; 不起於諸愛, 無量色集生, 貪欲恚害覺, 不能壞其心; 小長養眾苦, 漸次近涅槃, parallel to SN 35.95 at SN IV 74,22: *na so rajjati rūpesu, rūpaṃ disvā paṭissato* (C^e: *patissato*), *virattacitto vedeti, tañ ca nājjhosa* (C^e: *nājjhosāya*, S^e: *nājjhosā*) *tiṭṭhati. yathāssa passato rūpaṃ, sevato cā pi vedanaṃ, khīyati* (S^e: *khiyyati*) *no pacīyati* (S^e: *paciyati*). *evaṃ so caratī* (E^e: *carati*) *sato, evaṃ apacinato dukkhaṃ, santike nibbānaṃ vuccati* (B^e and S^e: *nibbāna vuccati*) and Up 4086 at D 4094 *ju* 242a1 or P 5595 *tu* 276a8: *gzugs rnams mthong nas dran ldan na, sems ni yang dag chags mi 'gyur, de las lhag par chags mi 'gyur, de las rang bzhin du ma yi, char* (P: *tshor*) *ba skye zhing 'byung mi 'gyur, brnab sems dang ni gnod sems kyis, sems 'di rnam par bcom mi 'gyur, gzugs dag nye bar mi stsogs* (P: *gsogs*) *na, mya ngan 'das pa zhes brjod do, sred zad mya ngan 'das pa zhes*; parts of his verses have also been preserved in SHT V 1311V, Sander and Waldschmidt 1985, 215–16, and SHT X 4097, Wille 2008, 265, although only for other sense doors, such as for the case of grasping the sign of taste, SHT V 1311V1–2: *smṛtir-muṣṭā priya-[n](imit)[t](aṃ ma)[na]sikurva[ta]* and then *saṃraktacitto vedayati tac-c-ādhyavasāya*

tiṣṭhati tasy-otpadyaṃte vedanā, with the result that *abhi(dhyābhir-vihiṃsābhi)ś-cittam-asy-opahanyate evam-ācinvato duḥkham-ārāṃ nirvāṇam-ucyate*, or else, on not grasping the sign of mental objects, SHT V 1311V3–4: *pratismṛtaḥ araktacitto veda[ya](ti tan-nādhyavasāya tiṣṭhati tasya n-otpadyaṃte vedanā*, and *abhidhyābhir-vihiṃsābhiś-cittaṃ n-āsy-opa(ha)nyate evam-apacinvato (duḥkhaṃ)*.

42. SN 35.95 at SN IV 76,17, SHT V 1311 R3–4, Sander and Waldschmidt 1985, 216, SHT X 4097 R3, Wille 2008, 265, SĀ 312 at T 2.99.90b26, and Up 4086 at D 4094 *ju* 242b2 or P 5595 *tu* 277a2.
43. Commenting on the expression "bare attention," Bodhi 2011, 28 points out that to employ the term "attention" to describe a form of mindfulness risks conflating what from the viewpoint of early Buddhism are two distinct mental functions. Attention (*manasikāra*) "occurs as soon as the object comes into the range of cognition. This act occurs automatically and spontaneously . . . Mindfulness, in contrast, does not occur automatically but is a quality to be cultivated."
44. DĀ 2 at T 1.1.15b2: 譬如故車, 方便修治得有所至, 吾身亦然, 以方便力得少留壽, 自力精進, 忍此苦痛. 不念一切相, 入無相定, 時我身安隱, 無有惱患; the phrase is based on emending 想 to read 相. As mentioned above in n. 8, the two characters 想 and 相 are frequently confused with each other; the present context clearly requires 相.
45. T 1.5.164c13: 不復持心思病.
46. T 24.1451.387b10: 以無相三昧觀察, 其身痛惱令息.
47. DN 16 at DN II 100,16: *sabbanimittānaṃ amanasikārā ekaccānaṃ vedanānaṃ nirodhā animittaṃ cetosamādhiṃ upasampajja viharati*; see also SN 47.9 at SN V 154,1.
48. Waldschmidt 1951, 194,5: *(e)katyā vedanā vīryeṇa pratiprasra(bhya) sarvanimittā(nām amanasikārād animittaṃ cetaḥsamādhiṃ kāyena sākṣīkṛtvopasampadya vyahārṣīt)*. The translation is based on the assumption that the instrumental *kāyena* serves in such contexts as an expression of "direct" realization rather than being about the physical body; see also Anālayo 2021e, 2391.
49. T 1.6.180a15: 即如其像正受三昧, 思惟不念眾相之定.
50. SN 36.6 at SN IV 208,11 and SĀ 470 at T 2.99.120a12.
51. See in more detail Anālayo 2016, 27–34.
52. EĀ 13.4 at T 2.125.573a9: 雖身有病, 令心無病; the first 身 is based on a 宋, 元, 明, and 聖 variant reading, as the Taishō edition rather has 雖心有病. Parallels are SN 22.1 at SN III 1,17: *āturakāyassa me sato cittaṃ anāturaṃ bhavissatī ti* and SĀ 107 at T 2.99.33a15: 於苦患身, 常當修學不苦患心, emending a reference to 身 to read 心, in line with the explanation of this statement given later on in the same discourse. This is thus the reverse of the error found in the Taishō edition of EĀ 13.4, showing that the shift from body to mind or mind to body could easily get confused.
53. SĀ 272 at T 2.99.72a26: 於四念處繫心, 住無相三昧, 修習, 多修習, 惡不善法從是而滅, 無餘永盡, parallel to SN 22.80 at SN III 93,22: *tayo akusalavitakkā kva* (C[e]: *taṃ kva*, S[e]: *taṃ*) *aparisesā nirujjhanti? catūsu* (C[e]: *catusu*) *vā satipaṭṭhānesu supatiṭṭhitacittassa* (B[e]: *suppatiṭṭhitacittassa*) *viharato animittaṃ vā samādhiṃ bhāvayato*.
54. SĀ 272 at T 2.99.72a29: 修習無相三昧, 修習, 多修習已, 住甘露門, 乃至究竟甘露涅槃.
55. SN 22.80 at SN III 93,26: *yāvañ c' idaṃ, bhikkhave, alam eva animitto samādhi bhāvetuṃ. animitto, bhikkhave, samādhi bhāvito bahulīkato mahapphalo hoti mahānisaṃso*.

56. SĀ 272 at T 2.99.72a28: 善男子, 善女人.
57. SN 5.2 at SN I 129,24: *itthibhāvo* (S^{e}: *itthībhāvo*) *kiṃ kayirā, cittamhi susamāhite?*, SĀ 1199 at T 2.99.326b6: 心入於正受, 女形復何爲?, and SĀ^{2} 215 at T 2.100.454a9: 女相無所作, 唯意修禪定; see in more detail Anālayo 2022d, 95–100.
58. Up 5010 at D 4094 *ju* 271a4 or P 5595 *thu* 14b4: *mtshan ma med pa bsgom byas nas, nga rgyal phra rgyas zhi bar 'gyur, de nas nga rgyal mngon rtogs nas, sdug bsngal tha mar byed par 'gyur*, with a Pāli parallel in SN 8.4 at SN I 188,23 (see also Sn 342): *animittañ* (E^{e}: *animittaṃ*) *ca bhāvehi, mānānusayam ujjaha, tato mānābhisamayā, upasanto carissasī ti*, which thus speaks of faring in peace and does not explicitly mention the making an end of *dukkha/duḥkha*, and a Chinese parallel in SĀ 1214 at T 2.99.331b6: 修習於無相, 滅除憍慢使, 得慢無間等, 究竟於苦邊. Another two parallels, SĀ^{2} 230 at T 2.100.458b14 and EĀ 35.9 at T 2.125.701a28, do not mention the signless, as the former instead presents the cultivation of right wisdom (正智慧) as the means to go beyond conceit, whereas the latter proceeds overall differently. The signless as the means to go beyond conceit does occur in a relevant quotation in the *Yogācārabhūmi*, Enomoto 1989, 25,19: *bhāvyatām animittaṃ ca mānānuśayanāśanaṃ, tato mānābhisamayād duḥkhasyāntaṃ kariṣyasi*; see also Enomoto 1994, 45.
59. SN 22.102 at SN III 155,15: *aniccasaññā, bhikkhave, bhāvitā bahulīkatā . . . sabbam asmimānaṃ* (C^{e} and E^{e} add *pariyādiyati*) *samūhanati* (C^{e} and E^{e}: *samūhanti*) and SĀ 270 at T 2.99.70c3: 無常想修習, 多修習, 能斷一切 . . . 慢, which thus speaks of conceit in general, whereas SN 22.102 takes up the more specific case of the conceit "I am." Both versions mention conceit as one of several detrimental states that can be overcome with perception of impermanence.
60. MĀ 82 at T 1.26.559a21: 或有一人得無相心定. 彼得無相心定已, 便自安住, 不復更求未得欲得, 不獲欲獲, 不作證欲作證. 彼於後時, 便數與白衣共會, 調笑, 貢高, 種種談譁. 彼數與白衣共會, 調笑, 貢高, 種種談譁已, 心便生欲. 彼心生欲已, 便身熱, 心熱. 彼身心熱已, 便捨戒罷道 (adopting twice the 宋 variant 相 instead of 想 and following an emendation of sequence given in the CBETA edition of 高貢 to read 貢高, in line with the reading found for the second instance). As explained in the introduction (see above p. 2), my use of the plural in translations is due to an attempt at gender-sensitive writing. The parallel AN 6.60 at AN III 397,11 reads: *ekacco puggalo sabbanimittānaṃ amanasikārā animittaṃ cetosamādhiṃ upasampajja viharati. so lābhī 'mhi animittassa cetosamādhissā ti saṃsaṭṭho viharati bhikkhūhi bhikkhunīhi upāsakehi upāsikāhi rājuhi* (B^{e}, E^{e}, and S^{e}: *raññā*) *rājamahāmattehi titthiyehi titthiyasāvakehi. tassa saṃsaṭṭhassa vissaṭṭhassa* (B^{e}: *vissatthassa*) *pākatassa* (E^{e} and S^{e}: *pākaṭassa*) *bhassam anuyuttassa viharato rāgo cittaṃ anuddhaṃseti. so rāgānuddhaṃsitena* (E^{e}: *rāgānuddhaṃsena*) *cittena sikkhaṃ paccakkhāya hīnāyāvattati*. AN 6.60 thus provides more details on the different persons such a practitioner could associate with but does not mention making fun, becoming conceited, and engaging in boisterous talk.
61. For a particularly telling instance see Anālayo 2016, 171–72.
62. MĀ 211 at T 1.26.792b12: 有二因, 二緣, 生無相定. 云何爲二? 一者不念一切相, 二者念無相界 (adopting throughout the 聖 variant 相 instead of 想, explicitly given only for the second of the two occurrences). The parallel MN 43 at MN I 296,32 reads: *dve kho, āvuso, paccayā animittāya cetovimuttiyā samāpattiyā: sabbanimittānañ ca amanasikāro, animittāya ca dhātuyā manasikāro*.
63. See Anālayo 2020d, 21, 60–61, 98, 201–3.

64. See in more detail Anālayo 2020a and above n. 43.
65. See Anālayo 2020d, 15.
66. This is the *Karmasiddhiprakaraṇa*, T 31.1609.784b19: 不思惟一切相, 及正思惟無相界. The Tibetan counterpart in Lamotte 1936, 196,24 just speaks of attention as such: *mtshan ma thams cad yid la mi byed pa dang mtshan ma med pa'i dbyings yid la byed pa'o.*
67. On *yoniso manasikāra* see Anālayo 2009f.
68. On unconsciousness as a meditative attainment and the corresponding cosmological realm see the discussion below p. 125.
69. MN 43 at MN I 297,2: *pubbe ca abhisaṅkhāro.*
70. MĀ 211 at T 1.26.792b25: 因此身及六處緣命根 (adopting the 宋, 元, and 明 variant 及 instead of 因).
71. MN 121 at MN III 108,26: *imam eva kāyaṃ paṭicca saḷāyatanikaṃ jīvitapaccayā ti*, MĀ 190 at T 1.26.737c15: 唯此我身, 六處, 命, and Skilling 1994, 176,11: *srog rkyen du byas pa'i skye mched drug gi lus de*. The Pāli version has the same phrase already earlier, at MN III 107,34, in relation to signless concentration. However, this part of the Pāli discourse appears to have suffered from textual corruption, which makes its presentation less reliable than the occurrence supported by the parallels; see below n. 128.
72. SĀ 502 at T 2.99.132b15: 作是念: 若有比丘不念一切相, 無相心正受, 身作證具足住, 是名聖住. 我作是念: 我當於此聖住, 不念一切相, 無相心正受, 身作證具足住, 多住. 多住已, 取相心生; the translation is based on the assumption, already mentioned above in n. 48, that 身 here renders an instrumental *kāyena*, which stands for "direct" realization. The assumption that the Chinese translation would have been based on such an instrumental receives support from a Sanskrit fragment parallel, Or.15009/563r5, Nagashima 2015, 392: *(amanasi)kār(ad ani)m(itta)ṃ (c)etaḥsamādhiṃ kāyena sā(kṣīkṛtvopasaṃpadya)*. The parallel SN 40.9 at SN IV 268,35 reads: *tassa mayhaṃ, āvuso, etad ahosi: idha bhikkhu sabbanimittānaṃ amanasikārā animittaṃ cetosamādhiṃ* (E^{e}: *cetosamādhim*) *upasampajja viharati, ayaṃ vuccati animitto cetosamādhī ti. so khvāhaṃ* (E^{e}: *kho ham*)*, āvuso, sabbanimittānaṃ amanasikārā animittaṃ cetosamādhiṃ upasampajja viharāmi. tassa mayhaṃ, āvuso, iminā vihārena viharato nimittānusāri* (C^{e}: *nimittānusārī*, E^{e}: *nimittānusari*) *viññāṇaṃ hoti.*
73. SN 40.1 to 40.8 at SN IV 262,28; see also AN 9.37, discussed below p. 41, where a concentration that appears to be of the signless type comes after the first three immaterial spheres.
74. MN 66 at MN I 455,18 and MĀ 192 at T 1.26.743b26 agree in describing a progression from the fourth absorption to the first immaterial sphere as part of a depiction of a successive surmounting of one concentrative experience by another that is superior. The same pattern also underlies listings of nine "successive" meditative abidings or attainments, which proceed through the four absorptions and the four immaterial spheres up to the attainment of cessation; see DN 34 at DN III 290,3 (=DN 33 at DN III 265,18), with parallels in Schlingloff 1962, 22 and T 1.13.240a5, or else AN 9.32 at AN IV 410,1, with a parallel in Up 2039 at D 4094 *ju* 70a4 or P 5595 *tu* 78b3. These presentations would imply that attaining the first immaterial sphere requires previous attainment of the fourth absorption; see also Anālayo 2020b, 574–75.
75. SĀ 501 at T 2.99.132a17.
76. MN 52 at MN I 350,10 (also AN 11.17 at AN V 343,19) and the parallels MĀ 217 at T 1.26.802b7 and T 1.92.916b17.

77. See above n. 60.
78. AN 5.29 at AN III 30,3, with parallels in EĀ^2 20 at T 2.150A.879a8 and T 4.212.755a16; see also Anālayo 2006a and 2022h.
79. DN 33 at DN III 249,15, Stache-Rosen 1968, 165 (which abbreviates and refers to the *Daśottara*, the relevant text of which can be found in Mittal 1957, 79), DĀ 9 at T 1.1.52a15 (yet another instance where 想 needs to be emended to 相), and T 1.12.232b13.
80. SN 48.50 at SN V 225,25: *vossaggārammaṇaṃ karitvā labhissati samādhiṃ, labhissati cittassa ekaggataṃ*.
81. Pande 1957, 477 comments on this type of position that it "is logically implied by the doctrine of karma which cannot postulate a first beginning without shifting the responsibility of human suffering from man to God or Chance."
82. This is the understanding of Spk III 234,9: *vossaggārammaṇaṃ karitvā ti nibbānārammaṇaṃ katvā*, a comment made in relation to another occurrence of this type of description in SN 48.9 at SN V 197,15. According to Bodhi 2002, 46n17, it seems that the *samādhi* described in this way "can be understood as a concentration aroused through the practice of insight meditation, aiming at the attainment of Nibbāna."
83. AN 1.19.1 at AN I 36,20.
84. See Anālayo 2022b.
85. AN 5.161 at AN III 186,1.
86. MN 20 at MN I 120,6: *tesaṃ vitakkānaṃ asati-amanasikāro āpajjitabbo* and MĀ 101 at T 1.26.588b13: 彼不念此念.
87. MN 10 at MN I 59,32, MĀ 98 at T 1.26.584a7, and EĀ 12.1 at T 2.125.568c24.
88. See in more detail Anālayo 2009a and 2015, 128.
89. MN 106 at MN II 263,26: *suññam* (E^e: *saññaṃ*) *idaṃ attena vā attaniyena vā ti*, MĀ 75 at T 1.26.542c18: 此世空, 空於神, 神所有, and Up 4058 at D 4094 *ju* 228b6 or P 5595 *tu* 261a6: *'jig rten ni stong pa'o . . . stong zhing bdag dang bdag gi dang bral ba'o*.
90. SĀ 557 at T 2.99.146a16: 若無相心三昧不涌, 不沒, 解脫已住, 住已解脫. The same type of question also occurs in SĀ 556 at T 2.99.145c22 and T 2.99.146a1 and in SĀ 558 at T 2.99.146b11, differing insofar as in the former case a group of nuns asks first the Buddha and then Ānanda, and in the latter case a monk asks Ānanda.
91. The **Mahāvibhāṣā*, T 27.1545.541b20: 若有獲得無相心定不沈, 不舉, 攝持諸行, 如水堤塘, 解脫故住, 住故解脫.
92. T 27.1545.541b24: 阿難告言: 佛說此定得解果報, 得解勝利. 解謂智生修道盡漏. 汝亦不久當得此事.
93. T 27.1545.541c2: 攝持諸行者: 多起加行, 多用功力. 極善作意得此定故.
94. See Anālayo 2009c and 2009e.
95. AN 9.37 at AN IV 428,4: *samādhi na cābhinato na cāpanato na ca sasaṅkhāraniggayhavāritagato* (C^e, E^e, and S^e: *sasaṅkhāraniggayhavāritavato*), *vimuttattā ṭhito, ṭhitattā santusito, santusitattā no paritassati*. AN 9.37 combines two different episodes, in the second of which Ānanda relates his previous encounter with the nun, whereas SĀ 557 reports the actual encounter and therefore has no parallel to the first part of AN 9.37 that precedes Ānanda's report of his exchange with the nun.
96. Bodhi 2012, 1828n1929 points out that other occurrences of this type of description, featuring in contexts related to awakening, suggest a shift of subject from the mind (*citta*) being freed, stable, and contented to the practitioner not being agitated. I have

decided not to follow this indication, because it seems to me that, unlike the case of the mind (which the early discourses regularly invest with agency), a shift of subject from *samādhi* to the practitioner is less natural.

97. Notably, in the case of a description in another Pāli discourse of a similar type of concentration practiced by the Buddha himself, the two Chinese parallels agree in not providing any reference to signlessness: SN 1.38 at SN I 28,31 (following the new PTS edition by Somaratne): *passa samādhiṃ subhāvitaṃ cittañ ca suvimuttaṃ, na cābhinataṃ na cāpanataṃ, na ca sasaṅkhāraniggayhavāritagataṃ* (C^{e} and E^{e}: *sasaṅkhāraniggayhavāritavataṃ*, S^{e}: *sasaṅkhāraniggayhacāritavataṃ*; see also Bodhi 2000, 371n88 for a discussion of the alternative readings *-vataṃ* and *-gataṃ*), with parallels in SĀ 1289 at T 2.99.355b15: 觀彼三昧定, 善住於正受, 解脫離諸塵, 不踊亦不沒, 其心安隱住, 而得心解脫 and SĀ^{2} 287 at T 2.100.474a13: 極爲善定, 終不矜高, 亦不卑下, 止故解脫, 解脫故止. In all versions the verse is spoken by one of several *deva*s who are eulogizing the Buddha's way of handling pain; in SN 1.38 the verse in question is spoken by the seventh *deva*, in SĀ 1289 by the fifth *deva*, and in SĀ^{2} 287 by the eighth. The two parallels do not have a counterpart to *sasaṅkhāraniggayhavāritavataṃ* (as is the case for SĀ 557, the parallel to AN 9.37); SĀ^{2} 287 does, however, have a reference to the reciprocally conditioning relationship between stability and being freed, which is not found in SN 1.38.
98. AN 9.37 at AN IV 426,25.
99. AN 7.53 at AN IV 78,18. A discourse quotation in the **Mahāvibhāṣā* gives the corresponding exposition on signlessness, T 27.1545.209b18.
100. Mp IV 200,3 (commenting on AN 9.37): *ayaṃ therī tālaphalaṃ yeva gahetvā idam phalaṃ kin nāmā ti pucchamānā viya arahattaphalasamādhiṃ gahetvā ayaṃ bhante ānanda samādhi kiṃphalo vutto bhagavatā ti pucchati*. Bodhi 2012, 1829n1931 points out a problem with the commentarial understanding of this passage as descriptive of an arahant's/arhat's fruition attainment, which is based on taking the phrase *kiṃphalo* as conveying the sense that the concentration described is the fruit of having previously reached arahantship, whereas occurrences of this type of phrase in other Pāli discourses convey the sense of a query about the fruit to be expected from the cultivation of the practice under discussion. Therefore, in the present case "this *samādhi* is not the fruit of final knowledge, but one that *yields* final knowledge." This sense also fits the query in SĀ 557 at T 2.99.146a17: 世尊說此何果, 何功德? In sum, it seems fair to conclude that the question is about the outcome of such concentration.

    The Pāli commentarial tradition regularly opts for the above explanation (except for the obvious case of AN 6.60, as a monastic who disrobes could hardly be an arahant/arhat; hence Mp III 402,10, when commenting on this discourse, speaks of a strong insight type of concentration: *animittaṃ cetosamādhin ti balavavipassanāsamādhiṃ*). For example, Ps II 352,14, commenting on the basic description of signless concentration in MN 43 (see above n. 62), takes the position: *animittāya ca dhātuyā manasikāroti sabbanimittāpagatāya nibbānadhātuyā manasikāro. phalasamāpattisahajātaṃ manasikāraṃ sandhāy' āha*. Such instances give the impression of a tendency to default to the idea of equating signlessness with Nirvana in a way that does not always do justice to the relevant discourse passages.

    This tendency as such does not seem to be confined to the Theravāda tradition, as the *Abhidharmakośabhāṣya* 8.24, Pradhan 1967, 449,10, correlates signless concentration to the third truth of cessation: *nirodhasatyākāraiḥ saṃprayuktaḥ samādhir ānimittaś caturākāraḥ*. The *Yogācārabhūmi* in turn defines signless concentration as mental stability and unification based on paying attention to the peace of the cessation of the five aggregates, Delhey 2009, 185,15: *animittaḥ [cetaḥsamādhiḥ] katamaḥ? teṣām evopādānaskandhānāṃ nirodhaṃ śāntato manasikurvato yā cittasya sthitir aikāgryam.*

Overall, there appears to be a trend in later exegesis to relate signless concentration predominantly in one way or another to Nirvana, without giving adequate room to its ordinary practice in the way suggested by the early discourses. This may be a reason contributing to a tendency in later traditions to refer to related forms of practice rather by way of nonattention (*amanasikāra*); see, e.g., Higgins 2006/2008 and Mathes 2008. Such terminological choice would avoid any potential conflict with the meaning attributed by authoritative exegesis to the signless concentration. Nonattention is indeed a key characteristic of signless concentration, which is but nonattention in relation to all signs, so that a shift to the alternative term would capture the practice well. Needless to say, this is just meant as a tentative suggestion; to explore this fully would take me far beyond the confines of the present study.

101. DN 34 at DN III 279,3: *ayaṃ samādhi santo paṇīto paṭippassaddhaladdho* (Se: *paṭippassaddhiladdho*) *ekodibhāvādhigato, na* (Ee and Se add *ca*) *sasaṅkhāraniggayhavāritagato* (Ce: *sasaṅkhāraniggayhavāritāvato*, Ee: *sasaṃkhāraniggayhavāritavato*, Se: *sasaṅkhāraṃ nigayha vāritavato*), with parallels in Mittal 1957, 70: *(ayaṃ samādh)i(ḥ śāntaḥ praṇ)ītaḥ pratipras(rabdhilabdha) ekotībhāvādhigata* and in DĀ 10 at T 1.1.53c26: 猗寂滅相, 獨而無侶 (as a qualification of 三昧), which thus combines a reference to tranquillity with the cessation of signs (in the case of another parallel, T 13, it is difficult to identify a counterpart). The concentration described in DN 34 recurs in AN 5.27 at AN III 24,17, of which no parallel appears to be known.

102. SĀ 1246 at T 2.99.341c21: 不爲有行所持, parallel to AN 3.100 at AN I 254,33: *so hoti samādhi santo paṇīto paṭippassaddhaladdho* (Be and Ce: *paṭippassaddhiladdho*, Ee: *paṭipassaddhaladdho*) *ekodibhāvādhigato na sasaṅkhāraniggayhavāritavato* (Be: *sasaṅkhāraniggayhavāritagato*, Ce: *sasaṃkhāraniggayhavāritavato*). See also the explanation offered in the *Yogācārabhūmi*, Delhey 2009, 226,12: *sacet samādhir na saṃskārābhinigṛhīto bhavatīti vistareṇa, iyaṃ cittasya karmaṇyatāviśuddhir abhijñeyeṣu dharmeṣu yatheṣṭapariṇāmanāt.*

103. Delhey 2009, 186,1: *yad uktam ānimittaś cetaḥsamādhir no cāvanata iti vistareṇa. tatra katham n[āva]nato bhavati nābhinataḥ? . . . tatra nimittāny amanasikurvaṃs teṣu na nirvidyate na vidūṣayati kevalam anabhisaṃskāram eva karoti. ato 'navanata ity ucyate. animittaṃ ca dhātuṃ manasikurvaṃs tatra na sajjate. tato 'nabhinata ity ucyate.*

104. Mp IV 199,15: *rāgavasena na abhinato, dosavasena na apanato . . . vimuttattā ṭhito ti kilesehi vimuttattā yeva ṭhito.*

105. See Anālayo 2017b, 48.

106. MN 113 at MN III 44,30: *nevasaññānāsaññāyatanasamāpattiyā pi kho atammayatā* (Se: *agammayatā*) *vuttā bhagavatā*. For a survey of the parallels, none of which has precisely the same formulation, see Anālayo 2011b, 643.

107. The need to cultivate *atammayatā* in relation to what are already unitary meditative experiences, evident in MN 113, shows that the main thrust of this term is not just about going beyond the subject–object duality, *pace* Pasanno and Amaro 2009, 110 and 122. In fact, unlike some later Buddhist traditions, early Buddhist thought does

not problematize duality; see Anālayo 2003b, 262–63 and 2022g. Instead, craving and clinging are problematized, whether that takes place in relation to dual or to unitary experiences, and the function of *atammayatā* is to counter this problem.

108. *Udānavarga* 15.4, Bernhard 1965, 214: *yasya syāt sarvataḥ smṛtiḥ, satataṃ kāyagatā hy upasthitā: no ca syān no ca me syān, na bhaviṣyati na ca me bhaviṣyati; anupūrvavihāravān asau, kālenottarate viṣaktikām*, with its Pāli parallel in Ud 7.8 at Ud 78,1: *yassa siyā sabbadā sati, satataṃ kāyagatā upaṭṭhitā: no c' assa no ca me siyā, na bhavissati na ca me bhavissati; anupubbavihārī tattha so, kālen' eva tare visattikan ti.*
109. See Anālayo 2009b, 212–14.
110. See in more detail Anālayo 2021c.
111. See in more detail Anālayo 2021g.
112. SN 22.55 at SN III 55,30: *no c' assa* (B^{e}, C^{e}, and S^{e}: *c' assaṃ*) *no ca me siyā, na bhavissati* (B^{e}: *nābhavissa*) *na me bhavissati*, whereas the parallel SĀ 64 at T 2.99.16c12 reads: 無吾我, 亦無有我所; 我既非當有, 我所何由生? A repetition of this dictum in the same discourse at T 2.99.16c21 reads: 非我, 非我所, 我, 我所非當有, which is considerably closer to the Pāli version, except for having the more affirmative part first. Hence the earlier formulation need not be taken to involve a substantially different perspective.
113. SĀ 64 at T 2.99.17a12: 識無所住故不增長, 不增長故無所爲作, 無所爲作故則住, 住故知足，知足故解脫，解脫故於諸世間都無所取，無所取故無所著，無所著故自覺涅槃, parallel to SN 22.55 at SN III 58,22: *tad appatiṭṭhitaṃ viññāṇaṃ avirūḷhaṃ anabhisaṅkhārañ ca* (C^{e} and S^{e}: *anabhisaṅkhacca*) *vimuttaṃ. vimuttattā ṭhitaṃ, ṭhitattā santusitaṃ, santusitattā na paritassati, aparitassaṃ paccattaññeva* (C^{e}: *paccattaṃ yeva*) *parinibbāyati*. In the preceding part, SN 22.55 indicates that consciousness is not established on any of the five aggregates, whereas SĀ 64 only makes such an indication for the other four aggregates.
114. SĀ 377 at T 2.99.103b1: 譬如, 比丘, 樓閣宮殿, 北西長廣, 東西牕牖. 日出東方, 應照何所? 比丘白佛言: 應照西壁. 佛告比丘: 若無西壁, 應何所照? 比丘白佛言: 應照虛空, 無所攀緣, parallel to SN 12.64 at SN II 103,13: *seyyathā pi, bhikkhave, kūṭāgāraṃ* (E^{e}: *kuṭāgāraṃ*) *vā kūṭāgārasālaṃ* (E^{e}: *kuṭāgārasālā*, S^{e}: *kūṭāgārasālā*) *vā uttarāya vā dakkhiṇāya vā pācīnāya vā vātapānā* (S^{e}: *pācīnavātapānā*). *suriye* (B^{e}: *sūriye*) *uggacchante vātapānena rasmi pavisitvā kvāssa* (E^{e}: *kvassa*) *patiṭṭhitā ti? pacchimāyaṃ* (C^{e}: *pacchimāya*), *bhante, bhittiyan ti. pacchimā* (S^{e}: *pacchimāya*) *ce, bhikkhave, bhitti nāssa kvāssa* (E^{e}: *kvassa*) *patiṭṭhitā ti? paṭhaviyaṃ* (B^{e} and E^{e}: *pathaviyaṃ*), *bhante ti. paṭhavī* (B^{e} and E^{e}: *pathavī*) *ce, bhikkhave, nāssa kvāssa patiṭṭhitā ti? āpasmiṃ, bhante ti. āpo ce, bhikkhave, nāssa kvāssa patiṭṭhitā ti? appatiṭṭhitā, bhante ti.*
115. SN 12.38 at SN II 66,1: *tad appatiṭṭhite viññāṇe avirūḷhe āyatiṃ punabbhavābhinibbatti na hoti* and its parallel SĀ 359 at T 2.99.100a27: 無攀緣識住故, 於未來世生, 老, 病, 死, 憂, 悲, 惱, 苦滅. SN 12.39 at SN II 66,27: *tad appatiṭṭhite viññāṇe avirūḷhe nāmarūpassa avakkanti na hoti* and its parallel SĀ 360 at T 2.99.100b7: 無攀緣識住故, 不入名色; both versions continue with the other links of dependent cessation in abbreviation. SN 12.40 at SN II 67,22: *tad appatiṭṭhite viññāṇe avirūḷhe nati na hoti, natiyā asati āgatigati na hoti, āgatigatiyā asati cutūpapāto na hoti* and its parallel SĀ 361 at T 2.99.100b17: 無攀緣識住故, 不入名色, 不入名色故, 則無往來, 無往來故, 則無生死; in this case as well both versions continue with the other links of dependent cessation in abbreviation.
116. SN 4.23 at SN I 122,12: *appatiṭṭhitena ca, bhikkhave, viññāṇena . . . kulaputto parinib-*

buto ti. The parallel SĀ 1091 at T 2.99.286b13 speaks instead of the protagonist having had a "mind" (*citta*) that is unestablished and relates that to the time of him committing suicide: 不住心, 執刀自殺. Another parallel, SĀ² 30 at T 2.100.383a12, mentions entry into Nirvana, followed by stating that there is no consciousness: 入涅槃, 無有神識; this version thus does not refer to the condition of not being established. SN 22.87 at SN III 124,12: *appatiṭṭhitena ca, bhikkhave, viññāṇena . . . kulaputto parinibbuto ti*. The parallel SĀ 1265 at T 2.99.347b11 specifies that his consciousness was unestablished at the time of committing suicide: 不住識神, 以刀自殺, whereas another parallel, EĀ 26.10 at T 2.125.643a10, qualifies his consciousness as being forever free from attachment: 神識永無所著; for a comparative study see also Anālayo 2011d.

117. Ud 8.1 at Ud 80,15; for the full passage see below n. 190.
118. SN 22.53 at SN III 53,15: *yo, bhikkhave, evaṃ vadeyya: aham aññatra rūpā aññatra vedanāya aññatra saññāya aññatra saṅkhārehi viññāṇassa āgatiṃ vā gatiṃ vā cutiṃ vā upapattiṃ vā vuddhiṃ* (Sᵉ: *vuḍḍhiṃ*) *vā virūḷhiṃ vā vepullaṃ vā paññāpessāmī* (Sᵉ: *paññapessāmī*) *ti, n' etaṃ ṭhānaṃ vijjati*, followed by referring at SN III 53,27 to *tad appatiṭṭhitaṃ viññāṇaṃ* (here as a result of the successful removal of lust for the five aggregates). The same pattern of proceeding from the impossibility of designating a consciousness apart from the other four aggregates followed by a reference to an unestablished consciousness holds for SN 22.54 at SN III 55,10+23 and SN 22.55 at SN III 58,9+22 (see above n. 113). Similarly, SĀ 39 (parallel to SN 22.54) states the impossibility of positing a consciousness apart from the other aggregates at T 2.99.9a11: 若離色, 受, 想, 行, 識有若來, 若去, 若住, 若生者, 彼但有言數, 問已不知, 增益生癡, 以非境界故, followed by describing an unestablished consciousness, T 2.99.9a15: 識無住處. The same holds for another parallel, Up 6019 at D 4094 *nyu* 11a2 or P 5595 *thu* 44a2: *gang zhig 'di skad du ngas gzugs las gzhan dang tshor ba dang 'du shes dang 'du byed las gzhan du rnam par shes pa 'gro ba'am 'ong ba'am gnas pa'am 'chi 'pho ba'am skye ba'am 'phel zhing rgyas pa dang yangs par 'gyur ba gdags par bya'o zhes smra na. de ni de'i tshig tsam dang dris pa'i lan yongs su mi shes shing lan la mgo rmongs bar byed pa ste. ji ltar yang de'i yul ma yin pa'i phyir ro*, followed at D 4094 *nyu* 11a7 or P 5595 *thu* 44a8 by *rnam par shes pa gnas pa 'phel zhing rgyas pa dang yangs par mi 'gyur te*. The parallel to SN 22.53, SĀ 40, abbreviates and thus would correspond to SĀ 39. The parallel to SN 22.55, SĀ 64, expresses the same basic situation in a slightly different manner, as after describing that consciousness relies on the other four aggregates, the exposition continues in this way at T 2.99.17a4: 若作是說: 更有異法, 識若來, 若去, 若住, 若起, 若滅, 若增進廣大生長者, 但有言說, 問已不知, 增益生癡, 以非境界故, followed at T 2.99.17a12 by referring to a consciousness that is unestablished anywhere: 識無所住 (see above n. 113).
119. Collins 1998, 202 comments that when some passages "speak of someone nirvanizing *apatiṭṭhena viññāṇena*, two renderings are possible: either 'with an unstationed consciousness' (= with consciousness, but an unstationed one), or 'without a stationed consciousness' (= with no consciousness-Aggregate stationed anywhere in *saṃsāra*). The former is ruled out by the fact that nirvana is the cessation of the Aggregates."
120. AN 3.163 at AN I 299,14: *suññato samādhi, animitto samādhi, appaṇihito samādhi* and its parallel EĀ 24.10 at T 2.125.630b3: 空三昧, 無願三昧, 無相三昧 (emending 想 to read 相). Whereas in this case the parallels agree, references to the types of contact that a practitioner will experience on emerging from the attainment of cessation vary

on the third. MN 44 at MN I 302,22 lists *suññato phasso, animitto phasso, appaṇihito phasso*, but the parallels have imperturbable and nothingness contact in addition to signless contact (strictly speaking these are actually parallels to MN 43); see MĀ 211 at T 1.26.792a19: 一者不移動觸, 二者無所有觸, 三者無相觸 and Up 1005 at D 4094 *ju* 9a6 or P 5595 *tu* 10a8: *mi g.yo ba dang cung zad med pa dang mtshan ma med pa gsum la'o*. The same difference recurs between SN 41.6 at SN IV 295,13 and its parallel SĀ 568 at T 2.99.150c3.

121. See in more detail Anālayo 2007.
122. Sn 1119: *suññato lokaṃ avekkhassu . . . sadā sato*.
123. Dhp 279: *sabbe dhammā anattā*, with Indic language parallels in the Gāndhārī *Dharmapada* 108, Brough 1962/2001, 134: *sarvi dhama aṇatva*, the Patna *Dharmapada* 374, Cone 1989, 203: *sabbadhaṃmā anāttā*, and the Sanskrit *Udānavarga* 12.8, Bernhard 1965, 194: *sarvadharmā anātmānaḥ*.
124. MN 112 at MN III 31,23 and MĀ 187 at T 1.26.733a2.
125. SĀ 80 at T 2.99.20b4: 若得空已, 能起無相, 無所有, 離慢知見者 (the discussion in SĀ 80 begins by mentioning 空三昧, making it reasonable to supplement "(concentration)" in the translation of the present extract), which has a parallel in T 2.103.500a10 (another parallel, T 2.104.500b22, proceeds differently). The presentation in the above quote could be related to an indication made in a Sanskrit fragment of a commentarial text, SHT V 1131V4, Sander and Waldschmidt 1985, 126: *yaḥ śunyatayā samanvāgata ānimitten-āpi saḥ yadi pratil(a)[bdh](aṃ)*.
126. SĀ 80 at T 2.99.20b8: 若比丘於空閑處樹下坐, 善觀色無常, 磨滅離欲之法. 如是觀察受, 想, 行, 識無常, 磨滅離欲之法. 觀察彼陰無常, 磨滅, 不堅固, 變易法; 心樂, 清淨, 解脫; 是名爲空. 如是觀者, 亦不能離慢, 知見清淨. 復有正思惟, 三昧, 觀色相斷, 聲, 香, 味, 觸, 法相斷; 是名無相. 如是觀者, 猶未離慢, 知見清淨. 復有正思惟三昧, 觀察貪相斷, 瞋恚, 癡相斷; 是名無所有. 如是觀者, 猶未離慢, 知見清淨. 復有正思惟, 三昧, 觀察: 我, 我所, 從何而生? 復有正思惟, 三昧, 觀察: 我, 我所, 從若見, 若聞, 若嗅, 若嘗, 若觸, 若識而生. 復作是觀察: 若因, 若緣而生識者, 彼識因, 緣, 爲常, 爲無常? 復作是思惟: 若因, 若緣而生識者, 彼因, 彼緣皆悉無常. 復次: 彼因, 彼緣皆悉無常, 彼所生識云何有常? 無常者, 是有爲行, 從緣起, 是患法, 滅法, 離欲法, 斷知法 (adopting a 宋, 元, and 明 variant that adds 我 before the first mention of 我所, in line with the formulation employed subsequently). Sanskrit fragment SHT I 106B, Waldschmidt, Clawiter, and Holzmann 1965, 90 has preserved counterparts to several aspects of the instruction in SĀ 80 (the fragment has been identified as a parallel to SĀ 80 by Tang Huyen in Bechert and Wille 1995, 239); see, e.g., B1: *(nimi)tte prahīnaṃ sama samanu[p]*, B2: *[ma]sy=ocyate ānimittaṃ evaṃ*, B3: *sa raga kiñca*, B5: *yat=punar=idam=ucyate ah(a)m=(a)vāma[m]*, and B6: *bhavati aham=asmi yad=yad=eva paśyāmi*.
127. Similar indications are made in the parallels: T 2.103.500a22: 除諸色相, 聲相, 香相, 以故謂言至於無相 (occurrences of 想 have been emended to 相), which only explicitly mentions the first three sense objects, and T 2.104.500c13: 觀諸色境, 皆悉滅盡, 離諸有相; 如是聲, 香, 味, 觸, 法亦皆滅盡離諸有相, 如是觀察名爲無相解脫門 (here, too, occurrences of 想 have been emended to 相), which relates such contemplation to the signless door to liberation. See also a discourse quotation in the **Mahāvibhāṣā*, T 27.1545.541c10: 觀色聲香味觸相，而捨諸相名無相定，彼觀境界相而捨有情相, which relates concentration on signlessness to abandoning all signs in relation to the five physical sense objects and then commends abandoning in particular the sign of a

sentient being when contemplating the signs of objects of the mind.

128. Anālayo 2012c, 32–36 and 2015, 134–36; see also Schmithausen 1981, 237.

129. MĀ 190 at T 1.26.737c1: 復次, 阿難, 比丘若欲多行空者, 彼比丘莫念無量識處想, 莫念無所有處想, 當數念一無相心定. 彼如是知: 空無量識處想, 空無所有處想, 然有不空, 唯一無相心定. 若有疲勞, 因無量識處想故, 我無是也; 若有疲勞, 因無所有處想故, 我亦無是; 唯有疲勞, 因一無相心定故. 若彼中無者, 以此故, 彼見是空. 若彼有餘者, 彼見真實有. 阿難, 是謂行真實空, 不顛倒也 (references to 無想心定 here and in the next note have been emended to 無相心定, which corresponds to the "signless concentration of the mind," *animitta cetosamādhi*, in MN 121 at MN III 107,28 and has its counterpart in the "signless element," *mtshan ma med pa'i dbyings*, in Skilling 1994, 172,5). The reference to "weariness," 疲勞, has its Pāli counterpart in *daratha*, for which Cone 2010, 375 lists "being hot or inflamed; distress; exhaustion." Particularly helpful for the present context appears to be an occurrence of the term in Nidd I 344,6, commenting on a reference in Sn 915 to *nibbāti*, which is glossed as *sabbe darathe . . . sameti upasameti vūpasameti nibbāpeti paṭipassambheti*. Another relevant occurrence would be Cp 142 at Cp 13,4: *sabbaṃ sameti darathaṃ, yathā sītodakaṃ viya*. Taking a lead from these occurrences in later texts invites opting for the nuance of "being hot or inflamed," understood in the present context as expressing an opposition to the coolness of Nirvana. In other words, rather than intending an actual "distress" or alternatively "disturbance," terminology which seems rather strong for the subtle and refined meditative experiences under description, in the present context the term *daratha* could be taken to convey that, however profound, these meditative experiences still fall short of the final goal of Nirvana; they still partake of the hotness of being conditioned and fall short of the coolness of the unconditioned.

130. MĀ 190 at T 1. 26.737c9: 彼作是念: 我本無相心定, 本所行, 本所思. 若本所行, 本所思者, 我不樂彼, 不求彼, 不應住彼.

131. Skilling 1994, 174,5: *de 'di snyam du sems te: mtshan ma med pa'i dbyings kyang mngon par 'dus byas shing sems pas mngon par bsams pa yin te. gang mngon par 'dus byas shing sems pas mngon par bsams pa de la ni mngon par dga' bar bya ba 'am, mngon par brjod par bya ba 'am, lhag par chags par bya ba 'am, lhag par chags shing gnas par bya bar mi rigs so.*

132. MN 121 at MN III 108,15: *ayam pi kho animitto cetosamādhi abhisaṅkhato* (E^e: *abhisaṃkhato*) *abhisañcetayito* (C^e: *abhisañcetasito*). *yaṃ kho pana kiñci abhisaṅkhataṃ* (E^e: *abhisaṃkhataṃ*) *abhisañcetayitaṃ* (C^e: *abhisañcetasitaṃ*) *tad aniccaṃ nirodhadhamman ti pajānāti*; notably the term *abhisaṅkhato/abhisaṃkhato* used in MN 121 corresponds to the terminology employed to describe the role of the aggregate of *saṅkhāras* in relation to other aggregates in SN 22.79, quoted above n. 35.

133. MN 121 at MN III 109,1: *paramānuttarā suññatāvakkanti* and Skilling 1994, 178,2: *stong pa nyid la 'jug pa bla na med pa*.

134. MN 26 at MN I 172,1: *amatam adhigataṃ*, MĀ 204 at T 1.26.777c16: 得 . . . 無死, and EĀ 24.5 at T 2.125.619a1: 已獲甘露善.

135. MN 26 at MN I 171,12: *āhañchaṃ* (S^e: *āhaññiṃ*; see also Skilling 2009, 89n33) *amatadundubhin ti*, MĀ 204 at T 1.26.777b26: 擊妙甘露鼓. Another discourse parallel, EĀ 24.5 at T 2.125.618c11, has instead a reference to the "medicine of the deathless," 甘露藥. References to the drum of the deathless occur also in a range of other sources

reporting this episode; see the *Udānavarga* 21.6, Bernhard 1965, 280,3: *haniṣye 'mṛtadundubhim*, the *Mahāvastu* of the Mahāsāṃghika-Lokottaravāda *Vinaya*, Marciniak 2019, 417,3 (see Senart 1897, 327,6): *āhaniṣyaṃ amṛtadundubhim*, the *Lalitavistara*, Lefmann 1902, 406,13: *tāḍayiṣye 'mṛtadundubhiṃ*, T 4.211.594b19: 擊甘露法鼓, and T 4.212.718a2 and T 4.213.787c5: 欲擊甘露鼓; for a Tocharian parallel see Sieg and Siegling 1933, 171. The *Saṅghabhedavastu* of the Mūlasarvāstivāda *Vinaya*, however, speaks instead of the "drum of Dharma," Gnoli 1977, 132,21: *āhantuṃ dharmadundubhim*.

136. MN 26 at MN I 169,24: *apārutā tesaṃ amatassa dvārā*. The whole episode of the Buddha's initial hesitation to teach is not found in the parallel MĀ 204; see in more detail Anālayo 2011a. Several of the sources that do report such a hesitation also have a reference to opening the door(s) of the deathless; see the *Mahāvastu* of the Mahāsāṃghika-Lokottaravāda *Vinaya*, Marciniak 2019, 406,2 (see Senart 1897, 319,3): *apāvṛtam me amṛtasya dvāraṃ*, the *Saṅghabhedavastu* of the Mūlasarvāstivāda *Vinaya*, Gnoli 1977, 130,8: *apāvariṣye amṛtasya dvāraṃ*, the Dharmaguptaka *Vinaya*, T 22.1428.787b2: 今開甘露門, the Mahīśāsaka *Vinaya*, T 22.1421.104a9: 甘露今當開, the *Lalitavistara*, Lefmann 1902, 400,18: *apāvṛtās teṣām amṛtasya dvārā*, T 3.189.643a22: 我今當開甘露法門 (which speaks of the "Dharma door of the deathless"), and T 3.190.806c26: 我今欲開甘露門.
137. MN 18 at MN I 111,14: *amatassa dātā*; the corresponding sections in the parallels MĀ 115 at T 1.26.604a18 and EĀ 40.10 at T 2.125.743b3 do not refer to the deathless.
138. SN 1.42 at SN I 32,14: *amataṃdado* (S^{c}: *amatandado*) *ca so hoti, yo dhammam anusāsatī ti*, with parallels in SĀ 998 at T 2.99.261b29: 以法而誨彼, 是則施甘露 and SĀ^{2} 135 at T 2.100.426c8: 如法教弟子, 能作如是施, 是名施甘露. Contrary to the assumption by Tamaki 1973, 1056, such reference to *amata* does not imply the ability "to attain the eternal life through realizing the transcendental dhamma."
139. See Kumoi 1969, 209 and Vetter 1995, 219; and on the ancient Indian conception of the deathless also, e.g., Collins 1982, 42–44 and Olivelle 1997.
140. AN 10.81 at AN V 152,8: *maraṇena . . . tathāgato nissaṭo visaṃyutto vippamutto vimariyādikatena cetasā viharati*. The other nine things are each of the five aggregates, birth, old age, *dukkha/duḥkha*, and defilements.
141. See Anālayo 2018b, 34.
142. Sn 1 to 17: *so bhikkhu jahāti orapāraṃ, urago jiṇṇam iva tacaṃ* (B^{e}: *ivattacaṃ*) *purāṇaṃ*.
143. Dhp 385: *yassa pāraṃ apāraṃ vā, pārāpāraṃ na vijjati*, with Indic language parallels in the Gāndhārī *Dharmapada* 35, Brough 1962/2001, 123, which has preserved *yasa pari avare ca, para*, the Patna *Dharmapada* 40, Cone 1989, 114: *yassa pāraṃ apāraṃ vā, pārāpāraṃ na vijjati*, and the Sanskrit *Udānavarga* 33.24, Bernhard 1965, 469: *yasya pāram apāraṃ ca, pārāpāraṃ na vidyate*.
144. MN 106 at MN II 265,30: *etaṃ amataṃ yadidaṃ anupādā cittassa vimokkho* (E^{e}: *vimokho*), with parallels in MĀ 75 at T 1.26.543b16: 若有無餘涅槃者是名甘露 and Up 4058 at D 4094 *ju* 230a5 or P 5595 *tu* 263a2: *'chi ba med pa gang zhe na? nye bar len pa spangs pa nges par byung ba, sred pa zad pa 'dogs chags dang bral ba 'gog pa ste*. Although differing in formulation, the parallels convey a similar sense.
145. SN 45.7 at SN V 8,17: *rāgakkhayo dosakkhayo mohakkhayo: idaṃ vuccati amataṃ*; the parallel SĀ 753 at T 2.99.199a16 relates the deathless to the eradication of the influxes: 甘露者界名說, 然我爲有漏盡者, 現說此名.

146. Vin I 41,2: *kacci nu* (C^e: *no*) *tvaṃ, āvuso, amataṃ* (S^e: *amatam*) *adhigato ti? āmāvuso, amataṃ* (S^e: *amatam*) *adhigato ti*, with Indic language parallels in the *Catuṣpariṣatsūtra*, Waldschmidt 1962, 382,8: *amṛt(aṃ tvayādhigatam? adhigatam āyuṣman)* and the *Mahāvastu* of the Mahāsāṃghika-Lokottaravāda *Vinaya*, Marciniak 2019, 71,14 (see Senart 1897, 61,16): *atha khalu te āyuṣman śāriputra amṛtam adhigataṃ amṛtagāmi vā mārgo? . . . amṛtam me āyuṣmān maudgalyāyana adhigata amṛtagāmī ca mārgo*.
147. AN 6.119 and AN 6.120 at AN III 450,22 and 451,17, which use the expression "seer of the deathless," *amataddaso*, qualified to be one who "proceeds having realized the deathless," *amataṃ sacchikatvā iriyati* (C^e: *irīyati*).
148. This helps correct the assumption by Sirimane 2016, 199 that "*Nibbāna* has not been fully experienced even by a trainee (*sekha*). A stream-enterer can also only 'deduce' it." This only holds for the less advanced type of trainee, the *dhammānusārin/dharmānusarin* or the *saddhānusārin/śraddhānusarin* (for a survey of textual references see Anālayo 2011b, 384f), who have indeed not yet experienced Nirvana and for this reason can only deduce it.
149. MN 140 at MN III 246,19: *muni kho pana, bhikkhu, santo na jāyati, na jīyati* (E^e and S^e: *jiyyati*), *na mīyati* (S^e: *miyyati*; missing in E^e), with a counterpart in one of its parallels, Up 1041 at D 4094 *ju* 41b4 and P 5595 *tu* 45a4: *thub pa zhes bya ba ni gang la skye ba med pa dang rga ba med pa dang 'chi ba med pa dang*. This type of statement is absent from the parallel MĀ 162 at T 1.26.692a29; see also Anālayo 2011b, 801n211.
150. Dhp 225: *te yanti accutaṃ ṭhānaṃ, yattha gantvā na socare*, with Indic language parallels in the Patna *Dharmapada* 240, Cone 1989, 165: *te yānti accutaṃ ṭṭhāṇaṃ, yattha gantā na śocati*, and the Sanskrit *Udānavarga* 7.7, Bernhard 1965, 157: *te yānti hy acyutaṃ sthānaṃ, yatra gatvā na śocati*.
151. Th 715: *na me hoti ahosin ti, bhavissan ti na hoti me; saṅkhārā vibhavissanti* (B^e and C^e: *vigamissanti*), *tattha kā paridevanā?* In an attempt to provide a poetic rendering in English, I have not done justice to the repetition of *na me hoti* as *na hoti me*. Regarding the reading *saṅkhārā vibhavissanti*, Norman 1969, 226 considers this to be preferable, as "the structure of the verse, with *bhavati* appearing four times in one form or another in the first line, seems to demand a compound of *bhavati* in the second line." Although in my translation I have adopted the reading *vibhavissanti*, I would nevertheless like to note that I think it is also possible that the occurrence of *bhavissāmī* in the preceding line led to an error during the course of oral transmission, whereby the reading *vigamissanti* was accidentally changed to become *vibhavissanti*.
152. AN 3.12 at AN I 106,21.
153. DN 33 at DN III 241,3 (also DN 34 at DN III 279,9 and AN 5.26 at AN III 21,8) and its parallels Stache-Rosen 1968, 149, DĀ 9 at T 1.1.51c3, and T 1.12.230c7; see also Collins 1992, 126–27, Anālayo 2009d, Pāsādika 2017, and Dhammadinnā 2021, 116–17.
154. SN 46.3 at SN V 68,1 and its parallels SHT I 533 V1+6, Bechert and Wille 1989, 215, and SĀ 724, where the relevant section is not fully preserved, for which see SĀ 723 at T 2.99.195a16; see also Anālayo 2021f, 8–9 and 2020/2022.
155. SĀ 729 at T 2.99.196a19: 依遠離, 依無欲, 依滅, 向於捨, parallel to SN 46.27 at SN V 87,15: *vivekanissitaṃ virāganissitaṃ nirodhanissitaṃ vossaggapariṇāmiṃ*.
156. See in more detail Anālayo 2013c, 219–21.

157. See Anālayo 2003b, 253–54.
158. An example is MN 56 at MN I 379,36 and its parallel MĀ 133 at T 1.26.630c4.
159. MN 56 at MN I 380,3: *seyyathā pi nāma suddhaṃ vatthaṃ apagatakāḷakaṃ sammad-eva rajanaṃ paṭiggaṇheyya* (Cᵉ and Eᵉ: *paṭigaṇheyya*) and its parallel MĀ 133 at T 1.26.630c8: 猶如白素, 易染為色.
160. For a survey of instances where parallels to Pāli versions of this pericope are not supported by their parallels see Anālayo 2011b, 327n87. In the present case, this appears to reflect an apparent tendency of relating such instances to the four noble truths. MN 56 at MN I 380,3 mentions just once "*dukkha*, its arising, its cessation, and the path" as the content of the teaching delivered by the Buddha, whereas its parallel MĀ 133 at T 1.26.630c7+8+10 mentions the same thrice: first as the content of the teaching given by the Buddha (corresponding to the formulation in MN 56) and two more times as the actual vision attained by the listener, for which MN 56 at MN I 380,6 instead employs the standard pericope about the arising of the Dharma-eye. At least in the present case, it seems possible that a fascination with the four noble truths, evident in a range of texts, led to a reformulation in MĀ 133.
161. SĀ 396 at T 2.99.106c21: 所有集法, 一切滅已, 離諸塵垢, 得法眼生; the discourse continues by describing the eradication of the three fetters, the certainty of not being reborn in lower realms as well as of reaching an end of *dukkha*/*duḥkha* within seven lives at most. Although all of this is standard in Pāli discourses, no actual parallel appears to be known for this discourse.
162. AN 3.91 at AN I 240,14: *tassa kho taṃ, bhikkhave, bhikkhuno n' atthi sā iddhi vā ānubhāvo vā: ajj' eva me anupādāya āsavehi cittaṃ vimuccatu sve vā uttaras' evā ti. atha kho, bhikkhave, hoti so samayo yaṃ tassa bhikkhuno adhisīlam pi sikkhato adhicittam pi sikkhato adhipaññam pi sikkhato anupādāya āsavehi cittaṃ vimuccati*; Sᵉ lacks the whole part from *adhisīlam* to the last instance of *sikkhato*, although it does refer to the three trainings elsewhere in the same discourse.
163. Sn 960: *gacchato agataṃ* (Eᵉ: *amataṃ*) *disaṃ*; see also Dhp 323: *gaccheyya agataṃ disaṃ*, in which case a different formulation occurs in the Indic language parallels extant in the Patna *Dharmapada* 92, Cone 1989, 127: *tāṃ bhūmim abhisaṃbhave*, and in the Sanskrit *Udānavarga* 19.8, Bernhard 1965, 259: *tāṃ bhūmim adhigacchati* (or alternatively *abhisaṃbhavet*). Although the reference in Dhp 323 to a region to which one has never gone does not receive support from its parallels, it is nevertheless an accurate reflection of the general position taken in early Buddhist thought, in contrast to the idea in some later traditions that awakening is in some form an intrinsic quality of the mind; see in more detail Anālayo 2022e, 92–113.
164. Dhp 383: *saṅkhārānaṃ* (Eᵉ: *saṃkhārānaṃ*) *khayaṃ ñatvā akataññū si*, with Indic language parallels in the Gāndhārī *Dharmapada* 10, Brough 2001, 120: *sagharaṇa kṣaya ñatva akadaño si*, the Patna *Dharmapada* 34, Cone 1989, 112: *saṃkhārāṇāṃ khayaṃ ñāttā akathaso si*, and the Sanskrit *Udānavarga* 33.60, Bernhard 1965, 494: *saṃskārāṇāṃ kṣayaṃ jñātvā hy akṛtajño bhaviṣyasi*.
165. Dhp 348: *muñca pure muñca pacchato, majjhe muñca bhavassa pāragū*, with Indic language parallels in the Gāndhārī *Dharmapada* 161, Brough 2001, 144: *muju pura muju pachadu, majadu muju bhavasa parako*, the Patna *Dharmapada* 150, Cone 1989, 142: *muñca pure muñca pacchato, majjhe muñca bhavassa pāragū*, and the Sanskrit *Udānavarga* 29.57, Bernhard 1965, 391: *muñca purato muñca paścato, madhye muñca bhavasya pāragaḥ*.

166. Sn 1098: *uggahitaṃ* (B^e and E^e: *uggahītaṃ*) *nirattaṃ vā, mā te vijjittha kiñcanaṃ.*
167. A detailed version of this simile can be found in the **Śūraṃgamasūtra*, T 19.945.111a9: 如人以手指月示人, 彼人因指當應看月. 若復觀指以爲月體, 此人豈唯亡失月輪, 亦亡其指. 何以故? 以所標指爲明月故, 豈唯亡指. The passage begins by clarifying that people use the finger of a hand to point out the moon so that another, on following that pointing, can see the moon. If that person instead were to look at the finger as if it were the moon, such a person misses the moon and also the finger, because the finger is mistaken for the moon. A shorter version can be found in T 17.842.917a27: 修多羅教如標月指, 若復見月, 了知所標畢竟非月, according to which the teachings in the *sūtra*s are like a finger pointing to the moon; once one has seen the moon, one understands that what marks it out is after all not the moon itself; see also, e.g., T 25.1509.125b1 and Lamotte 1944/1981, 538n2.
168. DN 9 at DN I 185,4: *yan* (B^e: *yaṃ*) *nūnāhaṃ na c' eva* (*c' eva* not in E^e) *ceteyyaṃ na ca* (*ca* not in E^e) *abhisaṅkhareyyan* (E^e and S^e: *abhisaṃkhareyyan*) *ti? so na c' eva ceteti, na ca* (*ca* not in E^e) *abhisaṅkharoti* (E^e and S^e: *abhisaṃkharoti*). *tassa acetayato anabhisaṅkharoto* (E^e and S^e: *anabhisaṃkharoto*) *tā c' eva saññā nirujjhanti, aññā ca oḷārikā saññā na uppajjanti, so nirodhaṃ phusati*, with parallels in Stuart 2013, 64: *ahaṃ cec cetayeyam abhisaṃskuryām, evam me iyaṃ ca saṃjñā nirudhyeta, anyā caudārikatarā saṃjñā prādurbhavet. sa na cetayate nābhisaṃskaroti, so 'cetayamāno 'nabhisaṃskurvaṃ samyag eva nirodhaṃ spṛśati* and in DĀ 28 at T 1.1.110b29: 我今寧可不爲念行, 不起思惟. 彼不爲念行, 不起思惟已, 微妙想滅, 麤想不生. 彼不爲念行, 不起思惟, 微妙想滅, 麤想不生時, 即入想知滅定. The last version thus relates this progression more specifically to the attainment of the cessation of perception and knowing; see also the discussion in Stuart 2013, 29.
169. SĀ 926 at T 2.99.236a11: 如是禪者, 不依地修禪, 不依水, 火, 風, 空, 識, 無所有, 非想非非想而修禪, 不依此世, 不依他世, 非日, 月, 非見, 聞, 覺, 識, 非得, 非求, 非隨覺, 非隨觀而修禪, parallel to AN 11.10 at AN V 324,28: *so n' eva paṭhaviṃ nissāya jhāyati, na āpaṃ nissāya jhāyati, na tejaṃ nissāya jhāyati, na vāyaṃ nissāya jhāyati, na ākāsānañcāyatanaṃ nissāya jhāyati, na viññāṇañcāyatanaṃ nissāya jhāyati, na ākiñcaññāyatanaṃ nissāya jhāyati, na nevasaññānāsaññāyatanaṃ nissāya jhāyati, na idhalokaṃ nissāya jhāyati, na paralokaṃ nissāya jhāyati, yam p' idaṃ* (S^e: *yam idaṃ*) *diṭṭhaṃ sutaṃ mutaṃ viññātaṃ pattaṃ pariyesitaṃ anuvicaritaṃ manasā, tam pi nissāya na jhāyati; jhāyati ca pana*, and SĀ^2 151 at T 2.100.430c28: 如是不依於彼地水火風, 亦復不依四無色定而生禪法, 不依此世, 不依他世, 亦復不依日月星辰, 不依見聞, 不依識識, 不依智知, 不依推求心識境界, 亦不依止覺知, 獲得無所, 依止禪; a Gāndhārī fragment parallel in Jantrasrisalai, Lenz, Qian, and Salomon 2016, 87–88, 77d+77b, r1–2 (see also v2) has preserved: *[y]o na pridhiv[i] n[iśrayo j̄]ayati na avo n[i]śrayo j̄ayati na teyo [ni](śrayo j̄ayati)* and *(na-)saña-na-asañayadano, na ima logo niśrayo j̄ayati n(a) [p](aralogo).*
170. AN 11.10 at AN V 325,25: *saññā vibhūtā hoti*, SĀ 926 at T 2.99.236a27: 能伏 … 想, with an alternative formulation at T 2.99.236b1: 悉伏彼想, and SĀ^2 151 at T 2.100.431a14: 皆虛僞, 都不見有真實, with an alternative formulation at T 2.100.431a17: 皆悉虛僞, 無有實法. For the significance of *vibhūta* in this context I follow Bodhi 2012, 1861n2211 and Ñāṇananda 2015, 354–55.
171. Mp V 80,13: *nibbānārammaṇāya phalasamāpattiyā jhāyati.*
172. AN 10.6 at AN V 8,7: *etaṃ santaṃ etaṃ paṇītaṃ yadidaṃ sabbasaṅkhārasamatho*

sabbūpadhipaṭinissaggo taṇhakkhayo (B^e: *taṇhākkhayo*) *virāgo nirodho nibbānan ti*, found similarly as an attainment of a concentration that is beyond all the known objects of perception in AN 11.7 at AN V 319,15, AN 11.8 at AN V 320,21, AN 11.19 at AN V 354,9, AN 11.20 at AN V 355,26, AN 11.21 at AN V 357,1, and AN 11.22 at AN V 358,14.

173. AN 11.8 at AN V 320,32.
174. Mp V 79,12: *aggapadasmin ti nibbāne.*
175. An instance of this reflection, as a way of inclining toward the deathless, occurs in a discourse quotation in the *Abhidharmakośavyākhyā*, Wogihara 1932, 273,19: *amṛte dhātāv upasaṃharati: etac chāṃtam etat praṇītaṃ, yad uta sarvopadhipratinisargas tṛṣṇākṣayo virāgo nirodho nirvāṇam iti.* This thus lacks a counterpart to *sabbasaṅkhārasamatho*. Such a counterpart is found, however, in a reference in the *Mahāvastu* of the Mahāsāṃghika-Lokottaravāda *Vinaya*, Marciniak 2020, 354,13 (see Senart 1890, 285,19): *etaṃ śāntaṃ etaṃ praṇītaṃ etaṃ yathāvad etaṃ aviparītaṃ yam idaṃ sarvopadhipratiniḥsargo sarvasaṃskārasamatho dharmopaccheda tṛṣṇākṣayo virāgo nirodho nirvāṇaṃ* (in this case together with some additional phrases) and in a discourse quotation in Up 3020 at D 4094 *ju* 113b7 or P 5595 *tu* 130b2: *'di ni zhi ba, 'di ni gya nom pa ste, 'di lta ste* (P lacks *'di lta ste*) *nye bar len pa thams cad las nges par 'byung ba sred pa zad pa 'dod chags dang bral ba 'gog pa'o zhes 'chi ba med pa'i dbyings la* (P: *las*) *gtong bar 'gyur ro*, which differs by referring to the deathless instead of to Nirvana.
176. MN 64 at MN I 435,36 and AN 9.36 at AN IV 423,2 introduce the maxim (formulated as in AN 10.6, quoted above in n. 172) with the phrase *amatāya dhātuyā cittaṃ upasaṃharati*. Both instances are based on a previous absorption attainment that is then contemplated with insight; for a comparative study see Anālayo 2011b, 357.
177. AN 3.32.1 at AN I 133,1: *idh' ānanda, bhikkhuno evaṃ hoti: etaṃ santaṃ etaṃ paṇītaṃ yadidaṃ sabbasaṅkhārasamatho sabbūpadhipaṭinissaggo taṇhakkhayo* (B^e: *taṇhākkhayo*; S^e: *gaṇhakkhayo*) *virāgo nirodho nibbānan ti. evaṃ kho, ānanda, siyā bhikkhuno tathārūpo samādhipaṭilābho yathā imasmiñ ca saviññāṇake kāye ahaṅkāramamaṅkāramānānusayā* (C^e throughout *ahiṅkāramamiṅkāramānānusayā*) *nāssu, bahiddhā ca sabbanimittesu ahaṅkāramamaṅkāramānānusayā nāssu; yañ* (C^e: *yaṃ*) *ca cetovimuttiṃ paññāvimuttiṃ upasampajja viharato ahaṅkāramamaṅkāramānānusayā na honti tañ* (C^e: *taṃ*) *ca cetovimuttiṃ paññāvimuttiṃ upasampajja vihareyya.* The parallel SĀ 983 at T 2.99.255c28 does not report the actual maxim.
178. This is the case for AN 11.7 at AN V 319,13, AN 11.8 at AN V 320,18, AN 11.19 at AN V 354,6, AN 11.20 at AN V 355,23, AN 11.21 at AN V 356,29, and AN 11.22 at AN V 358,11. The absence of such a reference thus appears to be specific to AN 10.6.
179. The same maxim recurs in AN 10.60 at AN VI 110,22+28 under the alternative headings of *virāgasaññā* and *nirodhasaññā*, confirming that it is indeed reckoned a "perception," even though it does not involve any of the otherwise known objects of perception. On the Tibetan parallel to AN 10.60 see Skilling 1993, 123–24 and Anālayo 2016, 100–104.
180. AN 11.9 at AN V 322,15.
181. AN 10.7 at AN V 9,24: *bhavanirodho nibbānaṃ.*
182. SN 35.117 at SN IV 98,3: *se* (E^e: *ye*) *āyatane veditabbe, yattha cakkhuñ* (B^e and S^e: *cakkhu*; E^e: *cakkhuṃ*) *ca* (not in S^e) *nirujjhati rūpasaññā ca virajjati* (B^e: *nirujjhati*), *se* (E^e:

ye) āyatane veditabbe . . . pe . . . yattha mano ca nirujjhati, dhammasaññā ca virajjati (B^e: *nirujjhati*), *se* (E^e: *ye*) *āyatane veditabbe.*

183. SĀ 211 at T 2.99.53b12: 於彼入處當覺知, 若眼滅, 色想則離, 耳, 鼻, 舌, 身, 意滅, 法想則離.
184. Spk II 391,3.
185. SN 35.117 at SN IV 100,11: *saḷāyatananirodhaṃ kho* (B^e: *no*) *etaṃ* (not in E^e)*, āvuso, bhagavatā sandhāya bhāsitaṃ* and SĀ 211 at T 2.99.53c2: 世尊略說者, 即是滅六入處.
186. See, e.g., the listing in Dhs 60,9 of the different mental factors and qualities considered to be present in the mind at the path-moment of stream-entry.
187. As an example to illustrate this tendency, Ñāṇananda 2015, 13 quotes the phrase *nibbānaṃ āgamma*; see, e.g., Vibh-a 53,4. Notably, on being pressed to provide a canonical authority for this phrasing, Vibh-a 54,10 gives the quotation *evaṃ avijjā ca taṇhā ca taṃ āgamma tamhi khīṇaṃ, tamhi bhaggaṃ . . .* As already noted by Ñāṇamoli 1956/1991, 824n16, this "quotation has not been traced." In fact, the phrase *nibbānaṃ āgamma* is only found in commentarial texts.

    The same holds for the idea of referring to the successful breakthrough to the deathless as an instance of "having entered the city of Nirvana"; see, e.g., Mil 333,2 or Spk II 83,14: *nibbānanagaraṃ pavisitvā*. Spk II 117,21–22 considers the city of Nirvana to be the implication of a reference to an ancient city in SN 12.65 at SN II 105,38. A problem with this proposal is that SN 12.65 at SN II 106,11 explicitly indicates that this city needs to be rebuilt or repaired. Such a need does not fit the unconditioned, which by its nature is beyond decay and hence also beyond a need for repairs. Had the intention of the reference to a city in SN 12.65 been to point to Nirvana, the detail about a need for repairs would not have been mentioned. Similarly unconvincing is the commentarial gloss on the simile of the seven chariots, assuming that the destiny of the seventh chariot, the city of Sāketa mentioned in MN 24 at MN I 149,13, can be identified with the city of Nirvana; see Ps II 157,12: *sāketanagaraṃ viya nibbānanagaraṃ*. The reference to Sāketa in MN 24 clearly intends the actual city and is not metaphorical. Moreover, in the original setting of the simile, although Sāketa is reached with the seventh chariot (= the seventh purification), this does not yet correspond to the full realization of Nirvana; see below n. 220). Yet another example of the notion of Nirvana as a city in Spk III 59,15 and 62,1 relies on introducing a second city, the *mahānagara*, in addition to the border town mentioned in the actual discourse, evidently being forced to do so since the border town is explained in the discourse itself to be a reference to the body made up of the four elements; see SN 35.204 at SN IV 194,27. Similar to the phrase *nibbānaṃ āgamma*, the idea of Nirvana as a city is clearly a later development.
188. For the case of the mind, SN 35.83 at SN IV 53,1 reads *n' atthi kho so . . . mano yena manena atīte buddhe parinibbute chinnapapañce chinnavaṭume pariyādinnavaṭṭe* (E^e: *pariyādiṇṇavaṭṭe*) *sabbadukkhavītivaṭṭe paññāpayamāno paññāpeyyā ti.*
189. MN 137 at MN III 218,29: *kadāssu* (B^e: *kudāssu*; C^e: *kudassu*) *nām' āhaṃ tad āyatanaṃ upasampajja viharissāmi yad ariyā etarahi āyatanaṃ upasampajja viharantī ti* and its parallels MĀ 163 at T 1.26.693a14: 我何時彼處成就遊, 謂處諸聖人成就遊 and Up 3069 at D 4094 *ju* 166b7 or P 5595 *tu* 192b4: *bdag nam zhig na mchog gi skye mched* (D: *mchod*) *bsgrubs shing nye bar gnas 'phags pa'i skye mched nye bar bsgrubs shing nye bar gnas zhes*; see also Dhammadinnā 2021, 116.

190. Ud 8.1 at Ud 80,10: *atthi, bhikkhave, tad āyatanaṃ, yattha n' eva paṭhavī* (B[e]: *pathavī*; C[e]: *paṭhavi*) *na āpo na tejo na vāyo na ākāsānañcāyatanaṃ na viññāṇañcāyatanaṃ na ākiñcaññāyatanaṃ na nevasaññānāsaññāyatanaṃ n' āyaṃ loko na paraloko na* (not in E[e]) *ubho candimasuriyā* (B[e] and E[e]: *candimasūriyā*). *tatrā pāhaṃ* (E[e]: *tad ahaṃ*; S[e]: *tam ahaṃ*), *bhikkhave, n' eva āgatiṃ vadāmi na gatiṃ na ṭhitiṃ na cutiṃ na upapattiṃ, appatiṭṭhaṃ appavattaṃ anārammaṇam ev' etaṃ* (E[e] and S[e]: *eva taṃ*), *es' ev' anto dukkhassā ti*. A similar passage in the Sanskrit *Udānavarga* 26.24, Bernhard 1965, 329, however, refers to a "place" instead of a "sphere": *abhijānāmy ahaṃ sthānaṃ, yatra bhūtaṃ na vidyate, nākāśaṃ na ca vijñānaṃ, na sūryaś candramā na ca, naivāgatir na ca gatir, nopapattiś cyutir na ca, apratiṣṭham anālambaṃ, duḥkhāntaḥ sa nirucyate.*
191. MĀ 115 at T 1.26.603b19: 若一切世間,天及魔,梵,沙門,梵志,從人至天,使不鬪諍... 是我宗本,說亦如是, parallel to MN 18 at MN I 108,26: *yathāvādī kho, āvuso, sadevake loke samārake sabrahmake sassamaṇabrāhmaṇiyā pajāya sadevamanussāya na kenaci loke viggayha tiṭṭhati . . . evaṃvādī kho ahaṃ, āvuso, evamakkhāyī ti*. Another parallel, EĀ 40.10 at T 2.125.743a10, proceeds differently; see Anālayo 2011b, 134–35.
192. DN 21 at DN II 288,21, Sanskrit fragment 581.102R, Waldschmidt 1932, 109, DĀ 14 at T 1.1.66a2, MĀ 134 at T 1.26.638c1, T 1.15.250a23, and T 4.203.477c16.
193. On the mental processing of data by way of name see also Anālayo 2020c.
194. Sn 872: *nāmañ ca rūpañ ca paṭicca phassā* (B[e] and S[e]: *phasso*) . . . *rūpe vibhūte na phusanti phassā*, a shift found similarly in T 4.198.181c9 from 名色 to mentioning just 色.
195. Gómez 1976, 161n34 reasons: "On the basis of 872 we must surmise that in 873–874 *rūpam* stands for *nāmarūpa*." Ronkin 2005, 247 comments on this verse: "What comes to a halt according to this description is but *nāmarūpa*," adding (252n8) that *rūpa* "here has the metaphysical sense of the representative of ordinary experience."
196. Sn 875 continues by mentioning the "purity of a *yakkha*," *yakkhassa suddhiṃ*, in reference to the realization described in the previous verse (the corresponding part in T 4.198.181c16 proceeds differently). The same term recurs in Sn 478 in evident reference to the final goal: *sarīrañ ca antimaṃ dhāreti, patto ca sambodhim anuttaraṃ sivaṃ; ettāvatā yakkhassa suddhi*. Another relevant passage is AN 10.29 at AN V 64,9, which mentions *paramatthavisuddhiṃ*, in which case S[e] (and a manuscript noted in E[e]) rather reads *paramayakkhavisuddhiṃ*; the reference in this case is to the fourth immaterial sphere. Although the variations between the editions and the qualification *parama* make this occurrence in AN 10.29 less directly relevant than Sn 478, perhaps the idea is that the speaker of Sn 875 has misunderstood the description in Sn 874 to refer to the fourth immaterial sphere, taking the references in this verse to *na saññasaññī* and *no pi asaññī* to intend *nevasaññānāsaññāyatana*. On this assumption, the reply given in Sn 876 does not directly contradict this assumption, perhaps for pedagogical reasons, but instead takes it up in the same terms as used by the questioner in order to lead the latter onward to a deeper understanding. Sn 876 then proceeds by confirming that there are indeed some who criticize the assumption that with the fourth immaterial attainment the final goal has been reached. This part could conveniently be read in the light of MN 102 at MN II 232,7 (for the Tibetan parallel see Skilling 1994, 332), which describes annihilationists who criticize other practitioners, including the proponents of the fourth immaterial attainment. MN 102 at MN II 233,4 then highlights the Tathāgata's insight into the conditioned nature of this position, similar to the Tathāgata's insight regarding those who promote the fourth imma-

terial attainment, reported in MN 102 at MN II 232,3. This insight would match the assessment in the first line of the final verse in Sn 877, *ete ca ñatvā upanissitā ti*, which appears to refer to those whose opinions are mentioned in the preceding verse, Sn 876, i.e., the promoters of the fourth immaterial sphere and those who criticize them. On this reading, Sn 877 would then clarify the apparent misunderstanding voiced in Sn 875, pointing out that the final goal requires going beyond all dependencies, be these based on *bhava* (= the fourth immaterial sphere) or its opposite (= annihilationism).

197. T 4.198.181c13: 不想想不色想, 非無想不行想, 一切想斷不著, 因想本戲隨苦; adopting the 宋, 元, and 明 variant 想斷不著 instead of 斷不著者 and assuming that 戲 is an abbreviated reference to 戲論. My rendering is also based on the assumption that, due to the need to keep the count of six characters in a line, the first negation 不 qualifies both 想想 and 不色想, and the negation 非 qualifies both 無想 and 不行想. For 不行, Hirakawa 1997, 41 gives the following possible Sanskrit equivalents: *apracarita, aprayoga, asamudācāra; agocara, acaritāvin, anadhyācaraṇa, avicāraṇā, avṛtti, nirāsa.* My translation of 不行 follows the common sense of this couplet to designate something that does not work and hence is "dysfunctional."

198. Sn 874: *na saññasaññī na visaññasaññī, no pi asaññī na vibhūtasaññī; evaṃ sametassa vibhoti rūpaṃ, saññānidānā hi papañcasaṅkhā* (E^e: *papañcasaṃkhā*).

199. Vin IV 110,7: *visaññī.*

200. AN 4.49 at AN II 52,19: *anicce niccasaññino, dukkhe ca sukhasaññino, anattani ca attā ti, asubhe subhasaññino . . . khittacittā visaññino.*

201. The first part of the verse reads as follows in the translation by Ñāṇaponika 1977, 187: "Nicht hat er das gewöhnliches Bewußtsein, noch ist es krankhaft. Er ist nicht unbewußt, noch hat er ein entkörpertes Bewußtsein." This could be rendered into English in this way: "He does not have consciousness that is normal, nor is it sick. He is not unconscious, nor does he have an incorporeal consciousness."

202. Sn 1113: *vibhūtarūpasaññissa.*

203. Nidd I 280,9 interprets the present verse as a reference to an attempt to attain the sphere of infinite space. As already pointed out by Gómez 1976, 161n45, such an interpretation "seems to ignore the fact that the *Kalahavivāda* is explicitly talking about the complete ending of becoming and sorrow." In the same vein, Ñāṇananda 2015, 234 comments on the position taken in Nidd I that "considerations of context and presentation would lead to a different conclusion. The extraordinary state alluded to by this verse seems to be a supramundane one . . . The transcendence of form, indicated here, is more radical than the transcendence in attaining to formless states. It is a transcendence at a supramundane level, as we may well infer from the last line of the verse, *saññānidānā hi papañcasaṅkhā*." Ñāṇananda 2015, 236 adds that the "verse beginning with *na saññasaññī* brings the entire analytical disquisition to a climax . . . Usually, such a disquisition leads up to a climax, highlighting *Nibbāna*. It is obvious, therefore, that the reference here is to the *Nibbānic* mind." Moreover, the ensuing verse Sn 875 indicates that some consider what has been described in Sn 874 to be supreme. As noted by Ñāṇananda 2015, 240, such a consideration would hardly arise in relation to an "intermediate stage between the fourth absorption and the first formless absorption," which "is of no account."

204. An illustrative example is the *Sotāpattisaṃyutta* (SN 55) and its Chinese counterpart (SĀ 833 to SĀ 860 and SĀ 1122 to SĀ 1135), which can be seen to place an overall

emphasis on the stream-enterer possessing four types of experiential confidence (*aveccap(p)asāda/avetyaprasāda*, rendered into Chinese as 不壞淨), rather than on having had a particular perceptual experience. As mentioned above in n. 147, references to the stream-enterer having had a vision of the deathless also occur in some discourses. But the overall highlight is clearly on the personal transformation that results from stream-entry. The same holds for arahants/arhats, where the emphasis is similarly on the successful destruction of the defilements. An example in case is a discourse entirely dedicated to verifying someone else's claim to being an arahant: MN 112 at MN III 29,24 and its parallel MĀ 187 at T 1.26.732a23, with a study in Anālayo 2008a.

205. Sn 884: *ekaṃ hi saccaṃ na dutīyam* (Cᵉ: *dutiyam*) *atthi, yasmiṃ pajā no vivade pajānaṃ*; see also T 4.198.182b10: 一諦盡二有無, 知是諦不顛倒, where the first part seems to reflect a similarly worded Indic original, whereas the result of knowing this truth is different, whether this is due to a difference in the original or due to the translator.

206. Nidd I 292,9: *ekaṃ saccaṃ vuccati dukkhanirodho nibbānaṃ, yo so sabbasaṅkhārasamatho sabbūpadhipaṭinissaggo taṇhakkhayo virāgo nirodho nibbānaṃ*; see also Vibh-a 86,6: *ekaṃ hi saccaṃ na dutiyam atthī ti ādisu paramatthasacce, nibbāne c' eva magge ca* (I take the reading *nibbāṇe* in Eᵉ to be a typographical error; in general, for quotes from Pāli exegetical works and commentaries I have been unable to consult different editions, due to not having direct access to these).

207. Sn 758: *amosadhammaṃ nibbānaṃ, tad ariyā saccato vidū* (Cᵉ: *vidu*), *te ve saccābhisamayā, nicchātā parinibbutā ti*.

208. MN 140 at MN III 245,15: *tassa sā vimutti sacce ṭhitā akuppā hoti . . . etaṃ hi . . . paramaṃ ariyasaccaṃ yadidaṃ amosadhammaṃ nibbānaṃ*.

209. MĀ 162 at T 1.26.692a13: 此解脫住真諦, 得不移動 . . . 成就彼第一真諦處 and Up 1041 at D 4094 *ju* 40b5 or P 5595 *tu* 44a5: *de'i rnam par grol ba bden pa'i byin gyis brlabs* (D: *gyi rlabs*) *mchog dang ldan par 'gyur ro . . . bden pa rnams kyi mchog ni 'di lta ste*; see also Stuart 2015, 282–85 and Dhammadinnā 2021, 108.

210. For a comparative study of a range of accounts, for the most part extant in Chinese, of what came to be known as the Buddha's first sermon see Anālayo 2012a and 2013a.

211. See Anālayo 2011c, 22–28.

212. Although at times such instances appear to be the result of some textual development; see Anālayo 2021b and 2022a.

213. *Pace* Harvey 2003, 307, who reasons that the four truths "are not something that Buddhists should respond to with 'belief.' To 'believe' the Four Truths is to mishandle them, not realize what they are"; see also the detailed argument by Harvey 2009 in support of understanding what has generally been taken to refer to a "noble truth" to convey much rather the sense of a "true reality for the spiritually ennobled."

214. Sn 839: *na diṭṭhiyā na sutiyā na ñāṇena . . . sīlabbatenā pi na suddhim āha, adiṭṭhiyā assutiyā añāṇā, asīlatā abbatā no pi tena* and its parallel, T 4.198.180b11: 亦見聞不爲黠, 戒行具未爲淨, 不見聞亦不癡, 不離行可自淨; see also Anālayo 2022i, 857.

215. Sn 839: *ete ca nissajja anuggahāya* and its parallel, T 4.198.180b13: 有是想棄莫受, where I would conjecture that perhaps 有是想 refers back to the preceding lines (quoted in my previous note), conveying the sense "possessing this discernment," which is then followed by "[one] lets go and does not cling." Bapat 1945, 208 translates the same as: "Leaving far such thoughts, by giving no shelter to them."

216. AN 4.175 at AN II 163,25: *vijjāya ce, āvuso, antakaro abhavissa, sa-upādāno* (Cᵉ and Eᵉ

throughout: *savupādāno) va samāno antakaro abhavissa. caraṇena ce, āvuso, antakaro abhavissa, sa-upādāno va samāno antakaro abhavissa. vijjācaraṇena ce, āvuso, antakaro abhavissa, sa-upādāno va samāno antakaro abhavissa. aññatra vijjācaraṇena ce, āvuso, antakaro abhavissa, puthujjano antakaro abhavissa. puthujjano hi, āvuso, aññatra vijjācaraṇena.*

217. AN 4.175 at AN II 163,31: *caraṇavipanno kho, āvuso, yathābhūtaṃ na jānāti na passati. caraṇasampanno yathābhūtaṃ jānāti passati. yathābhūtaṃ jānaṃ passaṃ antakaro hotī ti.*

218. Note also the similarity in reasoning between MN 24 at MN I 148,33: *aññatra ce* (E^e: *ca*), *āvuso, imehi dhammehi anupādā parinibbānaṃ abhavissa, puthujjano parinibbāyeyya. puthujjano hi, āvuso, aññatra imehi dhammehi* and the final part of AN 4.175 quoted above in n. 216.

219. MN 24 at MN I 149,35: *sīlavisuddhi yāvad eva cittavisuddhatthā, cittavisuddhi yāvad eva diṭṭhivisuddhatthā, diṭṭhivisuddhi yāvad eva kaṅkhāvitaraṇavisuddhatthā, kaṅkhāvitaraṇavisuddhi yāvad eva maggāmaggañāṇadassanavisuddhatthā, maggāmaggañāṇadassanavisuddhi yāvad eva paṭipadāñāṇadassanavisuddhatthā, paṭipadāñāṇadassanavisuddhi yāvad eva ñāṇadassanavisuddhatthā, ñāṇadassanavisuddhi yāvad eva anupādā parinibbānatthā*, MĀ 9 at T 1.26.430c28: 但以戒淨故, 得心淨, 以心淨故, 得見淨, 以見淨故, 得疑蓋淨, 以疑蓋淨故, 得道非道知見淨, 以道非道知見淨故, 得道跡知見淨, 以道跡知見淨故, 得道跡斷智淨, 以道跡斷智淨故, 世尊, 沙門瞿曇, 施設無餘涅槃也, and EĀ 39.10 at T 2.125.734c5: 戒清淨義者, 能使心清淨, 心清淨義者, 能使見清淨, 見清淨義者, 能使無猶豫清淨, 無猶豫清淨義者, 能使行跡清淨, 行跡清淨義者, 能使道清淨, 道清淨義者, 能使知見清淨, 知見清淨義者, 能使入涅槃義. On the somewhat differing terminology employed in the parallels for some of the stages of purification see Anālayo 2005.

220. Vism 672,7: *sotāpattimaggo sakadāgāmimaggo anāgāmimaggo arahattamaggo ti imesu pana catusu maggesu ñāṇaṃ ñāṇadassanavisuddhi nāma*; see also Anālayo 2021h, 96–97 (with references to my previous discussions of this issue). The usage of the term "path" here is based on the commentarial model that divides the experience of each level of awakening into consecutive momentary events, termed "path" and "fruit," both of which take Nirvana as their object and the latter of which automatically follows the former, whose function is to cut through the respective fetters (this usage differs substantially from the notion of the path in the early discourses; see Anālayo 2021h, 95–96).

221. DN 34 at DN III 288,24: *vimuttivisuddhi*, Schlingloff 1962, 18: *(vimuktiviśuddhiḥ)*, DĀ 10 at T 1.1.56a25: 解脫淨滅枝, and T 1.13.238c25: 度世 (which usually translates *lokuttara/lokottara*, but here presumably serves as a rendering of *vimutti/vimukti*; see Vetter 2012, 97). DN 34 additionally qualifies each purification as a *pārisuddhipadhāniyaṅga*. The term recurs in a fourfold listing in AN 4.194 at AN II 195,5, in which case the parallel SĀ 565 at T 2.99.148c18 just speaks of 清淨, but another parallel, Up 6082 at D 4094 *nyu* 48a2 or P 5595 *thu* 87b8, of *yongs su dag pa'i gtso bo*.

222. As pointed out by the commentary, Ps II 370,3, the passage involves two types of counterparts, one by way of opposition (such as what is pleasant in contrast to what is unpleasant) and one by way of being a similar counterpart (such as neutral feeling tone and ignorance).

223. MN 44 at MN I 304,19 and its parallels MĀ 210 at T 1.26.790a14 and Up 1005 at

D 4094 *ju* 11a1 or P 5595 *tu* 12a4. Another example is SN 48.42 at SN V 218,18, which pursues such a line of inquiry by identifying what each item takes recourse in, *paṭisaraṇa*. Yet another example is SN 23.1 at SN III 189,26, where the inquiry concerns the purpose of each item mentioned, *attha* (this part of SN 23.1 is without a counterpart in its parallel, SĀ 120).

224. Marciniak 2019, 253,2 (see Senart 1897, 201,16): *sayyathāpi nāma . . . gaṅgodakaṃ ca yamunodakaṃ ca saṃsyandamānaṃ saṃsyandati mahāsamudre, evam eva . . . saṃsyandati nirvāṇañ ca nirvāṇagāminī ca pratipadā*, with a parallel in DN 19 at DN II 223,10: *saṃsandati nibbānañ ca paṭipadā ca, seyyathā pi nāma gaṅgodakaṃ yamunodakena saṃsandati sameti*. With the corresponding similes in the two Chinese parallels, a gradual increase of emphasis on the ocean can be discerned, as a result of which the import of the simile takes on a somewhat different nuance; see DĀ 3 at T 1.1.30c24: 如恒河水, 炎摩水, 二水並流, 入於大海 and T 1.18.208c27: 譬如殑伽河水, 閻牟那河水, 流注大海, 增長無盡.

225. See Anālayo 2009b, 190–91.

226. DĀ 21 at T 1.1.94a3: 若比丘於六觸集, 滅, 味, 過, 出要, 如實而知, 則為最勝, 出彼諸見, parallel to DN 1 at DN I 45,17: *yato kho, bhikkhave, bhikkhu channaṃ phassāyatanānaṃ samudayañ* (C^e: *samudayaṃ*) *ca atthaṅgamañ* (C^e: *atthagamaṃ*; E^e: *atthagamañ*) *ca assādañ* (C^e: *assādaṃ*) *ca ādīnavañ* (C^e: *ādīnavaṃ*) *ca nissaraṇañ* (C^e: *nissaraṇaṃ*) *ca yathābhūtaṃ pajānāti, ayaṃ imehi sabbeh' eva uttaritaraṃ pajānāti*, Weller 1934, 64,12: *dge slong dag, gang tshun chad reg pa'i skye mched drug po dag ni kun 'byung ba nub pa dang ro myang ba dang nyes dmigs yang dag pa ji lta ba bzhin khong du chud pa; 'di ni 'di ltar lhag par yang dag par ji lta ba bzhin khong du chud pa yin no*, and Up 3050 at D 4094 *ju* 153a7 or P 5595 *tu* 177a2: *dge slong dag, gang gi phyir reg pa'i skye mched drug po dag gi kun 'byung ba dang mi snang ba dang nyes dmigs dang ro myang ba dang nges par 'byung ba yang dag pa ci lta ba bzhin du rab tu shes shing*, after which this version continues differently. Another parallel extant in Chinese, T 21, does not appear to have a corresponding indication at this juncture.

227. MN 102 at MN II 230,4: *atthi kho pana saṅkhārānaṃ* (E^e: *saṃkhārānaṃ*) *nirodho atth' etan ti iti viditvā tassa nissaraṇadassāvī tathāgato tad upātivatto*, with a Tibetan parallel in Skilling 1994, 318,7: *'di ltar 'du byed rnams yod na, 'du byed rnams kyi 'gog pa yang yod pas na, de bzhin gshegs pas de yod par thugs su chud nas, de las phyir ldog cing, de la zhi bar gzigs nges par 'byung bar gzigs zhing bzhugs so* and a Sanskrit parallel in the reconstructed formulation *viditvā śāntadarśī tatra tathāgato viharati niḥsaraṇadarśī tata eva upātivṛttaḥ*, which is based on bringing together the various smaller parts that have been preserved in SHT IV 33 fragments 4 v5, 5 Ab, and 7 v4, Sander and Waldschmidt 1980, 157–58, Or 15009/321 v1, Fukita 2009, 306, and Or 15009/642 r3, Kudo and Shono 2015, 445; see also Hartmann 1991, 223.

228. See, e.g., Sn 788: *diṭṭhena saṃsuddhi narassa hoti* and Sn 840: *diṭṭhiyā* (S^e adds *ca*) *eke paccenti suddhiṃ*; see also T 4.198.178a2: 信見諦及自淨 and T 4.198.180b16: 以見可誰有淨.

229. Up 3057 at D 4094 *ju* 157b6 or P 5595 *tu* 182a6: *de bzhin gshegs pa ni lta bar gyur pa spangs pa ste, 'on kyang de bzhin gshegs pa'i lta bar gyur pa spang ba* (P: *spangs pa*) *ci zhig lta ba ci zhe na*, with parallels in MN 72 at MN I 486,11: *diṭṭhigatan ti kho, vaccha, apanītam etaṃ tathāgatassa. diṭṭhaṃ* (B^e: *diṭṭañ*) *h' etaṃ, vaccha, tathāgatena*, SĀ 962

at T 2.99.245c21: 如來所見已畢 . . . 然如來見, and SĀ^2 196 at T 2.100.445b8: 諸有見者, 悉皆除捨, 都無諸見, 雖有所見, 心無取著.

230. MN 74 at MN I 497,26: *sabbaṃ me na khamatī* (B^e: *nakkhamatī*) *ti*, folio 162a5, Pischel 1904, 814: *sarvaṃ me na kṣamati,* SĀ 969 at T 2.99.249b3: 我一切見不忍 (the 宋, 元, 明, and 聖 editions do not have the 見 and would thus correspond more closely to the formulation in MN 74), and SĀ^2 203 at T 2.100.449a6: 於一切法悉不忍受; see also versions of this encounter in the *Avadānaśātaka*, Speyer 1909/1970, 187,10: *sarvaṃ me, bho Gautama, na kṣamata iti*, in the *Pravrajyāvastu* of the Mūlasarvāstivāda *Vinaya*, Eimer 1983, 96,13: *bdag ni thams cad mi bzod do* (with a considerably more detailed Chinese counterpart, T 23.1444.1028c5: 一切我法, 所有見等, 皆我不欲), the **Mahāvibhāṣā*, T 27.1545.509c9: 我一切不忍, and the **Mahāprajñāpāramitopadeśa* (大智度論), T 25.1509.62a3: 我一切法不受.

231. Sn 787: *adhosi so diṭṭhim idh' eva sabban* (E^e: *sabbā*) *ti*, Sn 800: *diṭṭhim pi so na pacceti kiñci*, and Sn 913: *sa vippamutto diṭṭhigatehi dhīro*. Here and elsewhere, I am not consistently providing references to parallel verses in T 198, as at times the text is too different and obscure. It remains uncertain to what degree such passages reflect a significant difference in the Indic original, given that, as already noted by Vetter 1990, 42, this "translation is, however, of a doubtful quality." Within the limitations of the present study, I am unable to follow up such passages in detail, hence I have to content myself with only noting those instances where the text seems relatively straightforward.

232. This assessment forms part of a critical reply to Burford 1991.

233. MN 22 at MN I 134,30 and its parallels MĀ 200 at T 1.26.764b19, EĀ 43.5 at T 2.125.760a13, and Up 8029 at D 4094 *nyu* 74b6 or P 5595 *thu* 119b7.

234. MN 22 at MN I 135,24: *kullūpamaṃ vo, bhikkhave, dhammaṃ desitaṃ* (E^e lacks *dhammaṃ desitaṃ*) *ājānantehi dhammā pi vo pahātabbā pageva adhammā*, with parallels in MĀ 200 at T 1.26.764c13: 若汝等知我長夜說栰喻法者, 當以捨是法, 況非法耶 and EĀ 43.5 at T 2.125.760a26: 善法猶可捨, 何況非法.

235. See also SN 35.197 at SN IV 175,16 and its parallel SĀ 1172 at T 2.99.313c22, which in turn relate the image of the raft to the eightfold path and the other shore to Nirvana.

236. MĀ 201 at T 1.26.767c5: 若汝等如是知, 如是見, 謂我此見如是清淨, 著彼, 惜彼, 守彼, 不欲令捨者, 汝等知我長夜說栰喻法? MN 38 at MN I 260,32: *imañ* (B^e and E^e: *imaṃ*) *ce tumhe, bhikkhave, diṭṭhiṃ evaṃ parisuddhaṃ evaṃ pariyodātaṃ allīyetha kelāyetha* (C^e and S^e: *keḷāyetha*) *dhanāyetha* (S^e: *dhaneyyātha*) *mamāyetha, api nu* (B^e adds *me*) *tumhe, bhikkhave, kullūpamaṃ dhammaṃ desitaṃ ājāneyyātha?*

237. Sn 152: *diṭṭhiñ ca anupagamma . . . dassanena sampanno.*

238. Sn 787: *attaṃ nirattaṃ* (B^e: *attā nirattā*) *na hi tassa atthi*; see also T 4.198.177c18: 已不著亦可離.

239. Sn 858: *attaṃ* (B^e and C^e: *attā*) *vā pi nirattaṃ* (B^e and C^e: *nirattā*) *vā, na tasmiṃ upalabbhati*, Sn 919: *n' atthi attā kuto nirattaṃ* (B^e and C^e: *nirattā*) *vā*, and Sn 954: *nādeti na nirassatī ti.*

240. Sn 795: *na rāgarāgī na virāgaratto* and Sn 813: *na hi so rajjati no virajjatī ti*; see also T 4.198.178a17: 婬不婬著污婬.

241. SN 22.79 at SN III 90,10: *n' evācināti* (S^e: *n' eva ācināti*) *na apacināti, apacinitvā ṭhito n' eva pajahati na upādiyati, pajahitvā ṭhito n' eva visineti* (E^e: *viseneti*) *na ussineti, visinetvā* (E^e: *visenetvā*) *ṭhito n' eva vidhūpeti na sandhūpeti, vidhūpetvā ṭhito* (on the significance of this passage for understanding the type of verses quoted in the preceding note

see Ñāṇananda 2015, 99–100), with parallels in SĀ 46 at T 2.99.11c24: 減而不增, 退而不進, 滅而不起, 捨而不取 (the first character involves an emendation of 滅 to read 減, following Yinshun 1983, 160n4) and Up 1014 at D 4094 *ju* 17a4 or P 5595 *tu* 19a2: *de nyams par byed cing mthu skyed par mi byed, 'grib par byed cing 'phel bar mi byed, mi gsal bar byed cing gsal bar mi byed, spong bar byed cing len par mi byed do.*

242. See, for example, DN 2 at DN I 84,11: *kataṃ karaṇīyaṃ*, with a Sanskrit parallel in *kṛtam karaṇīyaṃ*, Gnoli 1978, 251,12, and a Chinese parallel in 所作已辦, found in DĀ 27 (supplemented from DĀ 20 at T 1.1.86c8) and T 1.22.275c26.

243. An example is a listing of the "trainee" and the "non-trainee" (or less literally the "one beyond training") as two persons who are worthy of offerings; see AN 2.4.4 at AN I 63,6: *sekho ca asekho ca* and its parallels MĀ 127 at T 1.26.616a11: 一者學人, 二者無學人 (followed by an additional subdivision of each category that incorporates later ideas) and SĀ 992 at T 2.100.258c15: 學及無學.

244. The simile is inspired by a related illustration given in Mil 269,23 in order to explain how the unconditioned can be reached through a path that is conditioned.

245. Sn 853: *na saddho na virajjati.*

246. Dhp 97: *asaddho*, with Indic language parallels in the Patna *Dharmapada* 333, Cone 1989, 191: *aśraddho* and the Sanskrit *Udānavarga* 29.23, Bernhard 1965, 377: *aśraddhaś*. The whole poem employs double entendres of various types.

247. SN 48.44 at SN V 221,4: *yesaṃ* (S^{e}: *yesañ*) *hi taṃ* (B^{e}: *h' etaṃ*; C^{e} without *taṃ*), *bhante, aññātaṃ assa* (not in S^{e}) *adiṭṭhaṃ aviditaṃ asacchikataṃ aphusitaṃ* (B^{e} and C^{e}: *aphassitaṃ*, S^{e}: *apassitaṃ*) *paññāya, te tattha paresaṃ saddhāya gaccheyyuṃ.*

248. Sn 229: *yath' indakhīlo paṭhaviṃ sito* (B^{e}: *pathavissito*) *siyā, catubbhi vātehi* (S^{e}: *vātebhi*) *asampakampiyo, tathūpamaṃ sappurisaṃ vadāmi, yo ariyasaccāni avecca passati* with a counterpart in the *Mahāvastu*, Senart 1882, 292,14: *yathendrakīlo pṛthivīsanniśrito syā, catūrbhi vātehi asaṃprakampi, tathopamaṃ satpuruṣaṃ vademi, yo āryasatyāni sudeśitāni, gambhīra-arthāni avetya paśyati.*

249. Sn 1082: *sīlabbataṃ vā pi pahāya sabbaṃ, anekarūpam pi pahāya sabbaṃ, taṇhaṃ pariññāya anāsavāse* (S^{e}: *anāsavā ye*), *te ve narā oghatiṇṇā ti brūmi.*

250. MN 78 at MN II 27,11: *bhikkhu sīlavā hoti no ca sīlamayo, tañ ca cetovimuttiṃ paññāvimuttiṃ yathābhūtaṃ pajānāti, yatth' assa te kusalā sīlā* (C^{e} and E^{e}: *kusalasīlā*) *aparisesā nirujjhanti.*

251. MĀ 179 at T 1.26.721a16: 善戒何處滅無餘, 何處敗壞無餘? 若多聞聖弟子行戒不著戒, 此善戒滅無餘, 敗壞無餘.

252. MN 37 at MN I 255,26: *sabbe dhammā nālaṃ abhinivesāyā ti*. The reference here is to the third instance of this instruction, motivated by the fact that the corresponding third instruction in EĀ 19.3 is the most convenient one to take up. Unlike MN 37, which shows no variations, the three instances of this instruction in EĀ 19.3 differ considerably from each other; see also Anālayo 2011b, 247n204.

253. EĀ 19.3 at T 2.125.594c3: 解知: 一切諸法空, 無所有, 亦無所著.

254. SĀ 249 at T 2.99.60a16: 六觸入處盡, 離欲, 滅, 息, 沒已, 有餘耶? 此則虛言. 無餘耶? 此則虛言. 餘無餘耶? 此則虛言. 非有餘非無餘耶? 此則虛言. 若言: 六觸入處盡, 離欲, 滅, 息, 沒已, 離諸虛僞, 得般涅槃, 此則佛說, with a parallel in AN 4.175 at AN II 161,27: *channaṃ, āvuso, phassāyatanānaṃ asesavirāganirodhā atth' aññaṃ kiñcī ti iti vadaṃ appapañcaṃ* (S^{e} throughout: *apapañcaṃ*) *papañceti. channaṃ, āvuso, phassāyatanānaṃ asesavirāganirodhā n' atth' aññaṃ kiñcī ti iti vadaṃ appapañcaṃ*

papañceti. channaṃ, āvuso, phassāyatanānaṃ asesavirāganirodhā atthi ca n' atthi c' (Bᵉ: *ca*) *aññaṃ kiñcī ti iti vadaṃ appapañcaṃ papañceti. channaṃ, āvuso, phassāyatanānaṃ asesavirāganirodhā n' ev' atthi no n' atth' aññaṃ kiñcī ti iti vadaṃ appapañcaṃ papañceti. yāvatā, āvuso, channaṃ phassāyatanānaṃ gati tāvatā papañcassa gati; yāvatā papañcassa gati tāvatā channaṃ phassāyatanānaṃ gati. channaṃ, āvuso, phassāyatanānaṃ asesavirāganirodhā papañcanirodho* (Cᵉ adds *papañcanirodhā*) *papañcavūpasamo ti.*

255. Sn 1074: *accī yathā vātavegena khittā* (Eᵉ: *khitto*, Sᵉ: *khittaṃ*), *atthaṃ paleti na upeti saṅkhaṃ* (Eᵉ: *saṃkhaṃ*), *evaṃ munī nāmakāyā vimutto, atthaṃ paleti na upeti saṅkhaṃ* (Eᵉ: *saṃkhaṃ*).
256. Sn 1076: *atthaṅgatassa* (Cᵉ: *atthaṃgatassa*) *na pamāṇam atthi, yena naṃ vajjuṃ* (Eᵉ and Sᵉ: *vajju*) *taṃ tassa n' atthi, sabbesu dhammesu samūhatesu, samūhatā vādapathā pi sabbe ti*; for a quotation of a version of this verse see T 25.1509.85b10: 滅者即是不可量, 破壞因緣及名相, 一切言語道已過, 一時都盡如火滅 and Lamotte 1944/1981, 238.
257. Regarding the role of concepts, Ñāṇananda 1971/1986, 93 reasons: "Concepts, for all their vicious potency to delude us, are not to be blamed *per se* . . . They are not so much to be demolished, as to be comprehended and transcended"; see also Anālayo 2018c, 7–9 and 2021f.
258. AN 8.30 at AN IV 229,27: *nippapañcārāmass' āyaṃ dhammo nippapañcaratino* and its parallel MĀ 74 at T 1.26.541a11: 道從不戲, 樂不戲, 行不戲. In the case of the parallel T 1.46.835c23, the eighth thought of a great person has apparently become accidentally merged with a reference to the four absorptions that appears to belong to a later part of the exposition. In the case of another parallel, EĀ 42.6 at T 2.125.754b16, the relevant passage gives the impression of some reworking of the presentation to provide a relationship to progress toward Buddhahood; for a study of several instances reflecting the influence of Mahāyāna thought on the *Ekottarikāgama*, in the way it is now extant in Chinese translation, see Anālayo 2013b.
259. AN 6.14 at AN III 294,7 (also AN 6.15 at AN III 295,10): *yo ca papañcaṃ hitvāna, nippapañca pade rato, ārādhayī* (Eᵉ and Sᵉ: *ārādhayi*) *so nibbānaṃ, yogakkhemaṃ anuttaran ti*; on the term *yogakkhema/yogakṣema* see also Pontillo and Neri 2019.
260. SĀ 490 at T 2.99.126b3: 貪欲永盡, 瞋恚永盡, 愚癡永盡, 一切諸煩惱永盡, 是名涅槃, parallel to SN 38.1 at SN IV 251,19: *yo kho, āvuso, rāgakkhayo dosakkhayo mohakkhayo, idaṃ vuccati nibbānan ti*, which thus lists just the three root defilements, as is the case for both versions when defining an arahant/arhat (see next note).
261. SĀ 490 at T 2.99.126b22: 貪欲已斷無餘, 瞋恚, 愚癡已斷無餘, 是名阿羅漢, parallel to SN 38.2 at SN IV 252,15: *yo kho, āvuso, rāgakkhayo dosakkhayo mohakkhayo, idaṃ vuccati arahattan ti.* SĀ 490 adds the specification that these three have been eradicated "without remainder," something that can safely be assumed to be implicit in SN 38.2 as well.
262. Vism 508,14 (my presentation is a paraphrase intended to draw out the implications rather than an attempt at literally reflecting the wording of the *Visuddhimagga* passage).
263. See in more detail Anālayo 2010b, 26–27.
264. DN 29 at DN III 133,14: *abhabbo, āvuso, khīṇāsavo bhikkhu sañcicca* (Cᵉ: *saṃcicca*) *pāṇaṃ jīvitā voropetuṃ, abhabbo khīṇāsavo bhikkhu adinnaṃ theyyasaṅkhātaṃ* (Eᵉ: *theyyasaṃkhātaṃ*) *ādiyituṃ* (Eᵉ: *ādātuṃ*), *abhabbo khīṇāsavo bhikkhu methunaṃ dhammaṃ paṭisevituṃ, abhabbo khīṇāsavo bhikkhu sampajānamusā* (Sᵉ:

sampajānamusāvādaṃ) bhāsituṃ, with parallels in the Sanskrit *Dīrghāgama*, folio 285v5, DiSimone 2020, 212: *abh(av)yo 'rhadbhikṣuḥ kṣīṇāsravaḥ saṃciṃtya prāṇinaṃ jīvitād vyaparopayituṃ, [adattaṃ steyasaṃkhyātam ādātum,] abrahmacaryaṃ maithunaṃ dharmaṃ pratisevituṃ, saṃprajānaṃ mṛṣāvācaṃ bhāṣituṃ*, and in DĀ 17 at T 1.1.75b14: 若有比丘漏盡阿羅漢 . . . 一者不殺, 二者不盜, 三者不婬, 四者不妄. DN 29 and DĀ 17 proceed further to list altogether nine such impossibilities, whereas the Sanskrit version has only one more, corresponding to the fifth impossibility in DN 29.

265. The image of the mountain occurs in AN 6.55 at AN III 378,7 (also Vin I 184,27) and the metaphor of the column in AN 9.26 at AN IV 404,21. The parallel to AN 9.26, SĀ 499 at T 2.99.131b15+22+27, employs both similes (with two types of columns) to illustrate the freedom of the mind of an arahant/arhat from lust, anger, and delusion. Among the parallels to AN 6.55, the image of the mountain unshaken by winds as an illustration of mental imperturbability in regard to sense experience occurs in Sanskrit fragment 142 SB 35, Hoernle 1916, 169, Sanskrit fragment 412 folio 21V6, Waldschmidt 1968, 781, MĀ 123 at T 1.26.612c20, SĀ 254 at T 2.99.63a22 (see also T 2.99.63b6), the *Saṅghabhedavastu* of the Mūlasarvāstivāda *Vinaya*, Gnoli 1978, 146,6, and the Dharmaguptaka *Vinaya*, T 22.1428.844c25 (see also T 22.1428.845a8).
266. See also Anālayo 2015, 5–9.
267. AN 3.55 at AN I 159,19.
268. MN 51 at MN I 349,2: *sukhapaṭisaṃvedī* (B[e]: *sukhappaṭisaṃvedī*) *brahmabhūtena attanā viharati*. On the intriguing phrasing employed here see, e.g., Norman 1991, 195 (on compounds with *brahma-* in general), Collins 1993, 356, Schmithausen 2000, 6–7, Wynne 2007, 152n88 (criticizing the indeed unconvincing position taken by Pérez-Rémon 1980, 113–18), Gombrich 2009, 189–90, and the detailed study by Pontillo and Neri 2016.
269. DN 33 at DN III 217,19: *tayo aggī: rāgaggi dosaggi mohaggi*, with parallels in a Sanskrit fragment, Stache-Rosen 1968, 79: *trayo 'gnayaḥ: rāgāgnir dveṣāgnir mohāgniḥ*, DĀ 9 at T 1.1.50a23: 謂三火: 欲火, 恚火, 愚癡火, and T 1.12.228b11: 三火, 是佛所說, 謂貪火, 瞋火, 癡火.
270. SN 35.28 at SN IV 19,25 (also Vin I 34,16), with parallels in Waldschmidt 1962, 322,1, SĀ 197 at T 2.99.50b27, the *Saṅghabhedavastu* of the Mūlasarvāstivāda *Vinaya*, Gnoli 1977, 230,31, the Mahīśāsaka *Vinaya*, T 22.1421.109c1, and the Dharmaguptaka *Vinaya*, T 22.1428.797a24; see also Waldschmidt 1951/1967, 193 and Bareau 1963, 317–20.
271. The relationship between this nuance of the term and the extinction of the fires of defilements has been noted repeatedly; see, e.g., Johansson 1969, 58, de Silva 1987, 29, Norman 1994, 215, and Gombrich 1996, 65.
272. See, e.g., Schrader 1905, 167–68, with a critical reply in Hwang 2006, 58–60. The key passages quoted in support of this position are *Svetāśvatara Upaniṣad* 1.13, Radhakrishnan 1953/1992, 717, which explains that *vahner yathā yonigatasya mūrtiḥ na dṛśyate naiva ca liṅganāśaḥ*, "as the form of fire when latent in its source is not seen and yet its seed is not destroyed," and the *Maitrī Upaniṣad* 6.34, Radhakrishnan 1953/1992, 844, which indicates that *yathā nirindhano vahniḥ svayonāv upaśāmyate*, "even as fire without fuel becomes extinct in its own place" (or perhaps: "in its own source").
273. According to Hwang 2006, 62, "this fire image in the *Pārāyanavagga* seems to open the way to interpreting the state of an enlightened one after death not simply as mere

non-existence." It would indeed seem to put into perspective the assessment by, e.g., Childers 1875/1993, 266 that the Buddhist employment of the simile of "the extinction of a flame" in relation to the passing away of an arahant/arhat is "the strongest possible way of expressing annihilation intelligibly to all."

274. MĀ 162 at T 1.26.692a4: 受命最後覺, 則知受命最後覺, 身壞命終, 壽命已訖, 彼所覺一切滅息止, 知至冷也 . . . 譬如燃燈, 因油, 因炷. 彼若無人更增益油, 亦不續炷, 是爲前已滅訖, 後不相續, 無所復受, parallel to MN 140 at MN III 244,33: *so kāyapariyantikaṃ vedanaṃ vediyamāno* (B^{e} throughout: *vedayamāno*), *kāyapariyantikaṃ vedanaṃ vediyāmī* (B^{e} throughout: *vedayāmī*) *ti pajānāti; jīvitapariyantikaṃ vedanaṃ vediyamāno, jīvitapariyantikaṃ vedanaṃ vediyāmī ti pajānāti, kāyassa bhedā* (B^{e} adds *paraṃ maraṇā* and C^{e} *param maraṇā*) *uddhaṃ jīvitapariyādānā idh' eva sabbavedayitāni anabhinanditāni* (E^{e} and S^{e}: *abhinanditāni*) *sītibhavissanti* (B^{e} and C^{e}: *sītībhavissantī*) *ti pajānāti. seyyathā pi, bhikkhu, telañ ca paṭicca vaṭṭiñ ca paṭicca telappadīpo jhāyati; tass' eva telassa ca vaṭṭiyā* (E^{e}: *vattiyā*) *ca pariyādānā aññassa ca anupahārā anāhāro nibbāyati* and Up 1041 at D 4094 *ju* 40a6 or P 5595 *tu* 43b6: *lus kyi mthar rig cing tshor ba na, lus kyi mthar rig cing tshor ba'o zhes ji lta ba bzhin rab tu shes so. 'tsho ba'i mthar rig cing tshor ba na 'tsho ba'i mthar rig cing tshor ba'o zhes ji lta ba bzhin rab tu shes so. lus zhig ste* (P: *te*) *shi ba'i mthar 'di thams cad rig ste, thams cad ma lus par 'gags pa thams cad ma lus par nub pa, yongs su zad cing byang bar 'gro bar 'gyur ro. dper na til mar dang sdong bu las sgron ma 'byung bar 'gyur la, de la kha cig gis dus dus su* (not in P) *til mar* (not in P) *gyis ma gsos* (P: *g.yos*) *shing sdong bu la* (not in P) *nye bar ma bsdus na sgron ma'i nye bar len pa 'gags pas myur du 'chi bar 'gyur ro.*

275. AN 7.3 at AN IV 3,8: *yoniso vicine dhammaṃ, paññāyatthaṃ vipassati, pajjotass' eva nibbānaṃ, vimokkho hoti cetaso*; the same verse recurs in AN 7.4 at AN IV 4,25.

276. AN 3.89 at AN I 236,16: *viññāṇassa nirodhena, taṇhakkhayavimuttino* (B^{e} and C^{e}: *taṇhākkhayavimuttino*), *pajjotass' eva nibbānaṃ, vimokkho hoti cetaso*. The parallel SĀ 816 at T 2.99.210a20 does not directly relate the imagery of an extinct lamp to liberation of the mind: 正念不忘住, 其心得解脫, 身壞而命終, 如燈盡火滅. Another parallel does provide such a direct relationship between the extinction of the lamp and the liberation of the mind, Up 2080 at D 4094 *ju* 100a2 or P 5595 *tu* 114a7: *de dag srog dang bral gyur cing, rnam par sred zad rnam par grol, mar me shi bar gyur pa ltar, de yi sems ni* (P: *sems ni de yis*) *rnam par thar*.

277. DN 16 at DN II 157,14 (also SN 6.15 at SN I 159,5 and Th 906): *asallīnena cittena, vedanaṃ ajjhavāsayi* (C^{e}: *ajjhavāsayī*), *pajjotass' eva nibbānaṃ, vimokkho cetaso ahu*. For parallels to DN 16 see Waldschmidt 1951, 400,18: *asaṃlīnena cittena, vedanā adhivāsayan, pradyotasyeva nirvāṇam, vimokṣas tasya cetasaḥ* and T 1.7.205b23: 恬然絕思慮, 亦復無諸受, 如燈盡光滅, 如來滅亦然; and for parallels to SN 6.15 see SĀ 1197 at T 2.99.325b29: 其心不懈怠, 亦不住諸愛, 心法漸解脫, 如薪盡火滅 and SĀ^{2} 110 at T 2.100.414a10: 都捨於諸受, 如油盡燈滅, 滅有入涅盤, 心意得解脫; see also the *Avadānaśataka*, Speyer 1909/1970, 199,8: *asaṃlīnena cittena vedanā adhivāsayan, pradyotasyeva nirvāṇaṃ vimokṣas tasya cetasaḥ*, and the *Prasannapadā* (on *Mūlamadhyamakakārikā* 25.1), Vaidya 1960, 227,19: *asaṃlīnena kāyena, vedanām adhyavāsayat, pradyotasyeva nirvāṇaṃ, vimokṣas tasya cetasaḥ*. The same sense would also apply to the somewhat different formulation in the otherwise unrelated Sn 235: *nibbanti dhīrā yathāyaṃ* (C^{e}, E^{e}, and S^{e}: *yathāyam*) *padīpo*, with a counterpart in the *Mahāvastu*, Senart 1882, 293,15: *nirvānti dhīrā yatha tailadīpā*.

278. This basic situation appears to reverberate in one way or another in discussions of the abovementioned verse on the Buddha's passing away in later tradition. Abhidh-k 2.55, Pradhan 1967, 94,7, quotes the relevant statement in a debate on the nature of Nirvana and then takes the lamp simile to illustrate the liberation of the Buddha's mind: *pradyotasyeva nirvāṇaṃ vimokṣas tasya cetasa iti, yathā pradyotasya nirvāṇam abhāva evaṃ bhagavato 'pi cetaso vimokṣa iti*. The commentary on DN 16, Sv II 595,22, considers the lamp simile to illustrate that the Buddha's liberation was unobstructed by anything on approaching the utterly indescribable condition (i.e., final Nirvana), *kenaci dhammena anāvaraṇavimokkho sabbaso apaññattibhāvūpagamo*, which conveniently bridges the awakening and the final Nirvana (the same explanation recurs in Spk I 225,2). However, the commentary on Th 906, Th-a III 71,15 no longer brings in the Buddha's liberation of the mind and relates the lamp simile instead to the extinction of the aggregates, followed by quoting Sn 235 and Sn 1074. In fact, its gloss seems to be more influenced by these verses than by the actual wording of Th 906. The **Nyāyānusāra*, T 29.1562.432c23, also appears to take the lamp simile as illustrative of both the Buddha's liberation of the mind and the extinction of his aggregates: 如燈焰涅槃心解脫亦爾. 彼謂此說如燈涅槃, 唯燈焰謝無別有物, 如是世尊心得解脫, 唯諸蘊滅, 更無所有.

279. Thī 116: *tato sūciṃ gahetvāna, vaṭṭiṃ okassayām' ahaṃ; padīpass'* (S^{e}: *pajjotass'*) *eva nibbānaṃ, vimokkho ahu cetaso*. The imagery of the extinction of the lamp features among the reasons for my preferred choice of the translation "awakening" to render the term *bodhi*, instead of the alternative "enlightenment." Another and central reason is etymological, as in pre-Buddhist usage the term can stand for awakening or knowledge but not for enlightenment. In fact, in the *Ṛgveda* the meaning "awakening" is apparently the most prominent one; see Grassman 1955, 907 on *budh*: "Grundbegriff is 'erwachen, wachen' . . . Hieraus floss der Begriff 'geistig wachsam, regsam, achtsam sein'." Moreover, light-related imagery used in the early discourses in relation to the Buddha's role as the one who discovered the path to liberation tends to reflect his teaching activities and not the actual breakthrough to Nirvana on the night of his *bodhi* (see in more detail Anālayo 2021a and for a different perspective Bodhi 2020). It is this event of *bodhi* that turned him into a Buddha, and the same holds for Paccekabuddhas/Pratyekabuddhas, who by definition do not teach.

Besides, it also seems to me preferable to avoid possibly giving the mistaken impression that a realization of Nirvana is about encountering some form of inner light or luminosity, the experience of which, at least in early Buddhist thought, occurs instead in the context of tranquility meditation (see also Anālayo 2022e, 59–115). As the passages surveyed above would have conveyed, a realization of the deathless is preferably understood as a cessation experience, in the sense of a stepping out of the construction of experience as completely as possible, and thus is indeed comparable to a flame's or fire's going out, involving a major shift in reality comparable to waking up from a (lifelong) dream.

280. DN 2 at DN I 84,13 and its parallels in DĀ 20 at T 1.1.86c8 and in a discourse quotation in the *Saṅghabhedavastu* of the Mūlasarvāstivāda *Vinaya*, Gnoli 1978, 251,1.

281. AN 3.92 at AN I 242,20: *yato ariyasāvakassa virajaṃ vītamalaṃ dhammacakkhuṃ udapādi* (B^{e}: *uppajjati*), *saha dassanuppādā . . . ariyasāvakassa tīṇi saṃyojanāni* (C^{e} and S^{e}: *saññyojanāni*) *pahīyanti: sakkāyadiṭṭhi, vicikicchā, sīlabbataparāmāso*; see also

Sn 231: *sahā v' assa dassanasampadāya, tayassu dhammā jahitā bhavanti: sakkāyadiṭṭhi vicikicchitañ ca, sīlabbataṃ vā pi yad atthi kiñci*, with a counterpart in the *Mahāvastu*, Senart 1882, 291,23: *sarvaiva yasya darśanasaṃpadāyo, trayo sya dharmā jahitā bhavanti, satkāyadṛṣṭīvicikitsitaṃ ca, śīlavrataṃ cāpi yad asti kiṃcit*.

282. Sn 847: *saññāvirattassa na santi ganthā*; see also T 4.198.180c1: 捨不想無有縛, which Bapat 1945, 212 translates: "With no perceptions—which he has relinquished—fetters he has none." The formulation in the Chinese is indeed puzzling. Nevertheless, the proposed rendering does not work so well, since one who is free from fetters, be it an arahant or a Buddha, still has perceptions. Hirakawa 1997, 33 lists *nivṛtta* and *vinivṛtta* as possible Indic terms rendered by 不, which would fit the context better than a flat negation.

283. MN 1 at MN I 4,3: *nibbānaṃ nibbānato sañjānāti; nibbānaṃ nibbānato saññatvā, nibbānaṃ maññati, nibbānasmiṃ maññati, nibbānato maññati, nibbānam* (B^e and C^e: *nibbānaṃ*) *me ti maññati, nibbānaṃ abhinandati. taṃ kissa hetu? apariññātaṃ tassā ti vadāmi*, and its parallel EĀ 44.6 at T 2.125.766a25: 涅槃自知爲涅槃, 於中而自娛樂, 所以然者? 非智者之所說也; see also Anālayo 2011b, 23. The commentary, Ps I 38,27, takes this to refer to a conception of Nirvana held by non-Buddhists. As pointed out by Ñāṇananda 2015, 282, however, this commentarial interpretation "is at odds with the trend of this discourse, because the *sekha*," having already had an experience of Nirvana, will hardly have any interest in a non-Buddhist conception of Nirvana and would therefore not have any need to train in avoiding reification of such a conception.

284. MN 146 at MN III 275,12 and its parallels SĀ 276 at T 2.99.75b9, T 23.1442.793b16, and D 3 *ja* 56b2 or P 1032 *nye* 53b6; see also the *Yogācārabhūmi*, T 30.1579.748a6 and Schmithausen 1969a, 44,27.

285. Taking just the first case of the eye sense door, SN 35.191 at SN IV 164,26: *saṃvijjati kho, āvuso, bhagavato cakkhu, passati bhagavā cakkhunā rūpaṃ, chandarāgo bhagavato n' atthi* and its parallel SĀ 250 at T 2.99.60b17: 世尊眼見色若好, 若惡, 不起欲貪.

286. Th 116: *cha phassāyatane hitvā, guttadvāro susaṃvuto, aghamūlaṃ vamitvāna* (S^e: *vametvāna*), *patto me āsavakkhayo ti*.

287. SĀ 301 at T 2.99.85c26: 世間集如實正知見, 若世間無者不有. 世間滅如實正知見, 若世間有者無有. 是名離於二邊說於中道, 所謂此有故彼有, 此起故彼起, 謂緣無明行, 乃至純大苦聚集; 無明滅故行滅, 乃至純大苦聚滅, parallel to SN 12.15 at SN II 17,10: *lokasamudayaṃ* (C^e: *lokasamudayañ ca*; S^e: *lokasamudayaṃ ca*) *kho, kaccāna* (E^e throughout: *kaccāyana*), *yathābhūtaṃ sammappaññāya passato yā loke natthitā sā na hoti. lokanirodhaṃ kho, kaccāna, yathābhūtaṃ sammappaññāya passato yā loke atthitā sā na hoti . . . ete te, kaccāna, ubho ante anupagamma majjhena tathāgato dhammaṃ deseti: avijjāpaccayā saṅkhārā, saṅkhārapaccayā viññāṇaṃ . . . pe . . . evam etassa kevalassa dukkhakkhandhassa samudayo hoti. avijjāya tveva asesavirāganirodhā saṅkhāranirodho, saṅkhāranirodhā viññāṇanirodho . . . pe . . . evam etassa kevalassa dukkhakkhandhassa nirodho hotī ti* and a Sanskrit fragment parallel in Chung and Fukita 2020, 168: *lokasamudayaṃ kātyāyana yathābhūtaṃ samyakprajñayā paśyato yā loke nāstitā sā na bhavati. lok(a)nirodhaṃ yathābhūtaṃ saṃmyakprajñayā paśyato yā loke astitā sā na bhavati. ity etāv ubhāv aṃtāv anupagamya madhyamayā pratipadā tathāgato dharmaṃ deśayati: y(a)d uta asmin satīdaṃ bhavaty asyotpādād idaṃm utpadyate, yad uta avidyāpratyayā saṃskārā iti pūrvavad yāvat samudayo nirodhaś ca*

bhavati. The Chinese and Sanskrit version conclude by reporting that the teaching resulted in the listening monastic becoming an arahant/arhat.

288. See Anālayo 2018b, 6–9.
289. For a survey of several such instances and the related commentarial attempts to gloss over such depictions of the Buddha as subject to physical affliction see Anālayo 2011b, 35n55.
290. In the case of an arahant/arhat afflicted by intense pain from terminal disease, the early discourses do appear to envisage the possibility of suicide; see Anālayo 2010a, 2011d, and 2012b, 163–67. The relevant passages convey the impression that this should not be read as reflecting personal agitation but rather as a decision taken based on the sober assessment that to continue to endure physical pain serves no purpose at all.
291. SN 22.48 at SN III 47,9 and its parallels SĀ 55 at T 2.99.13b14 and Up 1009 at D 4094 *ju* 12a4 or P 5595 *tu* 13a8.
292. SN 22.85 at SN III 112,19 and its parallel SĀ 104 at T 2.99.31b12 explain the nature of an arahant/arhat after death in terms of each of the five aggregates having come to an end. As pointed out by Harvey 1995, 211, "a living Arahat still has some constructing activities . . . for S.III.112 refers to these as among the *dukkha* processes that end at his death."
293. See Anālayo 2008c, 405–6.
294. See in more detail Anālayo 2018b, 37–44 and 2022c.
295. SĀ 962 at T 2.99.246a7: 色已斷已知, 受, 想, 行, 識已斷已知, 斷其根本, 如截多羅樹頭, 無復生分, 於未來世永不復起. 若至東方, 南, 西, 北方, 是則不然; 甚深, 廣大, 無量, 無數, 永滅, parallel to MN 72 at MN I 487,31: *yena rūpena tathāgataṃ paññāpayamāno paññāpeyya, taṃ rūpaṃ tathāgatassa pahīnaṃ ucchinnamūlaṃ tālāvatthukataṃ anabhāvakataṃ* (B[e]: *anabhāvaṃkataṃ*; S[e]: *anabhāvaṅgataṃ*) *āyatiṃ anuppādadhammaṃ. rūpasaṅkhāvimutto* (B[e]: *rūpasaṅkhayavimutto*) *kho, vaccha, tathāgato gambhīro appameyyo duppariyogāho* (B[e] and S[e]: *duppariyogāḷho*) *seyyathā pi mahāsamuddo* (followed by rejecting the four options of the tetralemma as inapplicable and then repeating the same exposition for each of the other four aggregates), Up 3057 at D 4094 *ju* 158a5 or P 5595 *tu* 182b6: *de bzhin gshegs pas ngo bo gang gis gzugs su 'dogs shing nye bar 'dogs pa'i ngo bo de spangs shing yongs su shes la rtsa ba bcad cing shing ta la mgo bcad pa ltar skal ba mnyam pa phyis mi skye ba'i chos can du gyur to. gang dang gang gis tshor ba dang gang dang gang gis 'du shes dang gang dang gang gis 'du byed dang gang dang* (P does not have *gang dang*) *gang gis rnam par shes pa shes par 'dogs pa ngo bo nyid* (not in P) *de nyid kyi de bzhin gshegs pas sbyangs shing yongs su shes te. rtsa ba bcad cing shing ta* (P: *tā*) *la mgo bcad pa ltar skal ba mnyam par phyis mi skye ba'i chos can du 'gyur te. shar phyogs su ma song. lho dang nub dang byang phyogs su ma song ba ste zab cing rgya che la tshad med cing bgrang* (P: *'grang*) *du med pa'i mya ngan las 'das pa zhes bya'o*, and SĀ[2] 196 at T 2.100.445b25: 若言色是如來, 受, 想, 行, 識是如來者, 無有是處. 何以故? 如來已斷如斯色故, 受, 想, 行, 識亦復如是, 皆悉已斷. 譬如有人斷多羅樹, 斷已不生, 如來亦爾, 斷五陰已, 不復受生, 寂滅無想, 是無生法. Up 3057 and SĀ[2] 196 thus do not have a counterpart to the ocean simile in MN 72.
296. Hwang 2006, 57 comments that the "image of the extinguished fire was applied in this context together with the image of a palm uprooted. What is compared to a fire extinguished . . . ? As this discourse clearly shows, it is not nirvana itself but 'the material form (*rūpa*) of the *Tathāgata*' and . . . also the rest of the four aggregates."

297. SN 44.1 at SN IV 376,11: *atthi pana* (not in S^e) *te koci gaṇako vā muddiko vā saṅkhāyako vā yo pahoti mahāsamudde udakaṃ gaṇetuṃ* (C^e: *miṇituṃ*; E^e: *manituṃ*)*: ettakāni udakāḷhakāni iti* (C^e: *udakāḷhakānīti*) *vā, ettakāni udakāḷhakasatāni iti* (C^e: *udakāḷhakasatānīti*) *vā, ettakāni udakāḷhakasahassāni iti* (C^e: *udakāḷhakasahassānīti*) *vā, ettakāni udakāḷhakasatasahassāni iti* (C^e: *udakāḷhakasatasahassānīti*; E^e: *udakāḷhakasatasahassānī ti*) *vā ti? no h' etaṃ, ayye. taṃ kissa hetu? mahāyye* (S^e: *mahayye*)*, samuddo gambhīro appameyyo duppariyogāho* (C^e: *appariyogāho*) *ti. evam eva kho, mahārāja, yena rūpena tathāgataṃ paññāpayamāno paññāpeyya* (S^e: *paññapeyya*) *taṃ rūpaṃ tathāgatassa pahīnaṃ ucchinnamūlaṃ tālāvatthukataṃ anabhāvakataṃ* (B^e: *anabhāvaṃkataṃ*; S^e: *anabhāvaṅgataṃ*) *āyatiṃ anuppādadhammaṃ* (E^e: *anuppādakataṃ*)*. rūpasaṅkhāya* (C: *rūpasaṅkhaya*; S^e: *rūpasaṅkhyā*) *vimutto kho, mahārāja, tathāgato gambhīro appameyyo duppariyogāho* (C^e: *appariyogāho*)*, seyyathā pi* (S^e adds *mahārāja*) *mahāsamuddo. hoti tathāgato param* (here and below, B^e and S^e: *paraṃ*) *maraṇā ti pi na upeti, na hoti tathāgato param maraṇā ti pi na upeti, hoti ca na ca hoti tathāgato param maraṇā ti pi na upeti, n' eva hoti na na hoti tathāgato param maraṇā ti pi na upeti*; for a translation of the whole discourse see Anālayo 2022d, 26–29.

298. Oldenberg 1881/1961, 261 comments: "Wer Prädikate wie Sein und Nichtsein, gut genug für das Endliche, Bedingte, auf das schlechthin Unbedingte anwendet, der gleicht einem Mann, welcher . . . die Tropfen im Meer zu zählen versucht." On the ocean simile see also Robinson 1972, 320 and Harvey 1983, 35–36.

299. SN 22.35 at SN III 35,8: *yaṃ kho, bhikkhu, anuseti tena saṅkhaṃ gacchati*, with parallels in Sanskrit fragment Stein Kha.ii.10a, Chung 2008, 318,11: *yad anunīyate tenaiva saṃkhyāṃ ga(c)[ch](at)[i]* and SĀ 16 at T 2.99.3b16: 隨使使, 隨使死者, 則增諸數 (on 隨使死 see Schmithausen 1987/2007, 529n1426C).

300. Dhp 180: *taṃ buddham* (S^e: *buddhaṃ*) *anantagocaraṃ, apadaṃ kena padena nessatha*, with Indic language parallels in the Patna *Dharmapada* 277, Cone 1989, 175: *taṃ buddham anantagocaraṃ, apadaṃ kena padena nehisi*, and the Sanskrit *Udānavarga* 29.53, Bernhard 1965, 389: *taṃ buddham anantagocaraṃ, hy apadaṃ kena padena neṣyasi*, as well as in the *Saṅghabhedavastu* of the Mūlasarvāstivāda *Vinaya*, Gnoli 1977, 185,13: *taṃ buddham anantagocaram, apadaṃ kena padena neṣyasi.*

301. On several occasions the standard reference in Pāli discourses to *vibhavataṇhā* as one of three types of craving does not receive support from the respective parallel versions; see Anālayo 2011b, 70n216. Nevertheless, some listings of three types of cravings in Chinese *Āgama* discourses do mention craving for non-existence: see, e.g., DĀ 13 at T 1.1.60c13: 無有愛 and EĀ 49.5 at T 2.125.797c8: 無有愛.

302. DĀ 21 at T 1.1.93a26: 我身, 四大, 六入 . . . 然是無常, 必歸磨滅. 齊是名爲斷滅 (rather than adopting a literal translation of 我身 as "my body," my rendering in the present context reflects the impression that this phrase would be an affirmation that identifies the self with the body; the same also appears to underlie the last part in the otherwise closely similar formulation in T 28.1548.660a23: 齊是我斷滅), with discourse parallels in DN 1 at DN I 34,7: *yato kho, bho, ayaṃ attā rūpī cātummahābhūtiko* (B^e: *cātumahābhūtiko*) . . . *kāyassa bhedā ucchijjati vinassati, na hoti param* (B^e: *paraṃ*) *maraṇā, ettāvatā kho, bho, ayaṃ attā sammā samucchinno hoti*, T 1.21.269b9: 我色四大 . . . 身死在地 . . . 如是便滅盡, Weller 1934, 56,7: *bdag gzugs can ni 'byung ba chen po bzhi po . . . bdag ni nam zhig na yongs su chad par 'gyur ro*, and Up 3050 at D 4094 *ju* 151b3 or P 5595 *tu* 174b6: *ji srid du bdag gzugs can te rags pa* (P duplicates *rags pa*)

'byung ba chen po bzhi'i rgyu las byung ba . . . gang gi tshe bdag rgyun chad cing rnam par zhig la gcig nas gcig tu mi 'byung ba 'di tsam gyis na bdag yang dag par rgyun chad par 'gyur ro.

303. MĀ 200 at T 1.26.766a8: 諸沙門, 梵志誣謗我, 虛妄言不真實: 沙門瞿曇御無所施設, 彼實有眾生施設斷滅壞. 若此中無, 我不說, 彼如來於現法中說無憂, parallel to MN 22 at MN I 140,10: *yathā cāhaṃ* (C^e: *vāhaṃ*) *na vadāmi, tathā maṃ te bhonto samaṇabrāhmaṇā asatā tucchā musā abhūtena abbhācikkhanti: venayiko samaṇo gotamo, sato sattassa ucchedaṃ vināsaṃ vibhavaṃ paññāpetī ti. pubbe cāhaṃ, bhikkhave, etarahi ca dukkhañ c' eva paññāpemi, dukkhassa ca nirodhaṃ.* The succinct Pāli statement that the Buddha just teaches *dukkha* and its cessation recurs in SN 22.86 at SN III 119,5 (repeated in SN 44.2 at SN IV 384,14) but is absent from the parallel SĀ 106 at T 2.99.33a4.
304. MN 22 at MN I 140,6: *diṭṭhe vāhaṃ, bhikkhave, dhamme tathāgataṃ ananuvejjo* (B^e: *ananuvijjo*; S^e: *ananuvajjo*) *ti vadāmi* (the support of the consciousness appears to be implied, as it is mentioned just previously as *idaṃ nissitaṃ tathāgatassa viññāṇan ti*) and MĀ 200 at T 1.26.766a7: 如來是冷, 如來不煩熱, 如來是不異 (preceded by 如來是梵).
305. The same allegation has formed a prominent current among writings on Nirvana by Western scholars. An example is de La Vallée Poussin (1917, 377), who reasons that the "doctrine of annihilation was not an 'original purpose'; it was a result. That is to say, Śākyamuni (or the Church) did not start with such an idea of deliverance; this idea has been forced upon him (or upon them) because he has been rash enough to deny the existence of a soul."
306. AN 8.12 at AN IV 182,15 and its parallel MĀ 18 at T 1.26.441b21. The same type of exchange occurs in AN 8.11 at AN IV 174,19, in which case the parallels MĀ 157 and T 75 do not cover the accusation of being an annihilationist, leaving open the possibility that perhaps this part of AN 8.11 has been influenced by AN 8.12 during the course of textual transmission.
307. MĀ 215 at T 2.26.800c10+11 twice uses the phrase 實有眾生. DN 1 at DN I 34,11 and MN 102 at MN II 228,18 employ the phrase referring to the "annihilation of an existing sentient being," *sato (. . .) sattassa ucchedaṃ.*
308. An instance where the Buddha reportedly remained silent on the topic of the self, found in SN 44.10 at SN IV 400,17 and its parallels SĀ 961 at T 2.99.245b12, SĀ^2 195 at T 2.100.444c4, and Up 9031 at D 4094 *nyu* 88b6 or P 5595 *thu* 136a3, appears to be due to pedagogical reasons rather than the limitations of language; see in more detail Anālayo 2023.
309. MN 75 at MN I 508,30: *nibbānaṃ paramaṃ sukhaṃ* and its parallel MĀ 153 at T 1.26.672a29: 涅槃第一樂. The same statement recurs in Dhp 204: *nibbānaṃ* (C^e: *nibbāna*) *paramaṃ sukhaṃ*, with Indic language parallels in the Gāndhārī *Dharmapada* 162, Brough 2001, 145: *nivaṇa paramo suha*, the Patna *Dharmapada* 76, Cone 1989, 123: *nibbāṇaparamaṃ sukhaṃ*, and the Sanskrit *Udānavarga* 26.6, Bernhard 1965, 319: *nirvāṇaparamaṃ sukham.*

    The same phrase, *nibbānaṃ* (C^e: *nibbāna*) *paramaṃ sukhaṃ*, occurs also in the preceding Dhp 203, in which case, however, one of the Indic language parallels differs, namely the corresponding Sanskrit *Udānavarga* 26.7. The presentation in Dhp 203 is in fact not without some difficulties, as it provides a contrast to Nirvana as the supreme happiness with the phrase *saṅkhārā* (E^{e}: *saṃkhārā*) *paramā dukhā*. This appears to refer to *dukkha/duḥkha* as a general characteristic of conditioned phenomena (Norman 1997/2004, 30 renders *saṅkhārā* here as "conditioned things"). Yet, it is unclear to me in what sense this usage in Dhp 203 should be understood. Although room needs to be granted to poetic license, for the line to make sense the application of *parama* would require a contrast in something else that is less *dukkha/duḥkha* in comparison. In view of the broad scope of *saṅkhārā* as comprising all conditioned phenomena, such a contrast is difficult to find. The only possible contrast would be what is unconditioned, but that does not qualify at all as *dukkha/duḥkha*. The corresponding lines in the Sanskrit *Udānavarga* 26.7, Bernhard 1965, 319, read *saṃskārā duḥkham eva tu* and *nirvāṇaparamo bhavet*, which offer a more straightforward presentation by just qualifying conditioned phenomena as *dukkha/duḥkha* in general and employing the specification "supreme" or "foremost" only for Nirvana. This is not to take the position that the Sanskrit *Udānavarga* 26.7 version must necessarily be earlier, only that it makes more sense. In sum, for an evaluation of the idea of Nirvana as the supreme happiness, it seems to me preferable to rely on Dhp 204 rather than Dhp 203, as Dhp 204 has the support of all of its known Indic language parallels and does not involve what at least to my mind is a problematic proposition, found in Dhp 203.

310. AN 6.101 at AN III 442,20: *so vata, bhikkhave, bhikkhu* (E^{e}: *khikkhu*) *nibbānaṃ sukhato samanupassanto anulomikāya khantiyā samannāgato bhavissatī ti ṭhānam etaṃ vijjati; anulomikāya khantiyā samannāgato sammattaniyāmaṃ okkamissatī ti ṭhānam etaṃ vijjati; sammattaniyāmaṃ okkamamāno sotāpattiphalaṃ vā sakadāgāmiphalaṃ vā anāgāmiphalaṃ vā arahattaṃ vā sacchikarissatī ti ṭhānam etaṃ vijjatī ti*. This is preceded by describing the opposite case, when Nirvana is seen as *dukkha*, as a result of which it becomes impossible to attain any of the four levels of progress to awakening.

311. MN 51 at MN I 346,10 (moral conduct): *anavajjasukhaṃ*, MN I 346,23 (sense restraint): *abyāsekasukaṃ*, MN I 347,13 (first absorption): *vivekajaṃ pītisukhaṃ*, MN I 347,16 (second absorption): *samādhijaṃ pītisukhaṃ*, MN I 347,19 (third absorption): *sukhavihārī*, MN I 349,2 (liberation): *sukhapaṭisaṃvedī*.

312. Dhp 373: *amānusī ratī* (B^{e} and C^{e}: *rati*) *hoti, sammā dhammaṃ vipassato*, with Indic language parallels in the Gāndhārī *Dharmapada* 55, Brough 2001, 126: *amaṇuṣa radi bhodi, same dharma vivaśadu*, the Patna *Dharmapada* 60, Cone 1989, 119: *amānuṣā ratī hoti, sammaṃ dhammaṃ vipaśśato*, and the Sanskrit *Udānavarga* 32.9, Bernhard 1965, 433: *amānuṣā ratir bhavati, samyag dharmāṃ vipaśyataḥ*; see also Th 398: *pañcaṅgikena turiyena, na ratī* (E^{e} and S^{e}: *rati*) *hoti tādisī, yathā ekaggacittassa, sammā dhammaṃ vipassato* (also Th 1071).

313. MN 89 at MN II 121,20: *haṭṭhapahaṭṭhe udaggudagge abhiratarūpe* and its parallel MĀ 213 at T 1.26.796a28: 樂行端正, 面色悅澤; see also Anālayo 2011b, 514.

314. Th 35: *sukhaṃ sukhattho labhate*, Th 63: *sukhen' anvāgataṃ sukhaṃ* (C^{e} and S^{e}: *sukhan*), Th 220: *sukhena sukhaṃ laddhaṃ*, Th 227 and Th 263: *susukhaṃ vata nibbānaṃ*, Th 293: *sukhaṃ pappoti paṇḍito*, Th 545: *vimuttisukhena sukhito ramissāmi*, Th 888: *sukhaṃ sayāmi ṭhāyāmi, sukhaṃ kappemi jīvitaṃ*, Thī 24: *aho sukhan ti sukhato jhāyāmi*, and Thī 476: *nibbānasukhā paraṃ n' atthi*.

315. Th 1062 to Th 1065, which share the refrain: *te selā ramayanti maṃ*.

316. AN 3.34 at AN I 136,28: *sukham asayitthaṃ, ye ca pana loke sukhaṃ senti, ahaṃ tesaṃ aññataro*, with a parallel to the first part of this assertion in EĀ 28.3 at T 2.125.650a25:

快善眠也 and a partially preserved parallel to the second part in SHT V 1343V1, Sander and Waldschmidt 1985, 231: *ye ke[cil-loke su]*.

317. SN 4.18 at SN I 114,22: *susukhaṃ vata jīvāma . . . pītibhakkhā bhavissāma*, with a parallel in SĀ 1095 at T 2.99.288a25: 安樂而自活, 常以欣悅食.

318. MN 14 at MN I 94,29 and its parallels MĀ 100 at T 1.26.587c15 and T 1.55.851a3. See also Thī 44 and Thī 174, where nuns report sitting continuously for seven days in happiness.

319. This point can be illustrated with the example of the reasoning advanced by Jotikarāma 1995, 57–58 in support of the claim that just the "absence or cessation of suffering . . . is called the pleasure of Nibbāna." The example provided in support concerns a "miserable and wretched patient who is full of tumours, . . . groaning and moaning all day and night because of unbearable pains," who on being cured will consider the cure a source of pleasure or happiness. The happiness of Nirvana should be seen as similarly due to being cured of all-pervasive suffering. Hence, it is only "when every happening in the thirty-one planes is realized as . . . painful suffering . . . that . . . the pleasure of Nibbāna will be perceived. Exert [yourselves] to the utmost to perceive so!"

320. MN 102 at MN II 230,7: *samaṇabrāhmaṇā asaññiṃ attānaṃ paññāpenti* (B^{e}: *paññapenti*) *arogaṃ param* (B^{e}: *paraṃ*) *maraṇā* and Skilling 1994, 326,5: *dge sbyong dang bram ze gang dag 'du shes med par smra ba de dag kha cig de phan chad bdag 'du shes med par 'gyur ro zhes mngon par brjod pa mngon par brjod pa byed pa*.

321. Abhidh-k 2.41, Pradhan 1967, 68,11: *āsaṃjñikam asaṃjñiṣu nirodhaś cittacaittānāṃ* and Vism 559,28: (*arūpīnaṃ pana tayo va arūpino khandhā*) *asaññīnaṃ rūpato*; see also the discussion in Sharf 2014, 150–57.

322. AN 9.24 at AN IV 401,15: *santi, bhikkhave, sattā asaññino appaṭisaṃvedino, seyyathā pi devā asaññasattā* (S^{e}: *asaññisattā*).

323. DN 24 at DN III 33,25: *sant' āvuso, asaññasattā* (S^{e}: *asaññisattā*) *nāma devā, saññuppādā ca pana te devā tamhā kāyā cavanti* and DĀ 15 at T 1.1.69c23: 有眾生無想無知; 若彼眾生起想, 則便命終.

324. On the integration of the immaterial spheres into the Buddhist scheme of practice see also Anālayo 2021c, 1895–97.

325. MN 59 at MN I 400,19 (also in SN 36.19 at SN IV 228,18): *na kho, āvuso, bhagavā sukhaṃ yeva vedanaṃ sandhāya sukhasmiṃ paññapeti, api c'* (B^{e}: *ca*) *āvuso, yattha yattha sukhaṃ upalabbhati yahiṃ yahiṃ taṃ* (E^{e}: *tan*) *taṃ tathāgato sukhasmiṃ paññapeti*. The parallel SĀ 485 at T 2.99.124b14 instead explains the Buddha's position by distinguishing four types of happiness, one of which is the happiness of awakening: 有四種樂. 何等爲四? 謂離欲樂, 遠離樂, 寂滅樂, 菩提樂; see also SHT II 51(1)[41]R6–7, Waldschmidt, Clawiter, and Sander-Holzmann 1968, 11: *catvāry-udāyī sukhā(ni): n[ai]ṣkrāmyas(ukha)ṃ [vi]vekasukhaṃ saṃbodhisu(khaṃ nirvānasukhaṃ)* (the reading is based on a preliminary transcription as parts of the original fragment have been lost).

326. AN 9.34 at AN IV 415,3: *etad eva khv' ettha* (C^{e}: *khottha*), *āvuso, sukhaṃ yad ettha n' atthi vedayitaṃ*.

327. SN 36.1 at SN IV 204,18: *vedanānaṃ khayā bhikkhu, nicchāto parinibbuto ti*. Contrary to the assumption by Akanuma 1929/1990, 228, followed by Chung 2008, 134, as far as I can see SĀ 473 at T 2.99.121a2 does not appear to be a parallel to SN 36.1.

328. For the case of the fourth absorption see MN 59 at MN I 399,15 (also SN 36.19 at SN IV 226,28) and SĀ 485 at T 2.99.124b6, which abbreviates the relevant part, a

procedure also adopted in the parallel extant in Sanskrit, SHT II 51(1)[41]V8, Waldschmidt, Clawiter, and Sander-Holzmann 1968, 10 (see also above n. 325).

329. SN 36.29 at SN IV 236,9+22 presents such reflection of an arahant/arhat as the *nirāmisā nirāmisatarā pīti* and again the *nirāmisā nirāmisataraṃ sukhaṃ*. The parallel SĀ 483 does not cover the case of happiness at all and only has the case of more unworldly than unworldly joy, 無食無食樂, which according to T 2.99.123b8 is to be found in what appears to be the third absorption. This variation suggests that some textual confusion occurred, whereby the wording used in both versions to describe the more unworldly than unworldly liberation (*vimutti*/解脫) in terms of the mind of an arahant/arhat being free from the three root defilements (see SN IV 237,28 and T 2.99.123b17) was either replaced in the exposition of joy in SĀ 483 by a reference to a higher absorption, or else it replaced a different definition in the expositions of joy and of happiness in SN 36.29.

The former of these two alternatives receives support from the next discourse in the *Saṃyuktāgama*, as SĀ 484 at T 2.99.123c17, in agreement with its parallel AN 5.170 at AN III 202,28, indicates that the foremost type of joy is the one that leads to the eradication of the influxes, 如所生樂, 次第盡諸漏者, 是名樂第一. Although the terminology differs, the more unworldly than unworldly joy (or happiness) is clearly the supreme type recognized in SN 36.29, which makes the relationship established in this discourse between such joy (or happiness) and freedom from defilements the more convincing one.

330. DN 1 at DN I 36,24 and its parallels DĀ 21 at T 1.1.93b17, T 1.21.269c18, Weller 1934, 58,1, and Up 3050 at D 4094 *ju* 152a2 or P 5595 *tu* 175a6.

331. MN 75 at MN I 509,10: *paribbājako sakān' eva sudaṃ gattāni pāṇinā anomajjati: . . . idan taṃ nibbānaṃ, ahaṃ* (B^e: *ahañ*) *hi . . . etarahi arogo sukhī, na maṃ kiñci ābādhatī* (C^e: *ābādhayatī*) *ti* and MĀ 153 at T 1.26.672b5: 鬚閑提異學身 . . . 以兩手抆摸而作是說: 瞿曇, 此是無病, 此是涅槃.

332. A third sense noted by Rhys Davids and Stede 1921/1993, 362 is then "the dying out in the heart of the threefold fire or rāga, dosa & moha," and a fourth is "the sense of spiritual well-being, of security, emancipation, victory and peace, salvation, bliss." Both senses also convey indubitably positive connotations.

333. *Mahābhārata* 12.327.5, Belvalkar 1954b, 1869,2: *brahman nirvānaṃ paramaṃ sukham*. From the viewpoint of such similarity, it is also worthy of note that the *Mahābhārata* 12.171.51, Belvalkar 1954a, 980,1, presents the happiness of the destruction of craving as superior to sensual and celestial happiness, *yac ca kāmasukhaṃ loke, yac ca divyaṃ mahat sukham, tṛṣṇākṣayasukhasyaite, nārhataḥ ṣoḍaśīṃ kalām*. This closely corresponds to a Buddhist evaluation of happiness expressed in Ud 2.2 at Ud 11,22: *yañ* (E^e: *yaṃ*) *ca kāmasukhaṃ loke, yañ* (E^e: *yaṃ*) *c' idaṃ diviyaṃ sukhaṃ, taṇhakkhayasukhass' ete* (E^e and S^e: *taṇhakkhayasukhassa te*), *kalaṃ nāgghanti* (E^e: *n' agghanti*; S^e: *nagghanti*) *soḷasin ti* and in the Sanskrit *Udānavarga* 30.31, Bernhard 1965, 399: *yac ca kāmasukhaṃ loke, yac cāpi divijaṃ sukham, tṛṣṇākṣayasukhasyaitat, kalāṃ nārghati ṣoḍaśīm*. My referencing of such passages from the *Mahābhārata* is not meant to convey certainty about their precise dating vis-à-vis the early discourses. In fact, Gokhale 2020, 114n93 even proposes that the source of the above *Mahābhārata* conception of the destruction of craving as supreme happiness "is likely to be Buddhist."

334. *Mahābhārata* 4.21.22, Vira 1936, 100,5: *nirvāṇakāle dīpasya*.
335. Based on a survey of references to *nirvāṇa*, mainly in the *Mahābhārata*, Senart 1903, 102 comments: "Il est trop clair que le sens supposé de 'destruction' ne fournit pas le point de départ commun" for the Buddhist and Brahminical employment of the term.
336. SN 43.40–41 at SN IV 372,10: *dīpa* and *leṇa*, with its parallel in SĀ 890 at T 2.99.224b8: 覆蔭, 洲渚.
337. Sn 1094: *akiñcanaṃ anādānaṃ, etaṃ dīpaṃ anāparaṃ, nibbānaṃ iti naṃ brūmi, jarāmaccuparikkhayaṃ*; see also Anālayo 2022b, 1677.
338. Schopenhauer 1888, 698: "Wenn Nirwana als das Nichts definiert wird, so will dies nur sagen, daß der Sansara kein einziges Element enthält, welches zur Definition, oder Konstruktion des Nirwana dienen könnte." In a similar vein, Burns 1967, 18 argues: "Nirvana is nothing only in that it is no thing." The overall emphasis on negative description would be, as noted by Weeraperuma 2003, 170, simply because the "safer course is to state what Nirvana is *not* than what it actually *is*." Sobti 1985, 134 adds that it is also natural that "one who has experienced it . . . describes the state of *Nibbāna* negatively with reference to the state of affairs existing prior to the realization of *Nibbāna*. This is also, in a way, to inspire others."
339. For example, Singh 1989, 26 quotes the translation "there is an Unborn" as an example to show the metaphysical reality of Nirvana as "a different dimension of being. Some have tried to explain it away as a mere transformed state of personality. The logic of the words does not permit such an interpretation."
340. Norman 1994, 220 argues as follows: "Taken literally, the epithets *amata* and *ajāta* as applied to *nibbāna* could be interpreted as compounds of the past participles with the negative prefix *a*-, making negative possessive (*bahuvrīhi*) compounds: 'possessing nothing born,' 'possessing nothing dead.' I would suggest, however, that the grammatical explanation of these epithets, when they are applied to *nibbāna* to indicate the absence of birth and death, is that they are based upon past participles which are being used as action nouns, i.e. *jāta* = 'being born, birth,' *mata* = 'dying, death,' etc. From these action nouns, negative possessive adjectives are formed by prefixing *a*-: '(*nibbāna*) which has no birth, where there is no birth,' '(*nibbāna*) which has no death, where there is no death.' If this analysis of the epithets is correct, it enables us to suggest translations which avoid the difficulties which are present in renderings such as 'immortality,' 'unborn' and 'uncreated.' I have suggested that the correct translation for *amatapadaṃ* is 'the state where there is no death,' and we can translate the other epithets in a similar way; 'where there is no birth' (*ajāta*),' . . . 'where nothing has come into existence' (*abhūta*), 'where there is nothing made' (*akata*)."
341. Ud 8.3 at Ud 80,23: *atthi, bhikkhave, ajātaṃ abhūtaṃ akataṃ asaṅkhataṃ* (E[e]: *asaṃkhataṃ*). *no ce taṃ, bhikkhave, abhavissa ajātaṃ abhūtaṃ akataṃ asaṅkhataṃ, nayidha jātassa bhūtassa katassa saṅkhatassa nissaraṇaṃ paññāyetha. yasmā ca kho, bhikkhave, atthi ajātaṃ abhūtaṃ akataṃ asaṅkhataṃ, tasmā jātassa bhūtassa katassa saṅkhatassa nissaraṇaṃ paññāyatī ti*.
342. This is also the implication of a verse in the Sanskrit *Udānavarga* 26.21 that appears to be a distant counterpart to Ud 8.3, Bernhard 1965, 328: *ajāte sati jātasya, vaden niḥsaraṇaṃ sadā, asaṃskṛtaṃ ca saṃpaśyaṃ, saṃskṛtāt parimucyate*.
343. It 43 at It 37,19: *tassa nissaraṇaṃ santaṃ, atakkāvacaraṃ dhuvaṃ, ajātaṃ asamuppannaṃ, asokaṃ virajaṃ padaṃ, nirodho dukkhadhammānaṃ, saṅkhārūpasamo su-*

kho and Sanskrit *Udānavarga* 26.23, Bernhard 1965, 328: *tasya niḥsaraṇaṃ śāntam, atarkāvacaraṃ padam, nirodho duḥkhadharmāṇāṃ, saṃskāropaśamaṃ sukham.*

344. Ud 1.10 at Ud 9,4: *yattha āpo ca paṭhavī* (B^e: *pathavī*), *tejo vāyo na gādhati, na tattha sukkā jotanti, ādicco nappakāsati, na tattha candimā bhāti, tamo tattha na vijjati* and Sanskrit *Udānavarga* 26.25–26, Bernhard 1965, 330: *yatra nāpo na pṛthivī, tejo vāyur na gāhate, na tatra śuklā dyotanti, tamas tatra na vidyate, na tatra candramā bhāti, nādityo vai prakāśyate.* A to some degree comparable reference to the absence of the light provided by the sun, the moon, and the stars can be found in the *Kaṭha Upaniṣad* 2.2.15, the *Muṇḍaka Upaniṣad* 2.2.11, and *Śvetāśvatara Upaniṣad* 6.14 (although with different implications); see Radhakrishnan 1953/1992, 641, 685, and 747: *na tatra sūryo bhāti, na candratārakam, nemā vidyuto bhānti.*

345. See Anālayo 2017a, 12–20, republished with some revisions in Anālayo 2022e, 62–77. Although the former is quoted by Kuan 2020, 349, its contents do not appear to have been fully appreciated, as in particular the comparative perspective on DN 11 and MN 49 could have prevented mistaking the penetrative understanding of various objects, with which awakened ones are endowed as a result of their previous realization of Nirvana, to be itself a form of Nirvana. Descriptions of the direct knowledge of Buddhas and arahants, such as, e.g., in MN 1 and its parallels, do not use the term Nirvana to refer to such knowledge. The supposed problem identified by Kuan 2020, reflected in the title of his article: "Conscious of Everything or Consciousness Without Objects? A Paradox of Nirvana," is unfortunately the result of a misunderstanding.

346. DN 11 at DN I 223,13: *ettha āpo ca paṭhavī* (B^e: *pathavī*), *tejo vāyo na gādhati . . . ettha nāmañ ca rūpañ ca, asesaṃ uparujjhati, viññāṇassa nirodhena, etth' etaṃ uparujjhati*, parallel to Sanskrit fragment 389v7–8, Zhou 2008, 9: *atha pṛthiva āpaś ca, tejā vāyur nā gāhate . . . atra nāmarūpaṃ cāpy, aseṣaṃm uparudhyante*, DĀ 24 at T 1.1.102c14: 何由無四大, 地水火風滅? . . . 於此名色滅, 識滅餘亦滅, and Up 2027 at D 4094 *ju* 65a2 or P 5595 *tu* 72a7: *gang du sa chu me dang ni, rlung dag rjes su mi 'jug dang? . . . gang du ming dang gzugs dang* (D: dag) *ni, ma lus pa dag 'gag par 'gyur.* Although only DN 11 and DĀ 24 explicitly mention the cessation of consciousness, the same would be implicit in the other versions, since the cessation of name-and-form implies the cessation of consciousness due to the reciprocally conditioning relationship that obtains between them; see, e.g., the simile of the bundle of reeds in SN 12.67 at SN II 114,17 and its parallels in Sanskrit fragments, Chung and Fukita 2020, 109, and SĀ 288 at T 2.99.81b5.

347. SN 1.27 at SN I 15,16: *yattha āpo ca paṭhavī* (B^e and E^e: *pathavī*), *tejo vāyo na gādhati . . . ettha nāmañ ca rūpañ ca, asesaṃ uparujjhatī ti*, with parallels in SĀ 601 at T 2.99.160c25: 名色滅無餘, 薩羅小還流 and SĀ^2 176 at T 2.100.438a12: 名色都消盡, 如是池枯竭; see also SHT IV 50, Sander and Waldschmidt 1980, 236 (identified in Bechert and Wille 1995, 234).

348. DN 28 at DN III 105,20: *purisassa ca viññāṇasotaṃ pajānāti ubhayato abbocchinnaṃ idhaloke appatiṭṭhitañ ca paraloke appatiṭṭhitañ ca*, with parallels in Sanskrit, folio 293v2, DiSimone 2020, 334: *vijñānasrotaḥ pratyavekṣate, iha lok(e a)pratiṣṭhitam paraloke apratiṣṭhitam*, and in DĀ 18 at T 1.1.77b28: 觀識不在今世, 不在後世, which thus does not refer to consciousness as a stream. On the unestablished consciousness see also the discussion above p. 47.

349. SN 22.97 at SN III 148,18: *viññāṇaṃ n' atthi niccaṃ dhuvaṃ sassataṃ avipariṇāmadhammaṃ sassatisamaṃ tath' eva ṭhassati*, with a parallel in EĀ 24.4 at T 2.125.617b12: 無有 . . . 識, 恒在不變易, 久存於世者.
350. Sn 734: *yaṃ* (S^e: *yaṅ*) *kiñci dukkhaṃ sambhoti, sabbaṃ viññāṇapaccayā, viññāṇassa nirodhena, n' atthi dukkhassa sambhavo.*
351. Ud 8.9 at Ud 93,12: *abhedi kāyo nirodhi saññā, vedanā sītibhaviṃsu* (E^e: *pi 'tidahaṃsu* and S^e: *pīti dahaṃsu*) *sabbā, vūpasamiṃsu saṅkhārā, viññāṇaṃ attham āgamā* (C^e and E^e: *agamā*) *ti*, with a parallel in the *Prasannapadā* (on *Mūlamadhyamakakārikā* 25.1), Vaidya 1960, 227,14: *abhedi kāyo nirodhi saññā, vedanā pi ti dahaṃsu sabbā, vūpasamiṃsu saṃkhārā, viññāṇam attham agamā ti*; see also Anālayo 2012b. Contrary to the readings found in E^e and S^e, as well as in Vaidya's edition of the *Prasannapadā*, the notion that feelings tones become cool appears to be the appropriate one in the present context; see above n. 274 and a similar reference in the Mūlasarvāstivāda *Vinaya*, Dutt 1984, 258,8: *vedanā śītībhūtā*.
352. Ud 8.10 at Ud 93,25: *evaṃ sammāvimuttānaṃ, kāmabandhoghatārinaṃ, paññāpetuṃ gati n' atthi, pattānaṃ acalaṃ sukhan* (C^e: *sukhaṃ*) *ti*.
353. SĀ 1076 at T 2.99.280c13: 如是等解脫, 度煩惱淤泥, 諸流永已斷, 莫知其所之, 逮得不動跡, 入無餘涅槃, SĀ^2 15 at T 2.378b13: 得正解脫, 亦復如是, 已出煩惱, 諸欲淤泥, 莫能知彼, 所趣方所, and Indic language parallels in the *Udānavarga* 30.36, Bernhard 1965, 401: *evaṃ saṃyagvimuktānāṃ, kāmapaṅkaughatāriṇāṃ, prajñāpayituṃ gatir nāsti, prāptānām acalaṃ sukhaṃ*, and the Mūlasarvāstivāda *Vinaya*, Dutt 1984, 82,1: *tathā samyagvimuktānāṃ, kāmapaṅkaughatāriṇām, prajñaptaṃ vā gatir nāsti, prāptānām acalaṃ padam*; see also Enomoto 1994, 21.
354. On different nuances of silence and their implications in the early discourses see also Anālayo 2008b and 2023.
355. My translation of Oldenberg 1881/1961, 265: "es gibt einen Weg aus der Welt des Geschaffenen hinaus in die undergründliche Unendlichkeit. Führt es zu höchstem Sein? Führt es in das Nichts? Der buddhistische Glaube hält sich auf der Messerschneide zwischen beidem. Das Verlangen des nach Ewigem trachtenden Herzens hat nicht Nichts, und doch hat das Denken kein Etwas, das es festzuhalten vermöchte. In weitere Ferne konnte der Gedanke des Unendlichen, Ewigen dem Glauben nicht entschwinden, als hier, wo er, ein leiser Hauch, im Begriff sich in das Nichts zu tauchen, dem Blick zu entfliehen droht."
356. SN 2.17 at SN I 54,4: *nāññatra* (E^e: *na aññatra*) *sabbanissaggā, sotthiṃ passāmi pāṇinan ti*.
357. SĀ 596 at T 2.99.159c29: 無異一切捨, 而得見解脫 and Enomoto 1989, 26,7: *nānyatra sarvasaṃtyāgān, mokṣaṃ paśyāmi* (see also Enomoto 1994, 8). However, another parallel, SĀ^2 181 at T 2.100.439a17, proceeds differently and has only the distantly related 若捨於一切, 能除上諸患.
358. It 44 at It 38,5 and T 17.765.677a29. A distinction between two Nirvana elements can also be found in EĀ 16.2 at T 2.125.579a13. The explanation provided in the body of the discourse concerns the difference between a nonreturner and an arahant/arhat. Although the terms used to introduce this distinction are 有餘涅槃界 and 無餘涅槃界, the underlying Indic terminology need not have been the same as in It 44 (quoted below in note 363); see also Hwang 2006, 32. Whereas 有餘涅槃 (with or without a reference to "an element," 界) does not seem to recur in the same discourse collection,

無餘涅槃界 can elsewhere in the *Ekottarikāgama* also refer to the attainment of full awakening; see EĀ 28.3 at T 2.125.650b26: 便於無餘涅槃界而般涅槃: 生死已盡, 梵行已立, 所作已辦, 更不復受有, 如實知之.

Notably, the same standard description of the realization of full awakening occurs also in the discourse under discussion, EĀ 16.2 at T 2.125.579a19: 生死已盡, 梵行已立, 所作已辨, 更不復受有, 如實知之, 是謂無餘涅槃界 (the quotation is based on adopting three 宋, 元, and 明 variant readings: an addition of 所作已辨 and of 復, and a deletion of 爲 before 無餘). This parallelism would support the suggestion that the sense conveyed by EĀ 28.3 would also be relevant to EĀ 16.2.

Moreover, both of the Chinese phrases under discussion (without 界) feature in another discourse collection by a different translator in what is the counterpart to the query in Sn p. 59,19: *parinibbuto nu kho me upajjhāyo udāhu no parinibbuto ti*? The corresponding query in SĀ 1221 at T 2.99.333a7 reads: 我和上爲有餘涅槃? 無餘涅槃? The distinction drawn here is about the difference between a lesser level of progress to awakening and full awakening. Since the same holds for the actual content of EĀ 16.2, it seems probable that the terms 有餘涅槃 and 無餘涅槃 in this discourse carry connotations similar to those in SĀ 1221. For this reason, EĀ 16.2 is not of direct relevance to my present discussion.

359. Masefield 1979, 224 argues that the two Nirvana elements should "be understood not as successive stages in the attainment of release of one and the same individual . . . but as mutually exclusive means by which such release was to be attained by different individuals." An argument in support of this assessment concerns the contrast made in It 44 at It 38,26 between *saupādisesā bhavanettisaṅkhayā* and *anupādisesā pana samparāyikā, yamhi nirujjhanti bhavāni sabbaso*, which Masefield 1979, 219 takes to mean that the former is more advanced, since such a person "is said to have (already) abandoned all such becomings" and thus "advanced further than one enjoying the anupādisesa nibbānadhātu who will bring all becomings entirely to cessation (only) in the future." Yet, *bhavanetti* is a synonym for *bhavataṇhā*; see, e.g., Vin I 231,5, where the two occur together to convey the same meaning. Thus, *saupādisesā bhavanettisaṅkhayā* only refers to the abandoning of craving for becoming, whereas the bringing to cessation of all becomings, *nirujjhanti bhavāni sabbaso*, is a result of having previously overcome craving for becoming. Such actual bringing to cessation of all becomings is only associated with the *anupādisesā* Nirvana element.

Another argument concerns the reference in It 44 at It 38,18 to *tassa idh' eva, bhikkhave, sabbavedayitāni anabhinanditāni sītibhavissanti* (C^e: *sītī bhavissanti*), which Masefield 1979, 221 understands to imply that "the anupādisesa nibbānadhātu involves the becoming cool of all that is felt in this very existence rather than merely at death," which is then taken to imply that "we have here . . . not two stages in the release of the same individual but rather two mutually exclusive means to the attainment of such release." A reference to all that is felt becoming cool is a standard phrase in the early discourse for expressing the ending of feeling tones with the passing away of an arahant/arhat (see also above nn. 274 and 351). This could not happen before passing away, as fully awakened ones still experience *vedanā*. This finds illustration, for example, in references to the Buddha still experiencing back pain (see above p. 115).

More errors in Masefield 1979 could be taken up. However, for my present purposes it suffices to note these two substantial misunderstandings, which already show that the proposed understanding of the two Nirvana elements is not convincing.

360. See Th 702: *mahāgini* (S^e: *mahāggini*) *pajjalito, anāhāro 'pasammati, aṅgāresu ca santesu, nibbuto ti pavuccati* and the discussion in Ñāṇananda 2015, 399–400.

361. T 17.765.678a19: 云何名爲無餘依涅槃界? 謂諸苾芻得阿羅漢, 諸漏已盡, 梵行已立, 所作已辦, 已捨重擔, 已證自義, 已盡有結, 已正解了, 已善解脫, 已得遍知. 彼於今時一切所受無引因故, 不復希望, 皆永盡滅, 畢竟寂靜, 究竟清涼, 隱沒不現. 惟由清淨無戲論體. 如是清淨無戲論體, 不可謂有, 不可謂無, 不可謂彼亦有亦無, 不可謂彼非有非無; 惟可說爲不可施設究竟涅槃. 是名無餘依涅槃界; for a translation of the whole discourse see Anālayo 2022d, 214–17. The reference to 清淨 corresponds to the terminology employed in the **Śāriputrābhidharma*, T 28.1548.697b18, counterpart to a qualification of the mind as *pabhassara* in AN 1.6.1–2 at AN I 10,10; on possible Indic originals underlying 清淨 (including *prabhāsvara*) see Hirakawa 1997, 734 and on the notion of the luminous mind Anālayo 2022e, 59–115. However, in its general usage in T 765, 清淨 regularly conveys the notion of "purity." Examples are the standard description of the fourth absorption as endowed with purity of equanimity and mindfulness, T 17.765.679b5: 捨念清淨; the indication that sentient beings are purified due to the purity of their minds, T 17.765.687c10: 心清淨故, 有情清淨; or else a reference to accomplishing purity of both bodily and verbal activities, T 17.765.691a26: 成就清淨身, 語二業. This type of usage suggests "purity" as the most appropriate translation in the present context. The same would probably hold for a comparable statement in the 佛地經論, T 26.1530.312b11: 唯有轉依無戲論相離垢真, 如清淨法界, 解脫身在, 名無餘依般涅槃界; see also the 華嚴經探玄記, T 35.1733.113c17: 無餘依涅槃界中, 唯有清淨真如法界.

362. My translation of the German version of how Wittgenstein 1922, 91 introduces his *Tractatus Logico-Philosophicus*: "Was sich überhaupt sagen lässt, lässt sich klar sagen; und wovon man nicht reden kann, darüber muss man schweigen." As noted by Jayatilleke 1963/1980, 476, at the same time the early Buddhist position needs "to be distinguished from Agnosticism. It was not that there was something that the Buddha did not know, but that what he 'knew' in the transcendent sense could not be conveyed in words because of the limitations of language."

363. It 44 at It 38,15: *katamā ca, bhikkhave, anupādisesā nibbānadhātu? idha, bhikkhave, bhikkhu arahaṃ hoti khīṇāsavo vusitavā katakaraṇīyo ohitabhāro anuppattasadattho parikkhīṇabhavasaṃyojano sammadaññā vimutto. tassa idh' eva, bhikkhave, sabbavedayitāni anabhinanditāni sītibhavissanti* (C^e: *sītī bhavissanti*). *ayaṃ vuccati, bhikkhave, anupādisesā nibbānadhātu*.

364. SĀ 200 at T 2.99.51b26: 世尊, 我已於如上所聞法, 所說法, 獨一靜處, 思惟稱量, 觀察其義; 知此諸法皆順趣涅槃, 流注涅槃, 後住涅槃; see also Anālayo 2012d and 2021d. To repeat a disclaimer made earlier in relation to the tale of Bāhiya, my presentation is not meant to imply certainty about what happened on the ground in ancient India, instead of which I simply report the viewpoint of the reciters of the texts.

365. AN 8.19 at AN IV 203,7: (also Ud 5.5 at Ud 56,2, which only mentions *ayaṃ dhammo*, and Vin II 239,30) *ayaṃ dhammavinayo ekaraso: vimuttiraso*, with parallels in MĀ 35 at T 1.26.476c11: 我正法律亦復如是, 無欲爲味, 覺味, 息味及道味, which thus lists four different tastes related to liberation, and EĀ 42.4 at T 2.125.753a28: 我法中皆同

一味, 所謂賢聖八品道味, which mentions the single taste of the noble eightfold path (and also only refers to the Dharma, similar to Ud 5.5 in this respect).

366. See Anālayo 2006b.

367. This has already been noted by, e.g., McGovern 1872/1979, 87, Stcherbatsky 1923, 20, Rhys Davids 1936/1978, 324, and Karunaratne 1988, 118.

368. Abhidh-k 1.15 first refers to the canonical indication that the fourth aggregate comprises the six types of volition, Pradhan 1967, 10,19: *bhagavatā tu sūtre ṣaṭ cetanākāyā ityuktaṃ* (the reference is to an indication found in, e.g., SN 22.57 at SN III 63,32, SĀ 42 at T 2.99.10b17, and Up 6038 at D 4094 *nyu* 21a1 or P 5595 *thu* 55b3, in which case the reference to *'du shes* appears to be a copying error from the preceding passage and should be emended to *'du byed*) but then contrasts this to *ata evoktaṃ bhagavatā: saṃskṛtam abhisaṃskaroti, tasmāt saṃskārā upādānaskandha ity ucyata iti*, in reference to the above-discussed SN 22.79 at SN III 87,8, SĀ 46 at T 2.99.11c7, and Up 1014 at D 4094 *ju* 16b3 or P 5595 *tu* 18a7 (see n. 35). Vism 462,16 quotes the same passage, *yath' āha: saṅkhatam abhisaṅkharontī ti kho, bhikkhave, tasmā saṅkhārā ti vuccantī ti*, and then provides a long list of terms that on this reasoning can supposedly be included under the fourth aggregate, including, for example, mindfulness.

Such broadening of the scope of the fourth aggregate inevitably has repercussions on the understanding of the mental qualities that are now included under it. For example, Payutto 2017, 28 argues that because mindfulness "is a volitional response to sense objects it is classified as a mental formation (*saṅkhāra*)." A problem with this explanation is that the scope of mindfulness goes beyond volitional responses to sense objects. One example is a form of practice that ranges from sense restraint to bare awareness (see above pp. 8 and 17), where the task of mindfulness is to remain generally aware of the process of experience without reacting to specific sense objects. In such form of practice, mindfulness is established first and becoming aware of a particular sense object should not lead to any additional reaction other than just remaining continuously aware in general. Another example is the presence of mindfulness during absorption attainment, a form of practice which does not fit particularly well with the idea of volitionally responding to sense objects.

It is also unclear if the idea of being "a volitional response" really works for distinguishing the fourth aggregate from the others. Take the case of a hunter who sees a deer. The *body* raises the gun with pleasant *feeling tones* of excitement at the *perception* of the awaited target and with continuous eye-*consciousness* of the deer. In this example, each of the other four aggregates is part of "a volitional response" to a sense object.

This example reflects what is in fact a key problem, in that the role of *saṅkhāra*s comes to be broadened in a way that would also accommodate the other aggregates. The discourse passage quoted by traditional exegesis in support only indicates that volitional constructions are responsible for constructing each of the five aggregates into what they are (SN 22.79, SĀ 46, and Up 1014). If this is taken to imply a broadening of the compass of the fourth aggregate to include all that is constructed, then such broadening would have to comprise the other aggregates as well. In fact, these are explicitly mentioned in this passage as being constructed, unlike mindfulness, for example, which is not mentioned. That is, it would follow that all five aggregates should be subsumed under the fourth aggregate. This of course does not work, as the analysis into five aggregates loses much of its significance in this way. In sum, turning the fourth aggregate into an umbrella category for anything constructed involves a loss of meaning that prevents clearly setting this aggregate apart from the others.

369. See in more detail Anālayo 2019.

370. Applying this grid then calls for any instance of creating a sense of identity to be analyzed with the help of the scheme of the five aggregates of clinging. Take, for example, the famous dictum by the seventeenth-century philosopher René Descartes: *cogito, ergo sum*. This does not appear to be an instance of identifying with thought as such (that is, with *vitakka/vitarka*), as that would imply that his identity vanishes as soon as the thought is over. Instead, it must refer to the ability to think as a proof of his existence. This could then be understood to correspond either to the four mental aggregates taken in conjunction or else more specifically to perception and/or volition.

371. Spk II 308,11 relates the expression *asmīti*, used in the discourse, to conceit (as well as to craving etc.).

372. SN 22.83 at SN III 105,14: *upādāya asmīti hoti, no anupādāya*, with a parallel in SĀ 261 at T 2.99.66a8: 生法計是我, 非不生 (the phrasing appears to be due to a confusion between *uppāda/utpāda* and *upādāya*). In the case of the simile, the Pāli term *upādāya* could in principle also convey the sense that the person is looking into the mirror with an attitude of clinging. However, this sense would not work so well for the *anupādāya* part, as even without an attitude of clinging one would still be able to see oneself, as long as a mirror is there. For this reason, it seems to me that the indication *sakaṃ mukhanimittaṃ paccavekkhamāno upādāya passeyya no anupādāya* can be taken to intend the reliance on the mirror in order to be able to see oneself. This sense emerges more clearly in SĀ 261 at T 2.99.66a11, where the person "holds in the hand" (手執) the mirror, and the vision of oneself occurs "because" (故) of *utpāda/uppāda* (= *upādāya*) and not without it.

373. DN 22 at DN II 310,8, arrived at by detailing, for the case of each of the six senses, the arising of craving in relation to the sense, its object, the corresponding type of consciousness, contact, feeling tone, perception, intention, craving (!), thought, and pondering; see also Anālayo 2014, 91–100 and 2022f, 140–42. Each of the resultant sixty modes comes combined with the indication *etth' esā taṇhā pahīyamānā pahīyati, ettha nirujjhamānā nirujjhati*, which implies that each should be contemplated individually as an instance of the cessation of craving.

374. On the notion of *satipaṭṭhāna/smṛtyupasthāna* as a direct path to realization see Anālayo 2022e, 199–206.

375. See Jurewicz 2000.

376. Abhidh-k 3.20, Pradhan 1967, 131,9: *avidyā saṃskārāś ca pūrvānte jātir jarāmaraṇaṃ cāparānte, śeṣāṇyaṣṭau madhye*, Vism 578,32: *avijjā saṅkhārā cā ti dve aṅgāni atītakālāni, viññāṇādīni bhavāvasānāni aṭṭha paccuppannakālāni, jāti c' eva jarāmaraṇañ ca dve anāgatakālānī ti veditabbāni.*

377. See also Anālayo 2018b, 9–17.

378. Vism 532,10.

379. Vin I 40,28: *ye dhammā hetuppabhavā, tesaṃ hetuṃ tathāgato āha, tesañ ca yo nirodho, evaṃvādī mahāsamaṇo ti*, with Indic language parallels in the *Catuṣpariṣatsūtra*, Waldschmidt 1962, 378,13: *(ye dharmā hetuprabhavās, teṣāṃ hetuṃ tathāgata ā)ha, teṣāṃ ca yo nirodha, evaṃvādī (ma)h(ā)ś(ra)maṇ(aḥ)*. The *Mahāvastu* of the Mahāsāṃghika-Lokottaravāda *Vinaya* adopts a different formulation for the case of Sāriputta/

Śāriputra, Marciniak 2019, 71,2 (see Senart 1897, 61,3): *pratītyasamutpannānāṃ dharmāṇāṃ khalv āyuṣman śāstā upādāya pratiniḥsargaṃ vijñapeti*. However, when it comes to him repeating the teaching in front of Mahāmoggallāna/Mahāmaudgalyāyana, the same stanza is employed, Marciniak 2019, 72,8 (see Senart 1897, 62,8): *ye dharmā hetuprabhavā, hetuṃ teṣāṃ tathāgato āha, teṣāñ ca yo nirodha, evaṃvādī mahāśramaṇaḥ*. For other sources see, e.g., Lamotte 1949/1981, 631, Waldschmidt 1951/1967, 198–201, Migot 1952, 426–43, and Bareau 1963, 343–47; on inscriptional references see, e.g., Skilling 2003 and 2008.

380. In line with other developments discussed here, the importance of this reference to cessation is no longer evident with the Pāli commentarial tradition's suggestion that the first two lines of the teaching were already sufficient for the breakthrough to stream-entry; Mp I 159,6 (see also Dhp-a I 92,22, Th-a III 94,23, and Ap-a 211,8): *paribbājako paṭhamaṃ padadvayam eva sutvā sahassanayasampanne sotāpattiphale patiṭṭhahi, itaraṃ padadvayaṃ sotāpannakāle niṭṭhāpesi*. Hence, it is only natural for, e.g., Ñāṇaponika and Hecker 1997, 7 to report: "Upon hearing the first two lines, there arose in the wanderer Upatissa the dust-free, stainless vision of the Dhamma—the first glimpse of the Deathless, the path of stream-entry—and to the ending of the last two lines he already listened as a stream-enterer."

    Nevertheless, it could be noted that the actual report of his stream-entry in Vin I 40,30 indicates that this happened on having heard *imaṃ dhammapariyāyaṃ*, thereby using the same phrase with which the delivery of the whole verse by Assaji has been introduced just before, Vin I 40,26: *imaṃ dhammapariyāyaṃ*. This does not give the impression that the stream-entry should be related to hearing the first half of it only. The *Vinaya* commentary then relates each line to one of the four truths, with the third line corresponding to the third truth; see Sp V 975,19. This would not fit particularly well with the idea of the first two lines on their own being sufficient for the attainment of stream-entry, as it is the third truth that stands for the breakthrough to Nirvana.

381. SN 12.10 at SN II 10,3, with parallels in Sanskrit, Chung and Fukita 2020, 88, and in SĀ 285 at T 2.99.80a1. SN 12.65 at SN II 104,13, with parallels in Sanskrit, Chung and Fukita 2020, 95, Bongard-Levin, Boucher, Fukita, and Wille 1996 (see also Or.15009/85r8, Nagashima 2009, 154, Or.15009/175rb, and 15009/191v2, Melzer 2009, 215 and 223, and Or.15009/670r6 and v1–2, Kudo and Shono 2015, 467–68) and in SĀ 287 at T 2.99.80b26, EĀ 38.4 at T 2.125.718a17, T 16.713.826b13, T 16.714.827c6, and T 16.715.829a14.

382. SN 12.4 at SN II 5,10 to SN 12.9 at SN II 9 (abbreviated), with a parallel in SĀ 366 at T 2.99.101a18; see also DN 14 at DN II 30,26, Waldschmidt 1956, 134 or Fukita 2003, 126, DĀ 1 at T 1.1.7b4, and T 1.3.155c27.

383. SĀ 200 at T 2.99.51b29: 爾時世尊觀察羅睺羅心解脫智熟, 堪任受增上法, 告羅睺羅言: 羅睺羅, 一切無常.

384. SĀ 196 at T 2.99.50a25, which points out the impermanence of the eye, forms, consciousness, contact, and the three types of feeling tones arisen in dependence on contact, an analysis then applied similarly to the other five senses. The instruction continues by depicting a learned noble disciple who contemplates like this becoming liberated from the eye, etc., and thus becoming liberated from birth, old age, death, and other manifestations of *dukkha/duḥkha*.

385. MN 147 at MN III 278,11 (see also SN 35.121 at SN IV 106,3). The same examination

is then applied to visible forms, eye-consciousness, eye-contact, and feeling tone, perception, volitional constructions, and consciousness arisen in dependence on eye-contact, followed by repeating the same for the other five senses of the ears, the nose, the tongue, the body, and the mind.

386. See in detail von Rospatt 1995; see also Anālayo 2021h, 89–90.

387. The resultant need to distinguish Nirvana from ordinary cessation appears to have led to the additional qualification that, subsequent to such a type of cessation, there is no re-arising; see, for example, the discussion in Abhidh-k 2.55, Pradhan 1967, 92,17, regarding *yadi tarhi anutpāda eva nirvāṇam idaṃ* or the comments in Paṭis-a I 55,10: *dukkhassa vā anuppattinirodhapaccayattā dukkhanirodhan ti vuccati* or Paṭis-a III 546,22: *maggassa uppādakkhaṇe yeva kilese ca khandhe ca vosajjitattā ten' eva kāraṇena kilesā ca khandhā ca anuppattinirodhavasena nirujjhanti.* Hence there arises a need for, e.g., Ledi 2004, 6, to point out that Nirvana as cessation "does not mean cessation by way of vanishing . . . it means the overcoming of appearing . . . Differentiate the cessation by way of vanishing . . . from the cessation of Nibbāna."

388. Mahāsi 1980, 51 describes how, in the course of insight meditation, a practitioner comes to realize, in relation to all aspects of experience, "that they are all impermanent. Finally all sense-objects and consciousness of these sense-objects get dissolved. At this stage [s]he can look forward to *nibbāna.*" As noted by Mahāsi 1981/1992, 101, obviously "Nibbāna cannot be seen with the naked eye. It can [however] be seen inwardly as the cessation of all phenomena." That is, when "mind, matter, and mental formations cease . . . awareness of the[ir] cessation is Nibbāna" (95).

Aggacitta 1995, 7 provides a helpful survey of different cessation experiences from the viewpoint of the Mahāsi practice lineage, several of which are not at all related to Nirvana. That is, although the breakthrough to Nirvana involves a cessation experience, an experience of cessation need not be a breakthrough to Nirvana. According to his presentation, a genuine breakthrough to Nirvana "can only occur for a maximum of four times only" (21), namely when one of the four levels of awakening is attained. However, one who has reached one of these levels may repeatedly re-enter that experience, deliberately or involuntary, although such re-entry is not as powerful as the actual attainment.

389. Sanskrit *Udānavarga* 29.31, Bernhard 1965, 381: *śunyatā cānimittaṃ ca, samādhiś caiva gocaraḥ, ākāśaiva śakuntānāṃ, padaṃ teṣāṃ duranvayam*, with Indic language counterparts in Dhp 93 (see also Th 92): *suññato animitto ca, vimokkho* (E^{e}: *vimokho*) *yassa gocaro, ākāse va sakuntānaṃ, padaṃ* (S^{e}: *padan*) *tassa durannayaṃ* and the Patna *Dharmapada* 270, Cone 1989, 267: *śuṃñatā ānimitto ca, vimogho yesa gocaro, ākāśe va śakuntānāṃ, padaṃ tesaṃ durannayaṃ.*

References

Aggacitta, Bhikkhu. 1995. *Cessation Experiences and the Notion of Enlightenment: Tentative Findings of a Preliminary Research*. Petaling Jaya: Buddhist Wisdom Centre.

Agostini, Giulio. 2010. "'Preceded by Thought Are the Dhammas': The Ancient Exegesis on Dhp 1–2." In *Buddhist Asia 2: Papers from the Second Conference of Buddhist Studies Held in Naples in June 2004*, edited by Giacomella Orofino and Silvio Vita, 1–34. Kyoto: Italian School of East Asian Studies.

Akanuma Chizen. 1929/1990. *The Comparative Catalogue of Chinese Āgamas and Pāli Nikāyas*. Delhi: Sri Satguru.

Anālayo, Bhikkhu. 2003a. "Nimitta." In *Encyclopaedia of Buddhism, Volume 7*, edited by W. G. Weeraratne, 177–79. Sri Lanka: Department of Buddhist Affairs.

———. 2003b. *Satipaṭṭhāna: The Direct Path to Realization*. Birmingham: Windhorse Publications.

———. 2005. "The Seven Stages of Purification in Comparative Perspective." *Journal of the Centre for Buddhist Studies, Sri Lanka*, 3: 126–38.

———. 2006a. "Samādhi." In *Encyclopaedia of Buddhism, Volume 7*, edited by W. G. Weeraratne, 650–55. Sri Lanka: Department of Buddhist Affairs.

———. 2006b. "Saṅkhāra." In *Encyclopaedia of Buddhism, Volume 7*, edited by W. G. Weeraratne, 732–37. Sri Lanka: Department of Buddhist Affairs.

———. 2007. "Śūnyatā." In *Encyclopaedia of Buddhism, Volume 8*, edited by W. G. Weeraratne, 194–200. Sri Lanka: Department of Buddhist Affairs.

———. 2008a. "The Sixfold Purity of an Arahant According to the

Chabbisodhana-sutta and Its Parallel." *Journal of Buddhist Ethics*, 15: 241–77.
———. 2008b. "Tuṇhībhāva." In *Encyclopaedia of Buddhism, Volume 8*, edited by W. G. Weeraratne, 372–73. Sri Lanka: Department of Buddhist Affairs.
———. 2008c. "Upādāna." In *Encyclopaedia of Buddhism, Volume 8*, edited by W. G. Weeraratne, 402–8. Sri Lanka: Department of Buddhist Affairs.
———. 2009a. "The *Āneñjasappāya-sutta* and its Parallels on Imperturbability and on the Contribution of Insight to the Development of Tranquillity." *Buddhist Studies Review*, 26.2: 177–95.
———. 2009b. "Views and the Tathāgata: A Comparative Study and Translation of the Brahmajāla in the Chinese Dīrgha-āgama." In *Buddhist and Pali Studies in Honour of the Venerable Professor Kakkapalliye Anuruddha*, edited by K. L. Dhammajoti and Y. Karunadasa, 183–234. Hong Kong: Centre of Buddhist Studies, University of Hong Kong.
———. 2009c. "Vimokkha." In *Encyclopaedia of Buddhism, Volume 8*, edited by W. G. Weeraratne, 611–13. Sri Lanka: Department of Buddhist Affairs.
———. 2009d. "Vimuttāyatana." In *Encyclopaedia of Buddhism, Volume 8*, edited by W. G. Weeraratne, 613–15. Sri Lanka: Department of Buddhist Affairs.
———. 2009e. "Vimutti." In *Encyclopaedia of Buddhism, Volume 8*, edited by W. G. Weeraratne, 615–22. Sri Lanka: Department of Buddhist Affairs.
———. 2009f. "Yoniso manasikāra." In *Encyclopaedia of Buddhism, Volume 8*, edited by W. G. Weeraratne, 809–15. Sri Lanka: Department of Buddhist Affairs.
———. 2010a. "Channa's Suicide in the *Saṃyukta-āgama*." *Buddhist Studies Review*, 27.2: 125–37.
———. 2010b. *The Genesis of the Bodhisattva Ideal.* Hamburg: Hamburg University Press.
———. 2011a. "Brahmā's Invitation: The Ariyapariyesanā-sutta in the

Light of its Madhyama-āgama Parallel." *Journal of the Oxford Centre for Buddhist Studies*, 1: 12–38.

———. 2011b. *A Comparative Study of the Majjhima-nikāya*. Taipei: Dharma Drum Publishing Corporation.

———. 2011c. "Right View and the Scheme of the Four Truths in Early Buddhism: The Saṃyukta-āgama Parallel to the Sammādiṭṭhi-sutta and the Simile of the Four Skills of a Physician." *Canadian Journal of Buddhist Studies*, 7: 11–44.

———. 2011d. "Vakkali's Suicide in the Chinese Āgamas." *Buddhist Studies Review*, 28.2: 155–70.

———. 2012a. "The Chinese Parallels to the Dhammacakkappavattana-sutta (1)." *Journal of the Oxford Centre for Buddhist Studies*, 3: 12–46.

———. 2012b. "Dabba's Self-Cremation in the Saṃyukta-āgama." *Buddhist Studies Review*, 29.2: 153–74.

———. 2012c. "A Gradual Entry into Emptiness: Depicted in the Early Buddhist Discourses." *Thai International Journal of Buddhist Studies*, 3: 25–56.

———. 2012d. "Teaching and Liberation: Rāhula's Awakening in the Saṃyukta-āgama." In *Dharmapravicaya, Aspects of Buddhist Studies, Essays in Honour of N. H. Samtani*, edited by Lalji Shravak and Charles Willemen, 1–21. Delhi: Buddhist World Press.

———. 2013a. "The Chinese Parallels to the Dhammacakkappavattana-sutta (2)." *Journal of the Oxford Centre for Buddhist Studies*, 5: 9–41.

———. 2013b. "Mahāyāna in the Ekottarika-āgama." *Singaporean Journal of Buddhist Studies*, 1: 5–43.

———. 2013c. *Perspectives on Satipaṭṭhāna*. Cambridge: Windhorse Publications.

———. 2014. *The Dawn of Abhidharma*. Hamburg: Hamburg University Press.

———. 2015. *Compassion and Emptiness in Early Buddhist Meditation*. Cambridge: Windhorse Publications.

———. 2016. *Mindfully Facing Disease and Death: Compassionate Advice from Early Buddhist Texts*. Cambridge: Windhorse Publications.

———. 2017a. "The Luminous Mind in Theravāda and Dharmaguptaka

Discourses." *Journal of the Oxford Centre for Buddhist Studies*, 13: 10–51.
———. 2017b. *A Meditator's Life of the Buddha: Based on the Early Discourses*. Cambridge: Windhorse Publications.
———. 2018a. "The Bāhiya Instruction and Bare Awareness." *Indian International Journal of Buddhist Studies*, 19: 1–19.
———. 2018b. *Rebirth in Early Buddhism and Current Research*. Somerville, MA: Wisdom Publications.
———. 2018c. *Satipaṭṭhāna Meditation: A Practice Guide*. Cambridge: Windhorse Publications.
———. 2019. "How Mindfulness Came to Plunge into Its Objects." *Mindfulness*, 10.6: 1181–85.
———. 2020a. "Attention and Mindfulness." *Mindfulness*, 11.5: 1131–38.
———. 2020b. "A Brief History of Buddhist Absorption." *Mindfulness*, 11.3: 571–86.
———. 2020c. "The Five 'Fingers' of Name." *Insight Journal*, 46: 27–36.
———. 2020d. *Mindfulness in Early Buddhism: Characteristics and Functions*. Cambridge: Windhorse Publications.
———. 2020/2022. "The Qualities Pertinent to Awakening: Bringing Mindfulness Home." *Mindfulness*, 13.12: 2979–96.
———. 2021a. "Awakening or Enlightenment? On the Significance of *Bodhi*." *Mindfulness*, 12.7: 1653–58.
———. 2021b. "The Buddha's Awakening." *Mindfulness*, 12.9: 2141–48.
———. 2021c. "The Buddha's Pre-awakening Practices and Their Mindful Transformation." *Mindfulness*, 12.8: 1892–98.
———. 2021d. "The Buddha and His Son." *Mindfulness*, 12.2: 269–74.
———. 2021e. "Dimensions of the 'Body' in Tranquility Meditation." *Mindfulness*, 12.10: 2388–93.
———. 2021f. "Hearing, Reflection, and Cultivation: Relating the Three Types of Wisdom to Mindfulness." *Religion*, 21.441: 1–12.
———. 2021g. "An Inspired Utterance on Annihilation." *Sri Lanka International Journal of Buddhist Studies*, 7.1: 1–13.
———. 2021h. *Superiority Conceit in Buddhist Traditions: A Historical Perspective*. Somerville, MA: Wisdom Publications.
———. 2022a. "Abbreviation in the Ekottarika-āgama." *Annual Report of*

the International Research Institute for Advanced Buddhology at Soka University, 25: 61–71.

———. 2022b. "Being Mindful of What is Absent." *Mindfulness*, 13.7: 1671–78.

———. 2022c. "Beyond the Limitations of Binary Thinking: Mindfulness and the Tetralemma." *Mindfulness*, 13.6: 1410–17.

———. 2022d. *Daughters of the Buddha: Teachings by Ancient Indian Women*. Somerville, MA: Wisdom Publications.

———. 2022e. *Developments in Buddhist Meditation Traditions: The Interplay between Theory and Practice*. Barre: Barre Center for Buddhist Studies.

———. 2022f. *Early Buddhist Oral Tradition: Textual Formation and Transmission*. Somerville, MA: Wisdom Publications.

———. 2022g: "Nonduality in Early Buddhist Thought." In *Encyclopedia of Mindfulness, Buddhism, and Other Contemplative Practices*, edited by Nirbhay N. Singh. Cham: Springer. https://doi.org/10.1007/978-3-030-90465-4_75-1.

———. 2022h: "The Role of Absorption for Entering the Stream." *Journal of Buddhist Studies*, 19: 1–34.

———. 2022i: "Situating Mindfulness, Part 2: Early Buddhist Soteriology." *Mindfulness*, 13.4: 855–62.

———. 2023: "The Function of Silence in Āgama Literature." *Annual Report of the International Research Institute for Advanced Buddhology at Soka University*, 26: 67–76.

Bapat, P. V. 1945. "The Arthapada-Sūtra Spoken by the Buddha." *Visva-Bharati Annals*, 1: 135–227.

Bareau, André. 1963. *Recherches sur la Biographie du Buddha dans les Sūtrapiṭaka et les Vinayapiṭaka Anciens: De la Quête de l'Éveil a la Conversion de Śāriputra et de Maudgalyāyana*. Paris: École Française d'Extrême-Orient.

Bechert, Heinz and Klaus Wille. 1989. *Sanskrithandschriften aus den Turfanfunden, Teil 6*. Stuttgart: Franz Steiner.

———. 1995. *Sanskrithandschriften aus den Turfanfunden, Teil 7*. Stuttgart: Franz Steiner.

Beckh, Hermann. 1911. *Udānavarga, Eine Sammlung Buddhistischer*

Sprüche in Tibetischer Sprache, Nach dem Kanjur und Tanjur mit Anmerkungen Herausgegeben. Berlin: Reimer.

Belvalkar, Shripad Krishna. 1954a. *The Śāntiparvan, Part 3: Mokṣadharma, A; Being the Twelfth Book of the Mahābhārata, The Great Epic of India*. Poona: Bhandarkar Oriental Research Institute.

———. 1954b. *The Śāntiparvan, Part 3: Mokṣadharma, B; Being the Twelfth Book of the Mahābhārata, The Great Epic of India*. Poona: Bhandarkar Oriental Research Institute.

Bernhard, Franz. 1965. *Udānavarga, Band 1*. Göttingen: Vandenhoeck & Ruprecht.

Bodhi, Bhikkhu. 2000. *The Connected Discourses of the Buddha: A New Translation of the Saṃyutta Nikāya*. Somerville, MA: Wisdom Publications.

———. 2002. "The Jhānas and the Lay Disciple." In *Buddhist Studies, Essays in Honour of Professor Lily de Silva*, edited by P. D. Premasiri, 36–64. Sri Lanka: University of Peradeniya, Department of Pali and Buddhist Studies.

———. 2003. "Musīla and Nārada Revisited: Seeking the Key to Interpretation." In *Approaching the Dhamma: Buddhist Texts and Practice in South and Southeast Asia*, edited by Ann M. Blackburn and Jeffrey Samuels, 47–68. Seattle: Pariyatti Editions.

———. 2011. "What does Mindfulness Really Mean? A Canonical Perspective." *Contemporary Buddhism*, 12.1: 19–39.

———. 2012. *The Numerical Discourses of the Buddha: A Translation of the Aṅguttara Nikāya*. Somerville, MA: Wisdom Publications.

———. 2017. *The Suttanipāta: An Ancient Collection of the Buddha's Discourses, Together with Its Commentaries—Paramatthajotikā II and Excerpts from the Niddesa*. Somerville, MA: Wisdom Publications.

———. 2020. "On Translating 'Buddha.'" *Journal of the Oxford Centre for Buddhist Studies*, 19: 52–78.

Bongard-Levin, Grigorij Maksimovic, Daniel Boucher, Takamichi Fukita, and Klaus Wille. 1996. "The Nagaropamasūtra: An Apotropaic Text from the Saṃyuktāgama, A Transliteration, Reconstruction, and Translation of the Central Asian Sanskrit Manuscripts." In

Sanskrit-Texte aus dem buddhistischen Kanon, Folge 3, 7–103. Göttingen: Vandenhoeck & Ruprecht.

Brahmāli, Bhikkhu. 2009. "What the Nikāyas Say and Do Not Say about Nibbāna." *Buddhist Studies Review*, 26.1: 33–66.

Brough, John. 1962/2001. *The Gāndhārī Dharmapada: Edited with an Introduction and Commentary*. Delhi: Motilal Banarsidass.

Burford, Grace G. 1991. *Desire, Death, and Goodness: The Conflict of Ultimate Values in Theravāda Buddhism*. New York: Peter Lang.

Burns, Douglas M. 1967. *Nirvana, Nihilism and Satori*. Bangkok: World Fellowship of Buddhists.

Childers, Robert Caesar. 1875/1993. *A Dictionary of the Pali Language*. New Delhi: Asian Educational Services.

Chung Jin-il. 2008. *A Survey of the Sanskrit Fragments Corresponding to the Chinese Saṃyuktāgama*. Tokyo: Sankibo.

Chung Jin-il and Fukita Takamichi. 2020. *A New Edition of the First 25 Sūtras of the Nidānasaṃyukta*. Tokyo: Sankibo Press.

Collett, Alice. 2019. "Nirvāṇa in Early Buddhist Inscriptions." *Buddhist Studies Review*, 36.2: 221–47.

Collins, Steven. 1982. *Selfless Persons: Imagery and Thought in Theravāda Buddhism*. Cambridge: Cambridge University Press.

———. 1992. "Notes on Some Oral Aspects of Pali Literature." *Indo-Iranian Journal*, 35: 121–35.

———. 1993. "The Discourse on What is Primary (Aggañña-Sutta): An Annotated Translation." *Journal of Indian Philosophy*, 21: 301–93.

———. 1998. *Nirvana and Other Buddhist Felicities: Utopias of the Pali Imaginaire*. Cambridge: Cambridge University Press.

Cone, Margaret. 1989. "Patna Dharmapada." *Journal of the Pali Text Society*, 13: 101–217.

———. 2010. *A Dictionary of Pāli, Part II, G–N*. Bristol: Pali Text Society.

Conze, Edward. 1962. *Buddhist Thought in India: Three Phases of Buddhist Philosophy*. London: George Allen & Unwin.

Cousins, L. S. 1983. "Nibbāna and Abhidhamma." *Buddhist Studies Review*, 1.2: 95–109.

de La Vallée Poussin, Louis. 1917. "Nirvāṇa." In *Encyclopædia of Religion and Ethics, Volume IX, Mundas–Phrygians*, edited by James Hastings, 376–79. New York: Charles Scribner's Sons.

de Silva, Lily. 1987. "Nibbāna as Experience." *Sri Lanka Journal of Buddhist Studies*, 1: 29–50.

Delhey, Martin. 2009. *Samāhitā Bhūmiḥ: das Kapitel über die meditative Versenkung im Grundteil der Yogācārabhūmi*. Wien: Arbeitskreis für Tibetische und Buddhistische Studien, Universität Wien.

Dhammadinnā, Bhikkhunī. 2021. "Reflections on Truth and Experience in Early Buddhist Epistemology." In *Buddhism in Dialogue with Contemporary Societies*, edited by Carola Roloff, Wolfram Weiße, and Michael Zimmermann, 101–33. New York: Waxmann.

DiSimone, Charles. 2020. *Faith in the Teacher: The Prāsādika and Prasādanīya Sūtras from the (Mūla-)Sarvāstivāda Dīrghāgama Manuscript: A Synoptic Critical Edition, Translation, and Textual Analysis*. PhD thesis (revised), Ludwig-Maximilians-Universität, München.

Dutt, Nalinaksha. 1984. *Gilgit Manuscripts: Mūlasarvāstivāda Vinayavastu, Vol. III, Part 2*. Delhi: Sri Satguru.

Eimer, Helmut. 1983. *Rab tu 'byuṅ ba'i gźi. Die tibetische Übersetzung des Pravrajyāvastu im Vinaya der Mūlasarvāstivādins, 2. Teil: Text*. Wiesbaden: Otto Harrassowitz.

Enomoto Fumio. 1989. "Śarīrārthagāthā: A Collection of Canonical Verses in the Yogācārabhūmi." In *Sanskrit-Texte aus dem Buddhistischen Kanon: Neuentdeckungen und Neueditionen, Folge 1*, edited by Enomoto Fumio, Jens-Uwe Hartmann, and H. Matsumura, 17–35. Göttingen: Vandenhoeck & Ruprecht,

———. 1994. *A Comprehensive Study of the Chinese Saṃyuktāgama; Part 1: Saṃgītinipāta*. Kyoto: Kacho Junior College.

Feldman Barret, Lisa. 2017. *How Emotions are Made: The Secret Life of the Brain*. Boston: Mariner Books.

Fink, Charles K. 2015. "Clinging to Nothing: The Phenomenology and Metaphysics of Upādāna in Early Buddhism." *Asian Philosophy*, 25.1: 15–33.

Fukita Takamichi. 2003. *The Mahāvadānasūtra: A New Edition Based on Manuscripts Discovered in Northern Turkestan*. Göttingen: Vandenhoeck & Ruprecht.

———. 2009. "The Sanskrit Fragments Or. 15009/301–350 in the Hoernle Collection." In *Buddhist Manuscripts from Central Asia: The British Library Sanskrit Fragments, Volume II.1*, edited by Karashima Seishi and Klaus Wille, 298–330. Tokyo: International Research Institute for Advanced Buddhology, Soka University.

Gethin, Rupert. 1998. *The Foundations of Buddhism.* Oxford: Oxford University Press.

Gnoli, Raniero. 1977. *The Gilgit Manuscript of the Saṅghabhedavastu: Being the 17th and Last Section of the Vinaya of the Mūlasarvāstivādin, Part I.* Rome: Istituto Italiano per il Medio ed Estremo Oriente.

———. 1978. *The Gilgit Manuscript of the Saṅghabhedavastu: Being the 17th and Last Section of the Vinaya of the Mūlasarvāstivādin, Part II.* Rome: Istituto Italiano per il Medio ed Estremo Oriente.

Gokhale, Pradeep P. 2020. *The Yogasūtra of Patañjali: A New Introduction to the Buddhist Roots of the Yoga System.* London: Routledge.

Gombrich, Richard F. 1996. *How Buddhism Began: The Conditioned Genesis of the Early Teachings.* London: Athlone.

———. 2009. *What the Buddha Thought.* London: Equinox.

Gómez, Luis O. 1976. "Proto-Mādhyamika in the Pāli Canon?" *Philosophy East and West*, 26.2: 137–65.

———. 2004. "Nirvāṇa." In *Encyclopedia of Buddhism*, edited by Robert E. Buswell, 600–605. New York: Macmillan.

Grassman, Hermann. 1955. *Wörterbuch zum Rig-Veda.* Wiesbaden: Otto Harrassowitz.

Griffiths, Paul J. 1983: "Buddhist Jhāna: A Form-Critical Study." *Religion*, 13: 55–68.

———. 1986/1991. *On Being Mindless: Buddhist Meditation and the Mind–Body Problem.* Illinois, La Salle: Open Court.

Hamilton, Sue. 2000. *Early Buddhism: A New Approach, The I of the Beholder.* Richmond: Curzon.

Hartmann, Jens-Uwe. 1991. *Untersuchungen zum Dīrghāgama der Sarvāstivādins.* Habilitation thesis (unpublished), Göttingen: Georg-August-Universität.

Harvey, Peter. 1983. "The Nature of the Tathāgata." In *Buddhist Studies:*

Ancient and Modern, edited by Philip Denwood and Alexander Piatigorsky, 35–52. London: Curzon.

———. 1986. "'Signless' Meditations in Pāli Buddhism." *Journal of the International Association of Buddhist Studies*, 9.1: 25–52.

———. 1995. *The Selfless Mind: Personality, Consciousness and Nirvāṇa in Early Buddhism*. Richmond Surrey: Curzon.

———. 2003. "The Ennobling Realities of Pain and its Origin: Reflections on the First Two Ariyasaccas and Their Translations." In *Praṇāmalekhā, Essays in Honour of Ven. Dr. Medagama Vajiragnana*, edited by Ven. Wilaoye Wimalajothi, Ven. Mawatagama Pemananda, Ven. Udahawara Ananda, and Sanath Nanayakkara, 305–21. London: Buddhist Vihara.

———. 2009. "The Four Ariya-saccas as 'True Realities for the Spiritually Ennobled'—the Painful, its Origin, its Cessation, and the Way Going to This—Rather than 'Noble Truths' Concerning These." *Buddhist Studies Review*, 26.2: 197–227.

Higgins, David. 2006/2008. "On the Development of the Non-mentation (*Amanasikāra*) Doctrine in Indo-Tibetan Buddhism." *Journal of the International Association of Buddhist Studies*, 29.2: 255–303.

Hirakawa Akira. 1997. *Buddhist Chinese–Sanskrit Dictionary*. Tokyo: Reiyukai.

Hoernle, A. F. Rudolf. 1916. *Manuscript Remains of Buddhist Literature Found in Eastern Turkestan*. Oxford: Clarendon Press.

Horner, I. B. 1951/1982. *The Book of the Discipline (Vinaya-Piṭaka), Volume IV (Mahāvagga)*. London: Pali Text Society.

Hwang Soonil. 2006. *Metaphor and Literalism in Buddhism: The Doctrinal History of Nirvana*. London: Routledge.

Ireland, John D. 1990. *The Udāna: Inspired Utterances of the Buddha*. Kandy: Buddhist Publication Society.

Jantrasrisalai, Chanida, Timothy Lenz, Lin Qian, and Richard Salomon. 2016. "Fragments of an Ekottarikāgama Manuscript in Gāndhārī." In *Manuscripts in the Schøyen Collection: Buddhist Manuscripts, Volume IV*, edited by Jens Braarvig, 1–122. Oslo: Hermes Publishing.

Jayatilleke, K. N. 1963/1980. *Early Buddhist Theory of Knowledge*. Delhi: Motilal Banarsidass.

Johansson, Rune E. A. 1969. *The Psychology of Nirvana*. London: George Allen and Unwin.

Jotikarāma Sayādaw, Pyay (Bhaddanta Tejaniyābhivaṃsa). 1995. *Enlightenment on Nibbāna (Nibbānajotika)*. Translated by Tin Shwe. Yangon: Daw Zin Myint Maung.

Jurewicz, Joanna. 2000. "Playing with Fire: The *Pratītyasamutpāda* from the Perspective of Vedic Thought." *Journal of the Pali Text Society*, 26: 77–103.

Kabat-Zinn, Jon. 1990/2013. *Full Catastrophe Living: Using the Wisdom of Your Body and Mind to Face Stress, Pain, and Illness*. New York: Bantam Books.

Karunadasa, Y. 1991. "The Buddhist Critique of Ātmavāda and the Buddhist Ideal of Nibbāna." In *Studies in Buddhism and Culture in Honour of Professor Dr. Egaku Mayeda on His Sixty-Fifth Birthday*, edited by the Editorial Committee of the Felicitation Volume for Professor Dr. Egaku Mayeda, 49–67. Tokyo: Sankibo Busshorin.

———. 1994. "Nibbanic Experience: A Non-transcendental Interpretation." *Sri Lanka Journal of Buddhist Studies*, 4: 1–13.

Karunaratne, W. S. 1988. *Buddhism: Its Religion and Philosophy*. Singapore: Buddhist Research Society.

Kuan Tse-fu. 2020. "Conscious of Everything or Consciousness Without Objects? A Paradox of Nirvana." *Journal of Indian Philosophy*, 48: 329–51.

Kudo Noriyuki and Shono Masanori. 2015. "The Sanskrit Fragments Or. 15009/601–678 in the Hoernle Collection." In *Buddhist Manuscripts from Central Asia: The British Library Sanskrit Fragments, Volume III.1*, edited by Karashima Seishi, Nagashima Jundo, and Klaus Wille, 419–74. Tokyo: International Research Institute for Advanced Buddhology, Soka University.

Kumoi Shōzen. 1969. "Der Nirvāṇa-Begriff in den kanonischen Texten des Frühbuddhismus." *Wiener Zeitschrift für die Kunde Südasiens*, 12/13: 205–13.

Lamotte, Étienne. 1936. "Le Traité de l'Acte de Vasubandhu, Karmasiddhiprakaraṇa, Traduction, versions tibétaine et chinoise, avec un introduction et, en appendice, la traduction du chapitre xvii de la Madhyamakavṛtti." *Mélanges Chinois et Bouddhiques publiés par l'Institut Belge des Hautes Études Chinoises*, 4: 151–263.

———. 1944/1981. *Le traité de la grande vertu de sagesse de Nāgārjuna (Mahāprajñāpāramitāśāstra), Tome I.* Louvain-la-Neuve: Institut Orientaliste.

———. 1949/1981. *Le traité de la grande vertu de sagesse de Nāgārjuna (Mahāprajñāpāramitāśāstra), Tome II.* Louvain-la-Neuve: Institut Orientaliste.

Lefmann, S. 1902. *Lalita Vistara: Leben und Lehre des Çâkya-Buddha, Textausgabe mit Varianten-, Metren- und Wörterverzeichnis.* Halle: Verlag der Buchhandlung des Waisenhauses.

Ledi Sayādaw. 2004. *Nibbāna Dīpanī: The Manual of Nibbāna.* Translated by U Chit Tin. Yangon: Ministry of Religious Affairs.

Lenz, Timothy. 2003. *A New Version of the Gāndhārī Dharmapada and a Collection of Previous-Birth Stories: British Library Kharoṣṭhī Fragments 16 + 25.* Seattle: University of Washington Press.

Lin Qian. 2022. "On the Early Buddhist Attitude toward Metaphysics." *Journal of Indian Philosophy*, 50: 143–62.

Mahāsi Sayādaw. 1980. *To Nibbāna via the Noble Eightfold Path.* Translated by U Htin Fatt (Maung Htin). Rangoon: Buddha Sāsanā Nuggaha Organization.

———. 1981/1992. *On the Nature of Nibbāna (Nibbānapaṭisaṃyutta Kathā).* Translated by U Htin Fatt (Maung Htin). Selangor: Subang Jaya Buddhist Association.

Marciniak, Katarzyna. 2019. *The Mahāvastu: A New Edition, Vol. III.* Tokyo: International Research Institute for Advanced Buddhology at Soka University.

———. 2020. *The Mahāvastu: A New Edition, Vol. II.* Tokyo: International Research Institute for Advanced Buddhology at Soka University.

Masefield, Peter. 1979. "The Nibbāna-Parinibbāna Controversy." *Religion*, 9: 215–30.

Mathes, Klaus-Dieter. 2008. "Maitrīpa's Amanasikārādhāra ('A Justification of Becoming Mentally Disengaged')." *Journal of the Nepal Research Center*, 13: 1–30.

Matsumura Hisashi. 1985. "頼吒和羅経の展開の一断面." *Bukkyō Kenkyū*, 15: 39–62.

McGovern, William Montgomery. 1872/1979. *A Manual of Buddhist Philosophy*. Delhi: Nag Publishers.

Melzer, Gudrun. 2009. "The Sanskrit Fragments Or. 15009/151–200 in the Hoernle Collection." In *Buddhist Manuscripts from Central Asia: The British Library Sanskrit Fragments, Volume II.1*, edited by Karashima Seishi and Klaus Wille, 199–226. Tokyo: International Research Institute for Advanced Buddhology, Soka University.

Migot, André. 1952. "Un grand disciple du Buddha, Śāriputra, son rôle dans l'histoire du Bouddhisme et dans le développement de l'Abhidharma." *Bulletin de l'École Française d'Extrême Orient*, 46: 405–554.

Mittal, Kusum. 1957. *Dogmatische Begriffsreihen im älteren Buddhismus, I, Fragmente des Daśottarasūtra aus zentralasiatischen Sanskrit-Handschriften*. Berlin: Akademie Verlag.

Nagashima Jundo. 2009. "The Sanskrit Fragments Or. 15009/51–90 in the Hoernle Collection." In *Buddhist Manuscripts from Central Asia: The British Library Sanskrit Fragments, Volume II.1*, edited by Karashima Seishi and Klaus Wille, 128–59. Tokyo: International Research Institute for Advanced Buddhology, Soka University.

———. 2015. "The Sanskrit Fragments Or. 15009/501–600 in the Hoernle Collection." In *Buddhist Manuscripts from Central Asia: The British Library Sanskrit Fragments, Volume III.1*, edited by Karashima Seishi, Nagashima Jundo, and Klaus Wille, 347–418. Tokyo: International Research Institute for Advanced Buddhology, Soka University.

Ñāṇamoli, Bhikkhu. 1982. *The Path of Discrimination (Paṭisambhidāmagga)*. London: Pali Text Society.

———. 1956/1991. *The Path of Purification (Visuddhimagga) by Bhadantācariya Buddhaghosa*. Kandy: Buddhist Publication Society.

———. 1995/2005. *The Middle Length Discourses of the Buddha: A Translation of the Majjhima Nikāya*, edited by Bhikkhu Bodhi. Somerville: Wisdom Publications.

Ñāṇananda, Bhikkhu K. 1971/1986. *Concept and Reality in Early*

Buddhist Thought, An Essay on "Papañca" and "Papañca-Saññā-Saṅkhā." Kandy: Buddhist Publication Society.

——— 1974/1985. *The Magic of the Mind.* Kandy: Buddhist Publication Society.

———2015. *Nibbāna—the Mind Stilled, (Volumes 1–7). Library Edition. (The Nibbāna Sermons 1–33).* Sri Lanka, Mādhya Bhāraya: Pothgulgala Dharmagrantha Dharmasravana.

——— 2016. *The Law of Dependent Arising (Paṭicca Samuppāda): The Secret of Bondage and Release. Library Edition.* Sri Lanka: Kaṭukurunde Ñāṇananda Sadaham Senasun Bhāraya.

Ñāṇaponika, Thera. 1962/1992. *The Heart of Buddhist Meditation.* Kandy: Buddhist Publication Society.

———. 1968/1986. *The Power of Mindfulness.* Kandy: Buddhist Publication Society.

———. 1977. *Sutta-nipāta: Früh-buddhistische Lehr-Dichtungen aus dem Pali-Kanon, mit Auszügen aus den alten Kommentaren, übersetzt, eingeleitet, und erläutert.* Konstanz: Verlag Christiani.

Ñāṇaponika, Thera and Hellmuth Hecker. 1997. *Great Disciples of the Buddha: Their Lives, Their Works, Their Legacy.* Kandy: Buddhist Publication Society.

Narada Thera. 1987. *The Way to Nibbana.* Kuala Lumpur: Buddhist Missionary Society.

Norman, K. R. 1969. *The Elder's Verses I: Theragāthā, Translated with an Introduction and Notes.* London: Pali Text Society.

———. 1991. "Theravāda Buddhism and Brahmanical Hinduism: Brahmanical Terms in a Buddhist Guise." In *The Buddhist Forum II, Seminar Papers 1988–90*, edited by Tadeusz Skorupski, 193–200. London: School of Oriental and African Studies.

———. 1994. "Mistaken Ideas about Nibbāna." In *The Buddhist Forum III 1991–1993: Papers in Honour and Appreciation of Professor David Seyford Ruegg's Contribution to Indological, Buddhist and Tibetan Studies*, edited by Tadeusz Skorupski and Ulrich Pagel, 211–25, London: School of Oriental and African Studies.

———. 1997/2004. *The Word of the Doctrine (Dhammapada).* Oxford: Pali Text Society.

———. 2003. "The Aṭṭhakavagga and Early Buddhism." In *Jainism and Early Buddhism: Essays in Honor of Padmanabh S. Jaini*, edited by Olle Qvarnström, 512–22. Fremont: Asian Humanities Press.

Oldenberg, Hermann. 1881/1961. *Buddha: Sein Leben, Seine Lehre, Seine Gemeinde*. München: Wilhelm Goldmann Verlag.

Olivelle, Patrick. 1997. "Amṛtā: Women and Indian Technologies of Immortality." *Journal of Indian Philosophy*, 25.5: 427–49.

Palihawadana, Mahinda. 1984. "Dhammapada 1 and 2 and Their Commentaries." In *Buddhist Studies in Honor of Hammalava Saddhatissa*, edited by Gatare Dhammapāla, Richard Gombrich, and K. R. Norman, 189–202. Nugegoda: University of Jayewardenepura.

Pande, Govind Chandra. 1957. *Studies in the Origins of Buddhism*. Allahabad: University of Allahabad, Department of Ancient History, Culture and Archeology.

Park Jungnok. 2012. *How Buddhism Acquired a Soul on the Way to China*. Sheffield: Equinox Publishing.

Pāsādika, Bhikkhu. 2017. "Ancient and Modern Interpretations of the Pañcavimuttāyatana." *Journal of the Centre for Buddhist Studies, Sri Lanka*, 14: 139–47.

Pasanno, Ajahn and Ajahn Amaro. 2009. *The Island: An Anthology of the Buddha's Teachings on Nibbāna*. Redwood Valley, CA: Abhayagiri Monastic Foundation.

Payutto, Bhikkhu P. A. (Somdet Phra Buddhaghosacariya). 2017. *Buddhadhamma: The Laws of Nature and Their Benefits to Life*. Translated by Robin Philip Moore. Bangkok: Buddhadhamma Foundation.

Pérez-Rémon, Joaquín. 1980. *Self and Non-self in Early Buddhism*. The Hague: Mouton Publishers.

Pischel, Richard. 1904. "Bruchstücke des Sanskritkanons der Buddhisten aus Idyuktšari Chinesisch-Turkestān." *Sitzungsbericht der Königlich Preussischen Akademie der Wissenschaften, Berlin*, 25: 807–27.

Pontillo, Tiziana and Chiara Neri. 2016. "The Meaning of the Phrase 'To Become Brahman-' in Vedic and Sutta Piṭaka Sources." In *Vrātya Culture in Vedic Sources: Selected Papers from the Panel on 'Vrātya Culture in Vedic Sources' at the 16th World Sanskrit Conference (28 June–2 July*

2015) Bangkok, Thailand, edited by Tiziana Pontillo, Moreno Dore, and Hans Henrich Hock, 117–57. New Delhi: DK Publishers.

———. 2019. "The Case of *Yogakṣema/Yogakkhema* in Vedic and Suttapiṭaka Sources. In Response to Norman." *Journal of Indian Philosophy*, 47: 527–63.

Pradhan, P. 1967. *Abhidharmakośabhāṣya of Vasubandhu*. Patna: K.P. Jayaswal Research Institute.

Premasiri, P. D. 1972. *The Philosophy of the Aṭṭhakavagga*. Kandy: Buddhist Publication Society.

Radhakrishnan, S. 1953/1992. *The Principal Upaniṣads: Edited with Introduction, Text, Translation and Notes*. New York: Humanity Books.

Rhys Davids, T. W. and W. Stede. 1921/1993. *Pali–English Dictionary*. Delhi: Motilal Banarsidass.

Rhys Davids C. A. F. 1936/1978. *The Birth of Indian Psychology and its Development in Buddhism*. Delhi: Oriental Books.

Robinson, Richard H. 1972. "Some Methodological Approaches to the Unexplained Points." *Philosophy East and West*, 22.3: 309–23.

Ronkin, Noa. 2005. *Early Buddhist Metaphysics: The Making of a Philosophical Tradition*. London: Routledge Curzon.

Sander, Lore and Ernst Waldschmidt. 1980. *Sanskrithandschriften aus den Turfanfunden, Teil IV*. Wiesbaden: Franz Steiner.

———. 1985. *Sanskrithandschriften aus den Turfanfunden, Teil 5*. Wiesbaden: Franz Steiner.

Schlingloff, Dieter. 1962. *Dogmatische Begriffsreihen im älteren Buddhismus. Ia: Daśottarasūtra IX–X*. Berlin: Akademie Verlag.

Schmithausen, Lambert. 1969a. *Der Nirvāṇa-Abschnitt in der Viniścayasaṃgrahaṇī der Yogācārabhūmiḥ*. Wien: Kommissionsverlag der Österreichische Akademie der Wissenschaften.

———. 1969b. "Ich und Erlösung im Buddhismus." *Zeitschrift für Missionswissenschaft und Religionswissenschaft*, 53: 157–70.

———. 1970. "Zu den Rezensionen des Udānavargaḥ." *Wiener Zeitschrift für die Kunde Südasiens*, 14: 47–124.

———. 1981. "On some Aspects of Descriptions or Theories of 'Liberating Insight' and 'Enlightenment' in Early Buddhism." In *Studien zum Jainismus und Buddhismus, Gedenkschrift für Ludwig Alsdorf*, edited by Klaus Bruhn and Albert Wezler, 199–250. Wiesbaden: Franz Steiner.

———. 1987/2007. *Ālayavijñāna: On the Origin and the Early Development of a Central Concept of Yogācāra Philosophy*. Tokyo: The International Institute for Buddhist Studies.

———. 2000. "Ātman und Nirvāṇa im frühen Buddhismus." *Buddhismus in Geschichte und Gegenwart*, 4: 1–16.

Schopenhauer, Arthur. 1888. *Die Welt als Wille und Vorstellung: Siebente Auflage, herausgegeben von Julius Frauenstädt, zweiter Band, welcher die Ergänzungen zu den vier Büchern des ersten Bandes enthält*. Leipzig: F. A. Brockhaus.

Schrader, Otto F. 1905. "On the Problem of Nirvāṇa." *Journal of the Pali Text Society*, 5: 157–70.

Senart, Émile. 1882. *Le Mahāvastu: Texte sanscrit publié pour la première fois et accompagné d'introductions et d'un commentaire, Tome premier*. Paris: Imprimerie Nationale.

———. 1890. *Le Mahāvastu: Texte sanscrit publié pour la première fois et accompagné d'introductions et d'un commentaire, Tome deuxième*. Paris: Imprimerie Nationale.

———. 1897. *Le Mahāvastu: Texte sanscrit publié pour la première fois et accompagné d'introductions et d'un commentaire, Tome troisième*. Paris: Imprimerie Nationale.

———. 1903. "Nirvāṇa." In *Album-Kern: Opstellen Geschreven ter eere van Dr. H. Kern*, 101–4. Leiden: E. J. Brill.

Sharf, Robert H. 2014. "Is Nirvāṇa the Same as Insentience? Chinese Struggles with an Indian Buddhist Ideal." In *India in the Chinese Imagination: Myth, Religion, and Thought*, edited by John Kieschnick and Meir Shahar, 131–60. Philadelphia: University of Pennsylvania Press.

Sieg, E. and W. Siegling. 1933. "Bruchstück eines Udānavarga Kommentars (Udānālaṃkāra?) im Tocharischen." In *Festschrift Moriz Winternitz: 1863–23. Dez.–1933*, edited by Otto Stein and Wilhelm Gambert, 167–73. Leipzig: Otto Harrassowitz.

Singh, Jaideva. 1989. Introduction to *The Conception of Buddhist Nirvāṇa*

(With Sanskrit Text of Madhyamaka-kārikā), Part I, by Th. Stcherbatsky, 1–59. Delhi: Motilal Banarsidass.

Sirimane, Yuki. 2016. *Entering the Stream to Enlightenment: Experiences of the Stages of the Buddhist Path in Contemporary Sri Lanka*. Sheffield: Equinox Publishing.

Skilling, Peter. 1993. "Theravādin Literature in Tibetan Translation." *Journal of the Pali Text Society*, 19: 69–201.

———. 1994. *Mahāsūtras: Great Discourses of the Buddha*. Oxford: Pali Text Society.

———. 2003. "Traces of the Dharma, Preliminary Reports on Some ye dhammā and ye dharmā Inscriptions from Mainland South-East Asia." *Bulletin de l'École Française d'Extrême-Orient*, 90/91: 273–87.

———. 2007. "'Dhammas Are as Swift as Thought . . .': A Note on Dhammapada 1 and 2 and Their Parallels." *Journal of the Centre for Buddhist Studies, Sri Lanka*, 5: 23–50.

———. 2008. "Buddhist Sealings and the ye dharmā Stanza." In *Archaeology of Early Historic South Asia*, edited by Gautam Sengupta and Sharmi Chakraborty, 503–25. New Delhi: Pragati Publications.

———. 2009. "Ārādhanā Tham: 'Invitation to Teach the Dhamma.'" In *Peter Skilling: Buddhism and Buddhist Literature of South-East Asia, Selected Papers*, edited by Claudio Cicuzza, 80–89. Bangkok and Lumbini: Fragile Palm Leaves Foundation, Lumbini International Research Institute.

Smith, Douglas. 2015. "Was the Buddha an Anti-Realist?" *Journal of the Oxford Centre for Buddhist Studies*, 11: 143–78.

Sobti, Harcharan Singh. 1985. *Nibbāna in Early Buddhism: Based on Pāli Sources From 6th B.C. to 5th A.D.* Delhi: Eastern Book Linkers.

Speyer, J. S. 1909/1970. *Avadānaçataka: A Century of Edifying Tales Belonging to the Hīnayāna, Vol. II*. Osnabrück: Biblio Verlag.

Stache-Rosen, Valentina. 1968. *Dogmatische Begriffsreihen im älteren Buddhismus II: Das Saṅgītisūtra und sein Kommentar Saṅgītiparyāya*. Berlin: Akademie Verlag.

Stcherbatsky, Th. 1923. *The Central Conception of Buddhism and the Meaning of the Word "Dharma."* London: Royal Asiatic Society.

———. 1968/1989. *The Conception of Buddhist Nirvāṇa (With Sanskrit Text of Madhyamaka-kārikā), Part II.* Delhi: Motilal Banarsidass.

Stuart, Daniel M. 2013. *Thinking about Cessation: The Pṛṣṭhapālasūtra of the Dīrghāgama in Context.* Wien: Arbeitskreis für Tibetische und Buddhistische Studien, Universität Wien.

———. 2015. *A Less Traveled Path: Saddharmasmṛtyupasthānasūtra Chapter 2: Critically Edited with a Study on its Structure and Significance for the Development of Buddhist Meditation, Volume II.* Vienna and Beijing: Austrian Academy of Sciences Press/China Tibetology Publishing House.

Tamaki Koshiro. 1973. "The Fundamental Aspect of Dhamma in Primitive Buddhism." *Journal of Indian and Buddhist Studies,* 42: 1062–54.

Tilakaratne, Asaṅga. 1993. *Nirvana and Ineffability: A Study of the Buddhist Theory of Reality and Language.* Sri Lanka: University of Kelaniya, Postgraduate Institute of Pali and Buddhist Studies.

Vaidya, P. L. 1960. *Madhyamakaśāstra of Nāgārjuna, with the Commentary: Prasannapadā by Candrakīrti.* Darbhanga: The Mithila Institute of Postgraduate Studies and Research in Sanskrit Learning.

Vetter, Tilmann. 1990. "Some Remarks on Older Parts of the Suttanipāta." In *Earliest Buddhism and Madhyamaka,* edited by David Seyford Ruegg and Lambert Schmithausen, 36–56. Leiden: E. J. Brill.

———. 1995. "Bei Lebzeiten das Todlose Erreichen: Zum Begriff Amata im Alten Buddhismus." In *Im Tod gewinnt der Mensch sein Selbst: Das Phänomen des Todes in asiatischer und abendländischer Religionstradition,* edited by Gerhad Oberhammer, 43–74. Wien: Österreichische Akademie der Wissenschaften.

———. 2012. *A Lexicographical Study of An Shigao's and His Circle's Chinese Translation of Buddhist Texts.* Tokyo: The International Institute for Buddhist Studies.

Vira, Raghu. 1936. *The Virāṭaparvan: Being the Fourth Book of the Mahābhārata, The Great Epic of India.* Poona: Bhandarkar Oriental Research Institute.

von Helmholtz, Hermann. 1878/1927. *Die Tatsachen in der Wahrnehmung,* edited by H. Schneider. Leipzig: B. G. Teubner.

von Rospatt, Alexander. 1995. *The Buddhist Doctrine of Momentariness: A Survey of the Origins and Early Phase of this Doctrine up to Vasubandhu.* Stuttgart: Franz Steiner Verlag.

Waldschmidt, Ernst. 1932. *Bruchstücke Buddhistischer Sūtras aus dem zentralasiatischen Sanskritkanon, herausgegeben und im Zusammenhang mit ihren Parallelversionen bearbeitet.* Leipzig: F. A. Brockhaus.

———. 1951. *Das Mahāparinirvāṇasūtra: Text in Sanskrit und Tibetisch, verglichen mit dem Pāli nebst einer Übersetzung der chinesischen Entsprechung im Vinaya der Mūlasarvāstivādins, auf Grund von Turfan-Handschriften herausgegeben und bearbeitet.* Berlin: Akademie Verlag.

———. 1951/1967. "Vergleichende Analyse des Catuṣpariṣatsūtra." In *Von Ceylon bis Turfan: Schriften zur Geschichte, Literatur, Religion und Kunst des indischen Kulturraums, Festgabe zum 70. Geburtstag am 15. Juli 1967 von Ernst Waldschmidt*, 164–202. Göttingen: Vandenhoeck & Ruprecht.

———. 1956. *Das Mahāvadānasūtra: ein kanonischer Text über die sieben letzten Buddhas, Sanskrit, verglichen mit dem Pāli nebst einer Analyse der in chinesischer Übersetzung überlieferten Parallelversion, auf Grund von Turfan-Handschriften herausgegeben, Teil II: die Textbearbeitung.* Berlin: Akademie Verlag.

———. 1962. *Das Catuṣpariṣatsūtra: eine kanonische Lehrschrift über die Begründung der buddhistischen Gemeinde, Text in Sanskrit und Tibetisch, verglichen mit dem Pāli nebst einer Übersetzung der chinesischen Entsprechung im Vinaya der Mūlasarvāstivādins, auf Grund von Turfan-Handschriften herausgegeben und bearbeitet, Teil III.* Berlin: Akademie Verlag.

———. 1968. "Ein Beitrag zur Überlieferung vom Sthavira Śroṇa Koṭiviṃśa." In *Mélanges d'Indianisme à la Mémoire de Louis Renou*, edited by Louis Renou, 773–87. Paris: Éditions de Boccard.

———. 1980. "The Rāṣṭrapālasūtra in Sanskrit Remnants from Central Asia." In *Indianisme et Bouddhisme: Mélanges offerts à Mgr. Étienne Lamotte*, edited by André Bareau and Étienne Lamotte, 359–74. Louvain-la-Neuve: Institut Orientaliste.

Waldschmidt, Ernst, Walter Clawiter, and Lore Holzmann. 1965. *Sanskrithandschriften aus den Turfanfunden, Teil I*. Wiesbaden: Franz Steiner.

Waldschmidt, Ernst, Walter Clawiter, and Lore Sander-Holzmann. 1968. *Sanskrithandschriften aus den Turfanfunden, Teil II*. Wiesbaden: Franz Steiner.

Walshe, Maurice. 1987. *Thus Have I Heard: The Long Discourses of the Buddha*. London: Wisdom Publications.

Weeraperuma, Susunaga. 2003. *Nirvana: The Highest Happiness*. New Delhi: Vedams.

Welbon, Guy Richard. 1968. *The Buddhist Nirvāṇa and Its Western Interpreters*. Chicago: University of Chicago Press.

Weller, Friedrich. 1934. *Brahmajālasūtra: tibetischer und mongolischer Text*. Leipzig: Otto Harrassowitz.

Wille, Klaus. 2008. *Sanskrithandschriften aus den Turfanfunden Teil 10*. Stuttgart: Franz Steiner.

Wittgenstein, Ludwig. 1922. *Tractatus Logico-Philosophicus*. London: Kegan Paul, Trench, Trubner & Co.

Wogihara Unrai. 1932. *Sphuṭārthā Abhidharmakośavyākhyā by Yaśomitra, Part I*. Tokyo: The Publishing Association of Abhidharmakośavyākhyā.

Wynne, Alexander. 2007. *The Origin of Buddhist Meditation*. London: Routledge.

Yinshun 印順. 1983. 雜阿含經論會編. Taipei: 正聞出版社.

Zhou Chungyang. 2008. *Das Kaivartisūtra der neuentdeckten Dīrghāgama-Handschrift: Eine Edition und Rekonstruktion des Textes*. MA thesis, Georg-August Universität, Göttingen.

Zongtse, Champa Thupten. 1990. *Udānavarga, Band III: Der tibetische Text, unter Mitarbeit von Siglinde Dietz herausgegeben von Champa Thupten Zongtse*. Göttingen: Vandenhoeck & Ruprecht.

Index

F

R

S

W

Y

About the Author

BHIKKHU ANĀLAYO is a scholar of early Buddhism and a meditation teacher. He completed his PhD research on the *Satipaṭṭhānasutta* at the University of Peradeniya, Sri Lanka, in 2000 and his habilitation research with a comparative study of the *Majjhimanikāya* in the light of its Chinese, Sanskrit, and Tibetan parallels at the University of Marburg, Germany, in 2007. His over five hundred publications are for the most part based on comparative studies, with a special interest in topics related to meditation and the role of women in Buddhism.

What to Read Next from Wisdom Publications

Daughters of the Buddha
Teachings by Ancient Indian Women
Bhikkhu Anālayo

"Bhikkhu Anālayo makes a major contribution in furthering our understanding of early Buddhist nuns and female lay disciples by paying special attention to their spiritual journeys that were riddled with social prejudices and obstacles."
—Professor Hiroko Kawanami, author of *The Culture of Giving in Myanmar*

Early Buddhist Oral Tradition
Textual Formation and Transmission
Bhikkhu Anālayo

For hundreds of years after his death, the Buddha's teachings were transmitted orally, from person to person. In this volume, acclaimed scholar-monk Bhikkhu Anālayo examines the impact of such oral transmission on early Buddhist texts, be these monastic rules, verses, or prose portions of the early discourses.

Rebirth in Early Buddhism and Current Research
Bhikkhu Anālayo

"Bhikkhu Anālayo offers a detailed study of the much-debated Buddhist doctrine of rebirth and a survey of relevant evidence."
—Joseph Goldstein, author of *Mindfulness: A Practical Guide to Awakening*

About Wisdom Publications

Wisdom Publications is the leading publisher of classic and contemporary Buddhist books and practical works on mindfulness. To learn more about us or to explore our other books, please visit our website at wisdomexperience.org or contact us at the address below.

Wisdom Publications
132 Perry Street
New York, NY 10014 USA

We are a 501(c)(3) organization, and donations in support of our mission are tax deductible.

Wisdom Publications is affiliated with the Foundation for the Preservation of the Mahayana Tradition (FPMT).